Rhetoric, Innovation, Technology

Technical Communication and Information Systems
Ed Barrett, editor

The Nurnberg Funnel: Designing Minimalist Instruction for Practical Computer Skill, John M. Carroll, 1990

Hypermedia and Literary Studies, Paul Delany and George P. Landow, editors, 1991

Rhetoric, Innovation, Technology: Case Studies of Technical Communication in Technology Transfers, Stephen Doheny-Farina, 1992

Rhetoric, Innovation, Technology
Case Studies of Technical Communication in
Technology Transfers

Stephen Doheny-Farina

The MIT Press
Cambridge, Massachusetts
London, England

This book was set in Sabon and was printed and bound in the United States of America.

Library of Congress Cataloging-in-Publication-Data

Doheny-Farina, Stephen.
   Rhetoric, innovation, technology : case studies of technical
  communication in technology transfers / Stephen Doheny-Farina.
        p. cm. — (Technical communication and information systems)
  Includes bibliographical references and index.
  ISBN 0–262–04129–4
  1. Communication of technical information.   2. Technology   transfer.   I.
Title.   II. Series.
T10.5.D64   1992
338.9'26—dc20   91–36904
                                              CIP

Contents

Series Foreword

Technical communication is one of the most rapidly expanding fields of study in the United States, Europe, and the Pacific rim, as witnessed by the growth of professional societies and degree-granting programs in colleges and universities as well as the evolving status of documentation specialists in industry. The writer, and writing, are no longer mere servants of science and engineering but rather partners in the complex matrix of forces that go into the construction of knowledge and information. And the audience is not a passive but an active player in this transaction. Furthermore, computational science has delivered a powerful tool for the creation, presentation, exchange, and annotation of text—so powerful that we speak not in terms of a text but rather of a hypertext, of seamless information environments that integrate a variety of media.

The MIT Press Series in Technical Communication will present advanced research in all aspects of this rapidly expanding field, including hypertext and hypermedia systems, online documentation, information architecture, interface design, graphics, collaborative writing in distributed networks, the role of the writer in industry, scientific and engineering writing, training and education in technical writing. Only in addressing such a wide range of topics do we begin to understand the complexity and power of this field of expertise.

Ed Barrett

Preface

This book explores the rhetorical nature of the phenomena commonly labeled technology transfers and in the process uncovers some of the rhetorical barriers to successful technology transfers. At the same time, it attempts to deflate the myth of knowledge transfer by arguing that processes typically called information transfer and technology transfer are not transfers at all but instead series of personal constructions and reconstructions of knowledge, expertise, and technologies by the participants attempting to adapt technological innovations for social uses.

As such, this book is standing astride at least two disciplinary realms. On the one hand, it attempts to make some sense of what is being said and studied within "the field" of technology transfer studies. (I put quotation marks around "the field" because what I am referring to is a multidisciplinary amalgamation that resists simple classifications. I suppose that many whose work centers on technology transfers perceive a number of "fields" replete with subgroups, splinter groups, antigroups, and outsiders, like myself, attempting to make sense of these events we are calling technology transfers.) On the other hand, this book is a product of the relatively recent movement of rhetorical studies of scientific, technical, commercial, and professional enterprises, institutions, and disciplines.

Chapter 1 offers a critical review of the communication theory that underlies much research on technology transfer. I follow that review with a discussion of some examples of a small but growing body of rhetorically based research on rhetoric in scientific, technological, and professional contexts. A number of the ideas discussed in this chapter are explored in the remaining chapters, each of which is composed of lengthy case studies illustrating a variety of rhetorical issues in technology transfers.

Chapter 2 presents a case describing the development of an entrepreneurial start-up company. More important, it explores the constructive
and destructive power of a fledgling company's business plans, as well as
the social, political, and organizational factors that surrounded the writing of those texts. I first published this study in a considerably shortened
form in 1986 (Doheny-Farina 1986). The version in this book is more detailed and expansive, providing not only a more detailed picture of the
company but also a glimpse of the larger social-rhetorical environment
within which it arose. Furthermore, the case illustrates a number of issues
related to university-industry relationships in the development of innovative, start-up companies. Finally, it provides an analysis of an enterprise
attempting to evolve from a loosely to a more specified organizational
structure.

Chapter 3 analyzes the rhetorical barriers to the transfer of a new biomedical technology—an innovative, experimental artificial heart. In particular, the case explores the development of expertise across the transfer.
Because this case describes the relationship between a university research
hospital and a biomedical products manufacturer, it provides another
analysis of the challenges of university-industry collaboration in the development of technological innovations. At its center, chapter 3 is an examination of the development and use of several documents across the
transfer: from the technical developers to the writers to the users. This examination allows me to analyze some of the difficulties in crossing organizational structures. And, as such, it presents a series of problems that
contrast with those discussed in chapter 2, which focuses on an enterprise
attempting to establish, not overcome, organizational boundaries. Ultimately this chapter explores the contingent nature of new technologies—
the difficulties in establishing among participants just what a new technology is and does—and calls for a redefinition of the concept of technology transfer.

Chapter 4 carries on the analysis of the barriers that separate participants in technology transfers and presents two cases, each arguing that
expert practical rhetoricians—technical writers—need to become participants in new product development processes from the design stage on-
ward. As such, this chapter focuses on the difficulties in crossing
organizational barriers. In both cases, incremental advances in technologies and subsequent applications are the sources of new product develop-

ment projects that call for the inclusion of technical writers in order to adapt the applications to the users better.

Chapter 5 examines several key elements in the education of technical communicators, elements geared to help them constructively break down the walls between organizational and disciplinary divisions in order to become better collaborators with others of differing expertise. The book's appendix contains a brief discussion of specific classroom applications for technical communication courses, followed by a lengthy fictional case designed for the classroom to raise the issues of intraorganizational barriers to collaboration in a new product development process.

Some might criticize the inclusion of a chapter and appendix devoted to these educational issues. However, it is just as important to examine the pedagogical implications of the rhetorical nature of technology transfers as it is to examine the failures and successes of these processes in industry. If change is going to come, if the processes of adapting technologies to society are going to be improved, it is going to come, in part, through the performances of better educated, enlightened professionals.

Acknowledgments

I thank all of the participants with whom I worked in each case study. I cannot name them because of the need to render all participants anonymous. I have used pseudonyms throughout the case studies. I hope that they know how much I appreciate their cooperation.

There are, of course, some people I can name. My deepest thanks go to four colleagues: Bill Karis, Clarkson University, Mary Lay, University of Minnesota, Dorothy Winsor, GMI, and Jim Porter, Purdue University. Mary, Bill, and I worked together on a project that led me to one of the two case studies contained in chapter 4. Bill, Dorothy, and Jim read parts of the book and offered useful criticisms. Furthermore, Bill helped to foster many of the ideas in this book through the day-to-day, informal hallway discussions and debates that he and I have had over the last several years (that is, in between discussions of important things, like the Boston Celtics or our noontime faculty basketball games). Special thanks go to Judy Grant for helping me put the manuscript together and Brian and Nancy Harris for their gracious hospitality when I had to travel to their city to work on this project. I also thank Sandra Minkkinen, Beverly Miller, and Lorrie Lejeune for their editing and production work. Finally, Terry Ehling of the MIT Press and Ed Barrett, series editor, gave me the opportunity to produce this book. I am grateful to them.

Rhetoric, Innovation, Technology

1

Technical Communication and Technology Transfer

Scene 1: An Entrepreneurial Start-up

The start-up's executives sat around a table, and their lawyer bluntly described the company's desperate financial situation: "You are really a defunct corporation. You are bleeding to death." He then referred to the head of a venture capital firm (Hughes) who, two months earlier, had considered investing $450,000 in the company. But no such investment had ever materialized. "As Hughes said, you're not only looking at Chapter 11, you are there now."

At this point in the meeting, the company president reluctantly admitted there were other problems. His recent negotiations with a bank executive who arranged the first half of a $250,000 bank loan led the president to believe that the bank might not approve the remaining half of that loan. Apparently it appeared to the bank executive that the company, by its performance with the first installment, had not proved itself worthy of the rest of the loan. The lawyer told the executives what they knew too well: their biggest problem was continually missing production deadlines. If they had been "out to market" by now, they would not be in this trouble.

But they were, and they needed to find a way out of it. They decided that they had to write a new business plan and reshape the company.

Scene 2: The Fruits of a Biomedical Transfer

The patient had just gone through the main phase of heart surgery. The surgeons had completed the bypass, but the heart had not resuscitated sufficiently. A decision was made to use an assist pump—an artificial heart that would keep the patient alive until his heart revived or until he could undergo a heart transplant. Surgery was performed to attach him to the artificial heart, and shortly after, the artificial heart began to pump. But not long after giving the go-ahead to start the assist pump, the surgeon indicated that the patient was not responding well; the assist pump needed to perform more efficiently to keep the patient alive. The surgeon turned to the technician and said, "I'm not getting enough output. What can you do to increase the output of the pump?" At that moment, the technician could have made one or more of several adjustments to the device. Each adjustment could increase the output of the pump, but each would also have a physiological effect on the patient. A poorly chosen adjustment could hurt the patient's condition, tenuous at best at this point. Which adjustment or combination of adjustments should the technician make at that moment?

Scene 3: A Product Development Team

In 1988, ABC company was producing a large-scale software product. As part of that development project, the company installed the prototype for a customer as a prerelease test with the product slated for release to the market in October 1988. Unfortunately, in July of that year, some significant problems were revealed in the software when the new product was being tested. With the product scheduled to be released in two months, a crisis-response team was organized to solve the problems and keep the prerelease customer's operation afloat as the problems were being solved. The crisis-response team was multifunctional; it included programmers, marketers, technical writers, managers, field engineers, customer support personnel, and actual customers-users.

The team faced a challenge that involved the company's largest customers. Furthermore, the product in question was designed to precede a future product that was already in development and could not be completed and released without having the first product in place and working well. The flawed product involved a massive amount of software that was supporting a system that tied many different user sites and many levels of use. It involved complex hardware functions and equally complex software code. And it was this complexity of code that made problems difficult to analyze and fix. The team had a name for this difficulty. "We called it brittle code," said one technical writer, "because you made one change to it and it fell apart, causing 50 problems for every change you made." Ultimately, ten thousand lines of code were involved in the redesign.

When the problems started to occur, the company immediately moved in to the prerelease customer site and helped them to scaffold their system in order to keep it running effectively until the problems could be resolved. This quick-response action characterized the company's larger effort to fix its problems and produce what was ultimately a product of high quality. But it took an extraordinary effort by all involved to achieve that quality, and the stakes were high, as one of the technical writers on the team noted: "We were just about to make the product generally available, in field testing, the final phase of the product development. We were only two months from actually saying, 'Here world, here's this wonderful, new product.' If we had shipped [the flawed product], imagine the implications for our largest customers installing this product and having it fail. It would have been devastating." The challenges that faced the company's crisis-response team were many, and the technical writers on that team were about to plunge deeper into the technology than they had ever gone before.

These three scenarios focus on key moments in three of the case studies presented in this book. Each scenario represents differing facets of the dynamic and multidimensional processes that seemingly "transfer" technologies from laboratories to the marketplace.

Technology Transfer and Technical Communication

Technology transfer is an umbrella term that refers to an entire range of activities involved in developing new technologies and their applications for the marketplace. It involves creating and adapting prototypical developments so that they can be manufactured, marketed, and supported. In other words, it involves the development and commercialization of technological innovations.

A technological innovation becomes a product innovation when it becomes part of a commercial enterprise. (Not all technological innovations lead to a commercial venture and some R&D work may never result in a potentially marketable product.) Many product innovations are researched and developed by established corporations; others who research and develop product innovations launch new companies in order to reach the market with their innovation. These start-up companies are often entrepreneurial enterprises funded with venture capital, investments from outsiders who support the fledgling operations as they attempt to bring the innovations to market.

Since the mid-1970s, there has been a tremendous increase in the number of high-tech start-up companies and an equally dramatic increase in the analysis of technology transfers. Before that time, as Kozmetsky (1990) explains, most people thought that technological innovation, "the entire process from R&D in the laboratory to successful commercialization in the marketplace," was automatic: "Traditionally, we have thought that successful commercialization of R&D was the result of an automatic process that began with scientific research and then moved to development, financing, manufacturing, and marketing. . . . [Managers] did not necessarily need to be concerned with linkages in the technology commercialization process. Insufficient attention was paid to the connections between the myriad institutions involved in moving scientific research from the laboratory to the marketplace" (p. 23). But now, notes Kozmetsky, experts from a variety of disciplines and institutions in industry, government, and academia have devoted a great deal of energy trying to understand and improve technology transfers. At the same time the complexity of such ventures has increased because participant groups from all three entities (industry, government, and academia) are increasingly collaborating in technology transfers. Even within organizations, say within a corporation, diverse groups collaborate to develop and commercialize an innovation. Groups and subgroups (and sub-sub-groups, and . . .) from R&D to manufacturing to marketing to product support to customers and users are all participants in a variety of transfer processes.

And although it is typically not recognized as such in the technology transfer literature, these processes are highly rhetorical in nature. That is, *at their core* these processes involve individuals and groups *negotiating* their visions of technologies and applications, markets and users in what they all hope is a common enterprise. This means that the reality of a transfer does not exist apart from the perceptions of the participants. Instead, the reality—what the transfer *means* to the participants—is the result of continual conceptualizing, negotiating, and reconceptualizing. Thus, technology transfer is a rhetorical dynamic; it is, as Williams and Gibson (1990) argue, "a phenomenon of communication": "To make technology transfer successful requires overcoming the many barriers to communication encountered when individuals use different vocabularies, have different motives, represent organizations of widely differing cultures, and when the referents of the transactions may vary from highly abstract concepts to concrete products" (p. 10).

Leonard-Barton (1990) has implicitly classified technology transfers into two generic rhetorical situations: point-to-point, in which a source develops innovations for a highly specified purpose to a known audience-user, and diffusion, in which the source develops an innovation for a more general audience-user whose purposes may or may not be clearly known. In both types, the "receivers" (users) of the innovation can play a variety of roles "from superficial input late in the development process, when only minor alterations to the technology could be considered, to actual development partnership [with] technology sources . . . in the construction of innovations from the beginning" (p. 49).

The purposes of involving users, according to Leonard-Barton are to learn something about the user's needs, abilities, and attitudes so that the source can create a potentially usable and market-worthy product, and to gain "user buy-in"—involvement in the process that results in users being committed to the new product. In both situations, the cooperation and negotiation involve a "source" and a "receiver," and thus each is a communication-dominated enterprise. Nevertheless, we shortchange our conception of technology transfers if we assume they are based on a simple process of moving innovations from a source to one or more receivers. All we have to do is examine who the innovators may be in order to begin to question the validity of a simple source-to-receiver model of technology transfers. Users may play significant roles in the development of innovations. Indeed, often the users themselves are the principal innovators in technology transfers, undermining any simplistic notion that technology transfer begins with the technical developers and moves in a straight line to the users in the marketplace (Von Hippel 1988).

This view will not surprise experts in technology transfer; they all recognize the complex, reciprocal interactions that must occur among participant groups. But although many experts in the field have developed highly complex, interactive models of technology transfers, many of those models are based on a simplistic, information transfer model of communication—a model that I will counter in this chapter and the rest of the book. Before doing that, I present some views of technology transfer that are based on a far more complex perspective.

Rhetorical Approaches to Technology Transfer

Although he does not characterize his basic assumptions in terms of rhetorical theory, Bradbury's (1978) description of technology transfer clearly describes the centrality of practical rhetoric in the process:

Communication is vital for the innovator; how much more so for the technology transferor! The shift of context involved in technology transfer demands the shaping of the technology to fit the detail of the different system which comprises the new context. At every step in the operation of technology transfer there must be dialogue between those who would transfer and those who would adopt; dialogue concerning design, detail, specification detail, user need detail—contextual mapping to use the jargon of the morphological analysts. Such is the abstract nature of language that direct single step transfer of system description or user need by documentation must fail lamentably on sufficiency. It is only by the iterative process of verbal exchange with repeated readjustment of understanding and rephrasing of questions that the required degree of sufficiency of knowledge of context and specification can be achieved. (pp. 112–113)

Every aspect of technology transfers must be negotiated, constructed, and reconstructed in the minds of the participants. There is no clearly objective fact or physical entity that proceeds uninterpreted from the lab to the market. The entire process is one of interpretation, negotiation, and adjustment. Moreover, it engenders a reciprocal shaping as it develops; the innovators, the innovation, and the users of the innovation are all changed through the process. Additionally, what any one participant perceives as the technology or the innovation may be different from what others perceive: "The 'same technology' or the 'same innovation' has different meanings in different settings. The already-functioning social system and traditional practices in which the technology is placed have a tremendous impact on the ways the technology is understood and used. In fact, those who do adopt innovations are typically faced with a challenging task of resolving conflicts between old practices that derive from powerful situational constraints and imperatives of the new technology. As they resolve these conflicts, the original technology takes on multiple forms; the 'it' becomes 'them'" (Bruce and Peyton 1990, p. 172).

The conventional view of technology transfers is quite different; it holds that the innovation shapes the recipients and their actions. In other words, the innovation is a clearly delineated object and plan of action that in its idealized form will appear the same to all participants in the transfer. When differing participants see the innovation differently, they are either misperceiving or the innovation has been somehow distorted. If those who are implementing the transfer do the job correctly, the innovation will not suffer distortion. In fact, these so-called distortions are quite common:

> The prevalence of distortions of innovations is a clue that the conventional model of implementation is inadequate. The "distortions" arise because the innovation is not the only active element. . . . In reality, the innovation is but one small addition to a complex social system. Instead of seeing it as the primary instrument of change, it is better to see it as a bit of raw material that may stimulate the creation of something new.
>
> We are thus led to a different model for implementation of innovations. In this model, the active agents are not innovations, but the participants in the setting in which the innovation is placed. These participants first develop a perception of what the innovation is and then re-create it as they adapt it to fit with institutional and physical constraints, and with their own goals and practices. What they produce are different realizations of the original innovation . (Bruce and Peyton 1990, pp. 172–173)

Even the originators themselves may not agree on just what is the original innovation. From the sources to the users, technological innovations are part of complex social, organizational, institutional interactions, interpretations, and negotiations. And every participant along the way constructs and reconstructs the innovation based upon his or her experience and worldview.

I illustrate this view of technology transfer through case studies that show glimpses of the rhetorical nature of technology transfers. As Bradbury (1978) points out: "Such is the state of the art of technology transfer that scenarios and case studies must long remain the key to learning, be it of innovation or technology transfer; the theory and abstraction are not at the level at which numbers and mathematical models can be anything more than useful auxiliary aids to understanding" (p. 113). In other words, because of the contingent nature of this phenomenon, it is difficult to generalize across transfers. Accordingly, the case studies in this book are presented as slices of experiences, the analysis of which reveals that sophisticated rhetorical activity is central to the enterprise at hand.

Information Transfer: A Critique

The complex, rhetorical view of communication that implicitly underlies both Bradbury's and Bruce and Peyton's analyses is not evident in many other expert analyses of technology transfer. Although much of the technology transfer literature reveals sophisticated understandings of industry, R&D, manufacturing, marketing, and venture capital, many of these views are belied by a rather simplistic view of communication.

Some researchers of technology transfers have concentrated on studying networks and communication systems, creating models of such systems that show patterns, for example, of which subunits in an organization communicate with which other subunits and where in the system "uncertainty" will be most prevalent. Uncertainty is a key element in these models and central to technology transfer. It represents the difference between information needed to engage in a task and the information available. Clearly an overview of these networks and communication systems is essential to understanding the role of technical communication in technology transfers. We learn something about the patterns of within-group and group-to-group communication, as well as the nature of problem-solving tasks in R&D projects. Nevertheless, these approaches do not get to the heart of communication and communication problems because they base their analyses on the concept of information transfer.

This theory of communication separates knowledge from communication; it treats knowledge as an object that exists independently of the participants in the innovation venture. With this independent existence, information becomes an object that can be carried through channels, and thus the patterns of information transfer through these channels become important. So when communication means sending information through channels, we need to look at ways of better managing those channels to achieve better dissemination or diffusion of information; furthermore, clarity of information becomes vital: a "body of information, of objective facts, is just lying out there waiting to be communicated. When the communication is successful, the receiver is put in possession of those facts. The facts determine the communication, unless the originator interferes. The job of the originator is to move the facts from one place to another, handling them as little as possible so as not to tarnish them" (Dobrin 1989, p. 60).

Dobrin (1989) traces the concept of information transfer to a model that was used to explore the nature of telephony: "If we speak of technical communication as transferring information (reporting information, transmitting information, or communicating facts), we suggest to ourselves that we are like the telephone, which takes input and turns it into output almost invisibly. It encourages us in believing that, like the telephone receiver, the transmitter must function invisibly and that the success of the transmission can be measured by looking at what shape the facts are in when they arrive. Speaking this way obscures the fact that understanding, not facts, is being communicated" (p. 73). The information transfer view does not explain how information comes to mean something to a participant in communication activities, nor does it tell why people have difficulty communicating with one another. The concept of uncertainty indicates that the communication problem is not one of meaning but one of the availability of the correct information. That is, the communication problem we call uncertainty does not explain how individuals come to construct the meanings that they do; it explains a gap in knowledge and indicates that information must be gathered to fill in that gap.

This concept of uncertainty is analyzed by Miller (1990) in her critique of the rhetoric of Decision Science: "Uncertainty: . . . in terms of the disparity between the capacity of the human mind and the size of the decision problems implies that uncertainty lies in the discrepancy between information available and information needed; that is, uncertainty is wholly a problem of knowledge. Such uncertainty concerns events in the world that may have happened—if our information were more complete or our calculus more accurate, we could know with complete certainty whether it will rain today, whether the tossed coin will come up heads this time, whether Homer was blind, what the President knew and when he knew it" (p. 175). Uncertainty, then, is based on human ignorance. On the other hand, says Miller, an Aristotelian view of uncertainty does not concern knowledge but human actions: "Our imperfect knowledge, of course, makes deliberation about our actions more difficult, but, as Aristotle notes, we do not waste time deliberating about questions with only one possible answer, like whether New York is north of Rome. . . . Problems of knowledge presuppose no real conflict—except between people and the limits of available information. Problems of action involve conflict between people. . . . Problems of action are 'essentially contestable': problems of knowledge are not" (p. 175).

Any expert of technology transfer will say that transfer processes present problems of action, but many characterize communication in those processes as transferring information in order to lessen uncertainty. What is missing from many experts' views is this: each participant in technology transfers constructs meanings based on experience. Therefore, the amount and clarity of information will not necessarily lessen uncertainty. Membership in a group can mean adherence to a means of interpretation that may always clash with others adhering to another group's means of interpretation. No amount of rational information transfer will change that adherence. Indeed, lots of "high-quality" information may merely harden one's adherence to one's group in the light of this threat.

Understanding how individuals must mediate differing worldviews, or differing meaning-generating systems, is the key to understanding how people successfully or unsuccessfully collaborate. It is noteworthy that throughout the literature, researchers and analysts say that informal channels are the most effective channels of communication. Why does study after study describe verbal, informal communication as most often associated with effective communication? It is not because that type of communication is inherently more effective than, say, writing a report. The findings that promote informal communication are merely a symptom of what it actually takes to communicate sophisticated and complex issues: the development of shared worldviews that overcome interpersonal, political, and organizational barriers (which I will call rhetorical barriers). This is a process of negotiation and sharing of perspectives, values, language, knowledge, and so forth. It is not an exchange of objectified pieces of information but a development of relationships. Effective collaboration is not just shared information; it is shared relationships.

When one develops a more complex view—a rhetorical view—of communication in technology transfers, one begins to see that formal and informal, verbal and written forms of communication can be effective or ineffective depending on a variety of circumstances. The elements of the rhetorical situation influence the communicability of the moment.

The circumstances surrounding this critique are also subject to a rhetorical analysis, as well. For example, in the following section I highlight aspects of published research that illustrate what I see as a strain of information transfer that infects studies of technology transfer. I do this in part because it represents an accepted, if not expected, element of analytic scholarship: I am both associating myself with a tradition (rhetorical studies) and separating myself with another tradition (information transfer studies). With carefully selected and edited excerpts and paraphrases, I am making my argument that the following research should be interpreted as I see it. I am staking my claim to some small piece of analytical territory. Others may utterly reject my argument. They may say that I do not understand the research, that those researchers are speaking a different language and are basing their arguments on foundations that I know little or nothing about. So where is the meaning of that research? Is it in the texts that I read? In the conversations I may have had about the research? No. I am just one of many who have and will continue to construct meanings of that research. The extent to which others share my constructions is the extent to which my constructions will be judged valid or invalid. This, too, is the process of "communication of information" in technology transfers.

Technology Transfer and Rhetoric

Limited Views
Several issues stand out in the literature. Most of the following six analyses recognize:

- Uncertainty is prevalent in technology transfers.
- Communication is central to decreasing uncertainty.
- Within groups there will be common languages and common purposes.
- Across groups there may not be common languages and common purposes.
- Usually in technology transfers, communicating across groups is necessary.
- Individuals can serve as liaisons between groups to facilitate communication.
- Formal (written reports) and informal channels (spoken, face-to-face communication) are used in technology transfers.

Furthermore, each of the following concepts highlights differing aspects of what I am saying are limited views of communication.

Information transfer   In his analysis of information transfer in research and development in the Silicon Valley electronics industry, Rogers (1982) emphasizes the importance of information exchange in the development of technological innovations. He agrees with a body of research on innovation processes that sees uncertainty as the "central concept in innovation behavior." When faced with uncertainty, notes Rogers, individuals typically seek information: "Because innovation behavior always entails coping with a relatively high degree of uncertainty, such innovation is, most centrally, an informational process. Workers in a private firm pursuing innovation must devote most of their efforts to obtaining and using information: data about the performance of the innovation they are seeking to create, about the materials and components they are fabricating into the innovation; information about their competitors' products; about the nature of existing patents related to their proposed innovation; government policies affecting their proposed innovation; and the problems that consumers in their market face and how the proposed innovation might help solve some of these perceived problems" (p. 110). This view describes technology transferors as essentially information transferors, and most information transfer goes through informal channels, although in every firm there exist formal channels of communication (e.g., technical papers and reports).

The informal channels that are most important are the interpersonal, face-to-face communications among participants in innovation development enterprises. In the world that Rogers describes, the Silicon Valley electronics industry, this channel—though fraught with legal issues that sometime engender secrecy and intrigue—is seemingly an easy way to communicate because the R&D people throughout the industry are for the most part peers who have similar professional experiences and in many cases know each other personally. For example, much interfirm communication among technical professionals occurs in places like "the Wagonwheel Bar in Mountain View (a famous Silicon Valley watering hole for information exchange that is located near several major firms)" (p. 117).

Overall, Rogers paints a picture of a communication environment in which everyone is speaking the same language, motivated by similar goals, and involved in similar disciplines and technologies. In such an environment, it may seem obvious that information is something to be transferred among groups and individuals because the participants may all conceive of that information through similar worldviews.

Information processing A widely respected model of communication in R&D environments is the information processing model described by Tushman and Nadler (1980). A stated premise of their work is that technical communication can be managed in R&D labs and the effectiveness of that communication can determine the performance of those labs. Furthermore, they assume that R&D labs are open, social systems and are composed of subunits. The labs form networks of verbal communication, and "verbal interaction is a particularly important medium through which information is gathered, processed, and transferred" (p. 94). Overall, the labs "can usefully be seen as information processing systems. Information processing can be seen as an ongoing problem-solving cycle involving each area of the laboratory, the larger organization, and the external information world. For a particular task, a work area must effectively import technical and market information from the outside world; new and established information must be effectively processed within the work area" (p. 93).

Information processing then is central to the work of the lab. The authors' model assumes that uncertainty exists in the work of the lab. In order to lessen uncertainty, subunits must communicate externally. Unfortunately, such communication is difficult "due to contrasting coding and linguistic schemes which evolve as organizations develop specialized work areas. These coding and linguistic differences create a communication impedance which makes communication across organizational boundaries difficult and prone to bias and distortion" (p. 98). The goal of communicators is to overcome bias and distortion and communicate clearly. The process of achieving clarity, however, is only implied in the authors' information processing model.

In its most general form, this model is composed of two halves: on one side, the sources of uncertainty and the information required to overcome this uncertainty and on the other, the information processing capacity of the subunit, which involves the communication roles and structures in place in the subunit. The key to this model is the "fit" between the two sides: "The basic idea is that subunits face varying degrees of uncertainty and that to be successful they must match their information processing capacity to their information processing requirements" (p. 101). The model can be used by assessing the types of information that a project will demand, determining the communication patterns needed to achieve these requirements, and arranging the linkages between those who need information and the sources of information.

While I agree that it is useful to understand the concepts of uncertainty and the sources of uncertainty, the key to the success of any enterprise is tightly located in the word *fit*, the effective communication. How does one know if a fit is achieved? Who decides what meanings make a fit? Fit involves all of the vagaries of communication between and among differing groups and expertise. Thus, this model does not deal with the messy middle of it all: knowing what one needs in an innovative situation, constructing understandings of new information, understanding what others say and why they say it, what they may be holding back, and so on. The information processing approach assumes a rational system in which information is a commodity that can be transferred from a source to a destination.

Information gatekeeping   Given the problems in communicating from group to group within an R&D lab or from the group to outside the lab, Allen (1977) argues that information gatekeepers are particularly important communication roles.

> It is difficult to imagine a system better than that of the gatekeeper network for connecting the organization to its technical environment. Even if one were to attempt to design an optimal system for bringing in new technical information and disseminating it within the organization, it is doubtful that a better one could be produced than that which, in many cases, already exists. New information is brought into the organization through the gatekeeper. It can then be communicated quite readily to other gatekeepers through the gatekeeper network and disseminated outward from one or more points to other members of the organization. (p. 161)

Although this description assumes the transfer view of communication—information is an object that can be simply transferred and understood for what it is—Allen's description of gatekeepers belies this assumption. The gatekeepers are "high performers. They produce more papers for presentation at technical conferences, they are more frequently cited by management as 'key people,' and they receive higher ratings by peers and superiors" (p. 163). I think that it is safe to assume that these people are actually information managers who reconstruct what they learn outside their group and help others in their group to reconstruct that information, as well. Allen says as much when he differentiates between an "information officer" and a gatekeeper:

The information officer and gatekeeper are not identical functions, and they are not competing ones. They are really complementary functions. This is an important point and is one over which there seems to have been some misunderstanding. People have often interpreted the gatekeeper concept to mean that a person becomes intimately knowledgeable with the literature in a specific field and then directs his colleagues to appropriate sources. That, in a sense, is one function of an information officer. The gatekeeper may not be as knowledgeable about the various sources of information, but he does know far more of their content than the information officer does. In other words, while an information officer provides range, the gatekeeper provides depth. Moreover, the gatekeeper normally communicates content rather than direction to a source. He may do both, but his principal contribution comes by way of the translation that he can perform. He converts documentary information or information gained through personal contacts into terms that are both relevant to and understandable by the members of his organization. (p. 166)

On the one hand, Allen describes both the information officer and the gatekeeper roles in nonconstructive terms: the gatekeeper translates content and the officer directs colleagues to sources. But at the same time, Allen describes both as active agents that shape information as they learn it and present it to others by conceiving of the world of information that is appropriate for their colleagues and by selecting and interpreting the "information" that they see in that world.

Informal information   Like Tushman and Nadler, and Allen, Fischer (1980) argues on the basis of much research that technology transfers are based on the cooperation of differing groups and subgroups but that communication between groups is difficult: "There exists communication impedance at an organization boundary which reflects the unique coding schemes acquired by individuals in formal groups and which while facilitating the efficiency of communication internal to a group often impedes communication information sources external to the group" (p. 73).

Within-group communication is facilitated by unique within-group languages and purposes, but this serves to distort across-group communication. The latter can be overcome through effective liaisons between groups. And these liaisons are able to communicate most effectively through informal channels: "Because they are a prompt source of information, which in a sense is pre-digested, and because they allow instantaneous feedback, informal channels are a necessary complement to more formal channels of scientific and technical communication" (p. 73).

Formal communication channels grow obsolete, notes Fischer, so the best communication systems within an R&D operation are the informal ones that develop within the lab and between the lab and other groups (sources of information): "Sharing facilities such as coffee pots, rest rooms, or computer equipment might be an even easier, though more haphazard, approach to increasing intrafirm acquaintanceships" (p. 83). The reason, we must assume, is that it is through relationships that conceptions of knowledge can be shared. It may appear that information is transferred from a source to a destination but that information is "predigested," that is, interpreted and negotiated among participants in communicative activities.

Information interface   In a study of communication and "cross-functional teams" in new-product development, Pinto and Pinto (1990) note that communication is the vehicle "through which personnel from multiple functional areas share information that is so critical to the successful implementation of projects" (p. 201). That is, communication establishes an interface between groups. This vehicle must be managed so that a variety of participants can interact effectively. This work involves "acquiring" and "disseminating" information "in order to serve a number of distinct purposes, all related to improving the interactions among members of the project team and to the ultimate successful implementation of the project" (p. 202). The results of Pinto and Pinto's study show that teams that had a high degree of informal communication cooperated best: "Therefore, it behooves project managers to encourage unplanned or informal interactions among personnel working together on new program development projects" (p. 208). Again, although the authors characterize the research and the models in terms of information transfer, they keep discovering that the groups that interact personally work best. Why? Because they can negotiate the meanings and understandings that they must agree on to cooperate successfully. The interface is the relationship among individuals, not a channel through which information is acquired and disseminated.

Where knowledge resides   McDaniel et al. (1991) present a technology transfer system that prominently involves technical writers and technical documentation in the transfer of technology, an argument that I favor (chapter 4 of this book is dedicated to this argument). Unfortunately, McDaniel and her colleagues couch their system in information transfer terms.

Their argument says that the technical documentation for a new product is as much a part of the product innovation as any hardware or software components. The reason is that the thing being transferred is not just a physical product; it is also knowledge. Often the physical products are transferred, they note, but the knowledge is not: "The physical system is the apparent deliverable in technology-transfer projects; too often, it is all that participants receive. What is wanted by technology-transfer participants and is critical to pass on to them is the knowledge used to build and support these systems. This knowledge best resides in well-written, illustrated, and complete documentation" (p. 83). Well-written and -illustrated documents play an important role in the development and use of a technological innovation but the knowledge does not reside in the texts. The knowledge is not something existing outside the participants in the transfer, whether they are innovators, managers, marketers, or users. The knowledge is what the participants construct and agree upon.

Despite the information transfer arguments that some researchers and theorists may make, evidence in their work undercuts the approach that they claim. Throughout the literature, this double message is communicated. The following group of studies I examine present more complex views of communication in technology transfers, but these, too, are somewhat conflicted. Although they emphasize rhetorical approaches, in some ways they are still presenting communication technology transfers as information transfer.

More Complex Views

Improving relations   Ginn and Rubenstein (1986) investigated the working relationship between R&D and production in three strategic business units of a major chemical company: "In this interface region, there are multiple, dynamic interactions occurring among individuals and groups representing R&D, the pilot plant, manufacturing, marketing, and top management. . . . The degree of success or failure in advancing products through this interface has a direct bearing on the growth and productivity of manufacturing firms" (p. 158). Although the authors speak in terms of reducing uncertainty and transferring knowledge through an interface, they present a real-world picture that assumes a complex view of communication.

The researchers found that complex technology transfers generate high degrees of conflict, uncertainty, and exercises of power among collaborators: "The paradox is that, in the 'real world' of technological innovation, the more successful projects may have more uncertainty, conflict, and power associated with them than do less successful projects. . . . Thus we can anticipate and understand high levels of stress and dysfunctional conflict in 'real world' innovation projects which become technically and commercially successful" (p. 168). That is, successful projects face stiff barriers that need to be overcome.

Typically these types of barriers are bridged by people taking on linking roles (gatekeepers and boundary spanners). However, this may not be the most effective way to diminish the barriers between groups: "Establishment of linking or integrating roles does not appear to be as effective in moderating the conflict as one might predict. Integrators are hampered because of the fundamental differences in goal orientation which exist between R&D and Production. It is, therefore, recommended that efforts to improve interface relations should focus on organizational improvements to effectively reduce this fundamental barrier of goal incompatibility. This might be accomplished by bringing Manufacturing in earlier during the innovation process and by emphasizing participative decision making in goal setting and implementation" (p. 169).

What Ginn and Rubenstein discovered is that links between groups that hold fundamentally different ways of seeing the project may not be able to resolve differences. Passing information back and forth between groups or individuals with differing worldviews may do little to bring those two entities together. What must be done is to take steps—improve interface relations"—to meld worldviews among differing groups and individuals. (Issues such as these will be illustrated in each of the chapters of this book.)

Reconciling worldviews   A scheme that classifies different types of intergroup barriers has been developed by Souder (1988). In particular, Souder studied the misunderstandings and conflicts between R&D and marketing groups, which represent significant impediments to successful collaboration on new product ventures. Underlying this study is a complex, rhetorical approach to communication between groups.

Souder classified the characteristics of "states of harmony" or "disharmony" among collaborating groups. Disharmony can be mild or severe. Mild states of disharmony, according to Souder, have the following characteristics:

1. Lack of Interaction: In this state of affairs, there were very few formal and informal meetings between the R&D and marketing personnel. Both parties were deeply concerned with their own narrow specialties and neither saw any reason to learn more about the other's work. (p. 9)

2. Lack of Communication: In this state, the two parties purposely maintained verbal, attitudinal, and physical distances from each other. R&D purposely did not inform marketing about their new technologies until very late in the development cycle. Marketing purposely did not keep R&D informed about market needs. (p. 9)

3. Too Good Friends: In this state of affairs, the R&D and marketing personnel were too friendly and maintained too high a regard for each other. (9) [As a result of strong social connections, neither group thought it appropriate to interfere with the other's work.]

Severe states of disharmony have the following characteristics:

1. Lack of Appreciation: This state was characterized by strong feelings that the other party was relatively useless. Marketing felt that R&D was too sophisticated, while R&D felt that marketing was too simplistic. (p. 10)

2. Distrust: Distrust is the extreme case of deep-seated jealousies, negative attitudes, fears and hostile behaviors. In this state of affairs, marketing felt that R&D could not be trusted to follow instructions. R&D felt they were blamed for failures, but marketing was credited for successes. (p. 11)

Harmony was characterized by two types of relationships: dominant, characteristic of enterprises that did not develop complex technologies or respond to exacting customer demands, and equal, in which both parties saw themselves as sharing in the endeavors of both groups. All issues were open for both groups, and consensus was sought by both groups on issues.

Just as important was evidence that the participants in the equal partner cases had some basis of sharing worldviews: "Three features were common to all the Equal Partner cases. One, the marketing personnel were technically trained. They all had undergraduate degrees in science or engineering. Two, the marketing personnel had prior careers in R&D. Thus, personnel were often successfully exchanged or rotated between the R&D and marketing functions. Three, the R&D and marketing personnel had a strong sense of joint partnership" (p. 11). Note that the third feature is not a characteristic but a result of the shared view engendered by the first two features.

As a result of these findings, Souder makes recommendations that encourage open, collaborative work among participants in both groups—for example, "Managers should use teams of R&D and marketing employees at every opportunity [to] help avoid the natural impression that R&D and marketing are two separate organizational entities and cultures" (p. 18). Furthermore, it is clear that communication based on transferring information is not enough to overcome communication problems: "It appears that the institutionalized roles between R&D and marketing must be radically changed before new product development success rates can significantly increase. The only effective means to permanently avoid disharmonies is for the R&D and marketing parties to fully understand and appreciate their reciprocal roles, and to play out these roles in a true team setting. Moreover, it is essential that the R&D and marketing parties establish a team relationship that permits them to flexibly swap roles in response to evolving technologies, markets and customer needs" (p. 19).

The key is relationships geared toward reconciling worldviews. Passing information back and forth does not necessarily alter the meaning-generating systems that individuals bring to that information. Unfortunately, notes Souder, conflicts between R&D and marketing "continue to be surprisingly prevalent, chronic and disruptive to successful new product development. These findings are discouraging, in view of the obvious importance of the topic and an emerging awareness of it" (p. 19). Maybe if participants in such ventures became aware of the rhetorical demands of their work, more ventures would not be so afflicted with disharmony.

Souder's recommendations are implicitly based on an approach that recognizes the constructive nature of communication. But in a later article, he poses a model of the communication relationship between R&D and marketing that seems to be based on the information transfer approach to communication. Why? It may be that in the process of developing a model of the relationship, the focus moves away from the crux of communication—how individuals create the world through language and then attempt to communicate in terms of that world—and moves to patterns of communication activities within and across groups or subunits. (Recall Bradbury's statement that technology transfers are too dynamic to be modeled; it is more useful to view the phenomena through case studies.) Regardless, Moenaert and Souder (1990) propose a theoretical model and a set of testable propositions that attempt to answer two questions: "What role does information transfer play in integrating R&D and marketing functions, and what are the factors that induce and inhibit effective information exchange?"

The authors begin by noting that in technology transfers R&D groups and marketing groups must collaborate in order to develop successful new products: Furthermore, both groups are continually involved in information acquisition and processing in order to reduce uncertainty: "Activities like market research, business analysis, prototype development and prototype trials generate information necessary for the reduction of uncertainty. These activities are also roles that individuals or groups must perform in order to maximize information acquisition and processing. . . . We expect that the more the organization has reduced uncertainty, that is, the more the organization has closed the gap between the required and the possessed information, the better will be its decision making and implementation" (pp. 93–94).

During the development process, marketing personnel acquire information about such key issues as the prospective users and the competition, and those in R&D acquire, process, disseminate, and apply information about such key issues as technologies and applications. Through all of this information development, both groups will need to exchange information with each other. But, as we have seen, communication between differing groups is problematic: "The membership status of the individual in a particular subsystem has a bearing on his/her information processing and communication. Every subsystem develops its own 'technical' language that directs its perceptual exploration. These technical languages, which tend to increase the efficiency of intradepartmental communication, are responsible for the decrease of efficiency in interdepartmental communication" (p. 97). In order to break down the discursive walls that separate groups, the authors recommend an increasing amount of high-quality information exchange between groups. This exchange is described in the following seven propositions (followed by my interpretation of each) that together compose their model of information transfer.

Proposition 1: (a) The proficiency by which marketing (R&D) activities are executed (b) and, consequently, the uncertainty reduced by marketing (R&D) personnel, will be positively related to the amount and quality of information the marketing (R&D) personnel have received from R&D (marketing) personnel during the project's life-cycle. (p. 99)

The more that one group finds appropriate information for the other group, the better the other group will do its job.

Proposition 2: (a) The higher the mutual understanding by marketing and R&D personnel of each other's role, the higher the convergence of the uncertainty reduction by each of the subgroups. (b) This mutual understanding is positively related to the amount and quality of the information exchanged between marketing and R&D personnel during the project's life-cycle. (p. 99)

The more members of each group share worldviews, the more effectively they will communicate appropriately.

Proposition 3: The transfer of information from marketing to R&D is a positive function of (a) the quality of marketing resources, of (b) the uncertainty reduced by marketing and of (c) the quality and quantity of information provided by R&D. The same relations hold for the transfer of information from R&D to marketing. (p. 100)

If each group develops a lot of clear information that addresses the problems at hand, communication between groups will be more efficient.

Proposition 4: The transfer of information from marketing to R&D is negatively related to the level and amount of marketing and R&D resources applied. The same relations hold for the transfer of information from R&D to marketing. (p. 100)

If too many people from one group are producing information for too few people in the other group, communication may not be effective.

Proposition 5: The transfer of information from marketing to R&D will be maximized at some intermediate level of out-of-role behavior by marketing. The same relation holds for information transfers from R&D to marketing. (p. 101)

If some members of each group attempt to learn about the concerns of the other group, communication will be improved.

Proposition 6: The higher (a) the degree of task specification, and/or the more (b) self-contained the project structure and/or the more (c) harmonious the climate between marketing and R&D personnel, the higher the quantity and the quality of the information exchanged between marketing and R&D. (p. 101)

With a clear task, known colleagues, and good interpersonal working relationships, communication will be more effective.

Proposition 7: The allocation of human resources having an R&D education or experience to the marketing function will increase the information flows between the marketing and R&D functions. (p. 102)

If individuals share worldviews, communication will be more efficient.

The problem is not that the authors fail to understand the difficulties that exist between R&D and marketing; it is that their model either simplifies the keys to communication, by positing that passing on information is communication, or assumes the keys to communication, by stating that differing groups that share conceptions of tasks, roles, and meanings will communicate effectively. How do the differing individuals reach that stage? Not through simple information transfer. Models like this one build a highly complex view of the innerworkings of industry on a rather flimsy theory of communication.

Locating meaning in the minds of the participants   The most promising view of the nature of communication in technology transfers has been offered by Williams and Gibson (1990). After briefly reviewing previous attempts at modeling technology transfers that have dominated different eras, the authors pose what they call the "communication model":

First, successful technology transfer is an ongoing interactive process where individuals exchange ideas simultaneously and continuously. Feedback is so pervasive that the participants in the transfer process can be viewed as "transceivers," thereby blurring the distinction between the source(s) and destination(s).

The technology to be transferred often is not a fully formed idea and has no definitive meaning or value; meaning is in the minds of the participants. Researchers, developers, or users are likely to have different perceptions about the technology, which affects how they interpret the information. As a result, technology transfer is often a chaotic, disorderly process involving groups and individuals who may hold different views about the value and potential use of the technology. (p. 16)

This conception of the phenomenon is clearly based on a rhetorical, constructivist view of communication; however, a subsequent article by Gibson and Smilor (1991) still appears to validate limited views of communication in some key ways. For example, the authors separated acts of

communication from issues of cultural differences, complexity of technology, and the motivation of participants by positing four variables that
affect transfers: communication, distance, equivocality, and motivation.
The variable of distance includes not only physical distance but cultural
distances: "Cultural differences between the [technology transfer] con-
sortium and and shareholders loom as a more important dimension of
distance than geographical separation. . . . Each shareholder brings his or
her own values, attitudes, priorities, and ways of doing things to the con-
sortium" (p. 46). Motivation involves the shareholders' incentives in a
technology transfer enterprise. Equivocality involves the complexity of
the technology in the enterprise: "Highly equivocal technology is harder
to understand, more difficult to demonstrate and more ambiguous in its
potential applications" (p. 46).

Most important, the authors pose a two-tiered classification of communication: active communication links, involving interpersonal interactions among participants, and passive links, involving "research reports,
journal articles, computer tapes, and video tapes. Such media-based linkages are considered best for rapidly communicating the same message at
the same time to a widely dispersed audience" (p. 45). Thus, the authors
are assuming that reading texts, whether in printed form or other media,
is not a constructive activity but merely a reception of the same message
that everyone else who reads the same text will get.

The authors can attach an information transfer meaning to communication because they have separated facets of the rhetorical nature of technology transfer from communication. That is, issues of perceived
complexity, cultural and motivational differences, and mental constructions of texts are all rhetorical issues and should be considered as part of
one dimension, a dimension that they could call communication if they
wish. But by separating something called communication from those other factors, they return to the old concept of information transfer.

Rhetoric in Science and Technology

A growing body of research focuses on discursive practices and products
(e.g., writing processes and written texts) in organizations, institutions,
and disciplines; these studies are exploring the rhetorical nature of these

enterprises. Certainly there is a significant nondiscursive reality in these environments, but that reality is mediated through language use; it is mediated through rhetorical processes. The following studies illustrate the power of practical rhetoric in a variety of scientific and technical settings.

Producing Science

In Myers' (1990) study of biologists and the texts they produce, he is examining writing not merely as a process of reporting biological research but as a process of constructing scientific facts. Myers notes that the title of his study is *Writing Biology*, not *Writing about Biology* "because that would imply that biology is there before the writing and that the writing merely dresses it up" (p. xii). Instead, argues Myers, it is writing that produces biology. Such a process involves "getting others to see a phenomenon of animal behavior, making a claim about this phenomenon, negotiating the place and value of this claim in the structure of scientific knowledge, and determining the place of the authors in the scientific community." The purpose of his study is to provide analyses of scientific texts and their social contexts that illustrate "how texts produce scientific knowledge and reproduce the cultural authority of that knowledge" (p. ix).

In rejecting the idea that scientific texts are merely channels for information transfer, Myers argues that these texts are "structures for thinking and for social interaction" (p. x). Scientific discourse, says Myers, builds consensus in scientific communities. "It turns tensions, challenges, and even bitter controversies into sources of strength and continuity. Scientific texts help create the selectivity, communality, and cumulativeness that both scientists and nonscientists attribute to scientific thought" (p. x). The boundaries of scientific communities are drawn and redrawn through scientists' discursive activities.

Defining Disciplinary Boundaries

A text that has established the boundaries of a discipline is the focus of a study by McCarthy (1991). She studied the diagnostic processes and written texts of one child psychiatrist, Dr. Page, in order to explore the influences of a "charter document," the American Psychiatric Association's (APA) third edition of the *Diagnostic and Statistical Manual of Mental*

Disorders, commonly known as DSM-III. As a charter document, the manual shapes the collective knowledge of the discipline, and influences the actions of its members: "First, this manual shapes Dr. Page's understanding of what counts as relevant information about her patients and thus controls her gathering of data. Second, its diagnostic principles control her analysis of that information. In its role as a charter document, the DSM-III manual of mental disorders is closely linked to what Dr. Page knows about mental illness and how she writes about it" (p. 375).

McCarthy notes that experts in the profession recognized a need for such a document before it was produced. In response to a concern about the lack of diagnostic reliability, DSM-III was developed in the 1970s by an APA task force. Before the development of the text, there were no standardized definitions of mental disorders, so one disorder could have quite different meanings to different diagnosticians. It is in establishing a framework for interpretation that the book becomes a charter document:

The metaphor of a charter document has proven useful in looking at the meaning of DSM-III for Dr. Page. The charter document of a social or political group establishes an organizing framework that specifies what is significant and draws people's attention to certain rules and relationships. In other words, the charter defines as authoritative certain ways of seeing and deflects attention from other ways. It thus stabilizes a particular reality and sets the terms for future discussions. DSM-III is a charter document in psychiatry, and the particular reality that it stabilizes is the biomedical conceptual model of mental illness. (p. 359)

Thus, the charter document stabilizes the actions of the members of the discipline and the ways that they think about issues in the discipline.

A text that limited thinking in a multidisciplinary and multidimensional environment is the focus of a study by Karis (1989), who examined the process of producing a remedial action plan (RAP)—a document that would define the environmental pollution in a designated area and methods of remediating that area. In his study, Karis analyzed the way that prescribed discursive practices in environmental analysis procedures imposed a structure on the writing process. In this case, the practices were prescribed through a government document that listed types of "impaired beneficial uses" of water. This prescribed structure determined what was valid knowledge in this realm. If a writer did not conform to this structure (Karis borrows the term *schemata* from Michel Foucault), regardless of the local conditions, whatever the writer produced would be suspect. "To not conform to this schemata would run the risk of invalidating the chapter's conclusions" (p. 10).

Karis compares the imposition of the impaired uses document to McCarthy's analysis of the charter document in psychiatry. Both, he argues, shape what counts for knowledge: "In the same way that McCarthy's charter document can be said to have controlled her psychiatrist's discourse, so too has this list constrained the discourse of the RAP. In particular, it constrains it to the extent that it doesn't allow a fuller range of human concerns, e.g., religious or spiritual values, to become objects of discourse." The latter examples came into play when the RAP writing process involved local Native American cultures that were affected by both the pollution and the proposed remediation processes.

In both McCarthy's and Karis's work, science is constrained by charter documents. In the former, that constraint gives shape to a discipline; in the latter, it attempts to delineate the limits of scientific issues in the study of water quality and pollution.

Socializing Individuals into Groups

In their study of writing in an R&D division of Exxon ITD, Paradis, Dobrin, and Miller (1985) note that writing in that environment was commonly viewed as "a pragmatic routine of transferring and archiving information" (p. 281). But neither the managers nor the R&D employees could see how the writing that they did so frequently on the job played the significant role that it did in the organization:

At ITD, the personal or social functions of writing were virtually unrecognized. Yet personal interviews made it clear that individuals often wrote for reasons that had nothing whatever to do with passing along technical information. Several individuals told us, for example, that their writing forced them to stay abreast of other developments, in order to coordinate their work with that of other employees. Conversely, the writing in any given week constituted an important updating process by which work completed was now made available to the community. Hence, the activity of writing demanded that its practitioners develop a kind of social consciousness of the organizational environment. In addition, writing made individuals take the measure of their own fit in the R&D organization, because it made them evaluate their work, their attitudes, and their relationships with colleagues. One's documents also kept one's profile up among colleagues, giving writers the opportunity to show their accomplishments to their colleagues. (p. 293)

Writing served both managers and engineers as a way to archive and communicate but also as "a means of self-analysis and self-projection" (p. 293). It thus becomes part of the process of developing an organizational identity; it becomes part of the process of group membership. This phenomenon is both a source of strength and a weakness in organizations, as the following study of communication failures indicates.

Herndl, Fennel, and Miller (1991) examined the role of communication failures between intraorganizational groups in a study of the Three Mile Island nuclear reactor accident and the explosion of the shuttle *Challenger*. The authors note that both events involved communication failures among professionals during the routine performances of their jobs. In the study, the failures were examined in terms of the differing communication practices among differing groups within the organizations: "The notion that subgroups within an organization may be differentiated not only by their work relationships but also by the way they use language suggests a possible reason for miscommunication within such an organization. Communication failures may be caused, at least in part, by the differentiation of discourse along the lines of social structure" (p. 280).

The authors find that two types of communication failures can be attributed to the differentiation of discourse along subgroup lines: miscommunication "due to the lack of a common language or to faulty communication procedures within an organization," and misunderstanding, which "is detected through substantive analysis of what people say or write and what they must share to interpret discourse as it was intended. Put simply, miscommunication revolves around the how of communication, while misunderstanding revolves around the what" (p. 303).

Issues of miscommunication and misunderstanding also involve the failures of texts to mediate technology to users. The following study of legal liability and instructional manuals explores this function of written texts.

Mediating Technology and Users
The rhetorical nature of operator's manuals for a stud gun, a specialized construction tool, is the subject of a study by Paradis (1991). This tool, used to fire nails and other fastening devices into different types of materials, is based on an old firearms technology adapted to a new environ-

ment. The occasions for the analysis were two product liability cases that involved this technology: "In effect, the inquiry sought to determine, in the context of tort law and legal liability, the rhetorical role of operator's manuals in the social construction of a technology. This question ultimately touched on the role of written discourse in constructing a world of 'reasonable' actions that could resolve the polarities inherent in almost any technology between mechanical function and social purpose" (p. 257–258).

Operators' manuals serve to mediate between the world of technological expertise in research and development and the novice users in the marketplace. The difficulty lies in the increasing complexity of technology for an increasingly larger market composed of more and more novice or naive users. As technologies become more complex, the rhetorical effort that is necessary to adapt that complexity to the market becomes increasingly demanding: "The technical object must be rescued from the control of the specialist and related to the broad social environment. . . . This question is a significant one for all individuals involved in the processes of production—the designers, the producers, and the writers. In the operator's manual, we shift from the initial design and manufacturing orientation toward objects to a new orientation toward human thought and behavior" (p. 276). It is a rhetorical process through which technology is manifested in the world. Such is the focus of the case studies in this book.

The Worth of a Rhetorical Examination of Technology Transfers

In the conclusion to his study of the rhetoric of science, Charles Bazerman (1988) compares the relative worth of math and rhetoric to the work of scientists. He notes that scientists in different disciplines, specialties, and subspecialties use differing facets and complexities of mathematics. He also notes some of the differing facets of rhetoric that are involved in the work of scientists. Some scientific fields, notes Bazerman, are highly restricted, slowly developing, and comprise adequate rhetorical practices: "A thorough practical command within the regularized domain may need to be supplemented only by an analysis of the implications and a cursory knowledge of basic rhetorical concepts. Then, if the rhetorical problems heat up, the individual scientist can at least recognize the problem and know where to begin looking for answers" (p. 331). But in more volatile, interdisciplinary fields, ones in which the participants work in rapidly evolving theoretical environments, the participants may need a better understanding of the rhetorical nature of events. Participants may require far greater understanding of complex argumentation and a far greater ability to analyze the rhetorical dynamics of the field.

The problem with this projection of rhetorical necessities and its comparison to math requirements, says Bazerman, is that the necessity of mathematics is explicitly accepted as a matter of course, but the role of rhetoric is largely unknown: "Scientists, however, are unlikely to recognize difficulties in framing successful investigations and claims as rhetorical, unlikely even to be aware of rhetoric as a relevant field. Even if they are aware that their claim making can be fruitfully conceived in rhetorical terms, they may have little idea of what the relevant branches of rhetoric are, what books to read, or whom to talk to. Finally, even if they find a willing rhetorician to talk to, very few of those rhetoricians have had any experience in talking to scientists and applying rhetorical knowledge to problems of scientific communication" (p. 332).

Therein lies my vantage point with this book: the rhetorician/outsider attempting to understand and talk about the rhetorical nature of a technological-commercial enterprise. The subject is a worthy one because, like the volatile fields that Bazerman describes, the varied, sometimes murky, and frustrating thing commonly called technology transfer is a locus of sophisticated rhetorical activity. Those who will participate in or study technology transfers, the commercialization of innovations, the dissemination or diffusion of ideas from labs to markets should come to some understanding of the rhetorical processes that are ever-present in these enterprises.

2

From Investment to Production: The Role of Two Business Plans in a New High-Tech Venture

In January 1982, the United States was deep into a recession, but a small group of what the popular press commonly calls whiz kids were starting an enterprise in the same spirit as the legendary start-ups that fueled Silicon Valley and the Massachusetts Miracle. They were graduate and undergraduate students from a highly respected northeastern university, and they were going to exploit the pending microcomputer revolution, creating a dynamic, high-tech company out of a class project. They were going to be another example of the golden connection between the innovative technologies they were studying in the university and the lucrative potential of the marketplace. They were all going to get rich.

This chapter tells their story and in doing so explores how the process of developing a technology and a business to exploit that technology was a rhetorical enterprise. Most people who study technology transfers focus on business, legal, technological, and managerial issues; few have considered the process from a rhetorical perspective. This chapter, by taking on this perspective, will provide some insight into the processes of entrepreneurial leadership, the creation of innovative start-up companies, and the so-called transference of expertise from the university to the marketplace.

The 80s, Computers, Entrepreneurs, and the American Dream

Reducing decades to cultural clichés seems to be a quick and dirty way to make sense of common experiences, and we are already seeing the recently departed 80s characterized as the decade of yuppie greed. While many of those who did get rich in the 80s did so on Wall Street, some made their fortunes by developing new, innovative, computer-based technologies. Indeed, if we split what we commonly think of as the 80s (which actually ended psychologically in October 1987 with the stock market crash, just like the 60s did not really end until the early 70s with Watergate and the first oil embargo) into an early and late period, we might come up with two different icons for the decade. The icon in 1986 would be the young Wall Street wizards or corporate raiders making obscene amounts of money with junk bonds and leveraged buyouts. The icon in 1983, however, might be any one of a number of computer entrepreneurs, such as Steve Jobs of Apple, Bill Gates of Microsoft, or Mitch Kapor of Lotus. *Time* magazine named the computer Man of the Year in 1983. By 1984 mass market books were already telling the stories of the computer and electronics revolution; Kidder's *Soul of a New Machine* was published in 1981, followed in 1984: *Fire in the Valley* by Frieberger and Swaine, *The Computer Entrepreneurs* by Levering, Katz, and Moskowitz, and *Silicon Valley Fever* by Rogers and Larson.

The most visible component of this quickly romanticized boom in technology was the microcomputer because it was the first type of computer that could capture mass market sales. That became evident with the early success of Apple Corporation, and it seemed ensured when IBM began selling lots of personal computers in 1982. At that time, the market appeared to be wide open, as the following examples show:

• An October 25, 1982, article in *Business Week* entitled, "A Business that Defies Recession" stated "Unemployment may have hit more than 10 percent of the work force and the auto and housing industries may be facing the worst recession since World War II. But manufacturers of microcomputers costing anywhere from $200 to $10,000 are having what could only be described as a romp" (p. 30).

• An earlier article in *Business Week* (August 2, 1982) "The Incredible Explosion of Startups," compared the microcomputer boom to the minicomputer boom of the 1970s: "Startup fever is sweeping the information processing industry for the second time in 15 years. As a result the minicomputer establishment that sprang up in the early 1970's is coming under competitive fire from a battery of newcomers. Lured by a ready supply of venture capital and new, more cost-effective technology, those entrepreneurs are now offering low-cost computers that can more economically do the jobs once handled by the pricier models from the minicomputer producers" (p. 53).

• In their book *High Tech Ventures* (1991), Bell and McNamara discuss the success of Autodesk corporation, which began with a proposal by

John Walker in January 1982. Citing Walker's own account of the company's beginnings (Walker 1987), the authors note the timing of his venture: "Autodesk was funded ($59,030) by its founders, a group of talented programmers who built applications programs and marketed them through retail dealers whom they knew. The company vision was that a PC revolution would occur and that this group would simply capitalize on it. . . . When Autodesk went public in June 1985, each $1 initially invested was worth $165, and in mid-1990, the firm's value was over $1 billion" (p. 43).

In America, the legend goes, a person with a dollar, an idea, some talent, and fortuitous timing can make it big. Those who made it in the early 1980s became the heroes of the microcomputer boom.

These heroes were the young, computer industry entrepreneurs. They seized upon new technologies and new applications and not only made money but also changed the world in a variety of ways. What made this whole computer boom scenario so appealing to technologists and, most important, to investors, was (get ready for a barrage of American Dream clichés) the ground-floor, grass-roots, rags-to-riches potential of the technology. A lot of people with money to invest thought that if Jobs and Wozniak could do it in their garage, maybe some other kid with ingenuity and an electrical engineering degree could make the next leap into the pantheon of successful electronic entrepreneurs.

The success of many of these start-ups was seemingly based on what Robert Reich (1987) calls the "myth of the entrepreneurial hero," but, in truth, most of these businesses were the results of the collective effort of teams. The problem, argues Reich, is that there is a clear disparity between the popular image and the reality. Certainly the image of the entrepreneur is that of the lone, ambitious, charismatic visionary who leads a new company to become established and profitable and then leaves or is forced out whenever steady-state management must take over. The literature on entrepreneurship is full of such descriptions. For example, in an analysis of entrepreneurial leadership in established corporations (when an innovative enterprise is carried out within a company as opposed to within a start-up), Knight (1987) characterizes the corporate entrepreneurs, who must be working with others before, during, and after the enterprise is launched, as lone product champions: "(1) He/she is ideally chosen by self-selection. He should choose himself, rather than being delegated. (2) There are no hand-offs. He runs with the idea all the way, but with support from team members. (3) The doer decides. He has the final say and does it his way" (p. 289). Reich likens characterizations like these to a long history of mythic characters that American culture has revered. But, he argues, we can no longer afford such hero worship: "To the extent that we continue to celebrate the traditional myth of the entrepreneurial hero, we will slow the progress of change and adaptation that is essential to our ecomonic success. If we are to compete effectively in today's world, we must begin to celebrate collective entrepreneurship, endeavors in which the whole of the effort is greater than the sum of individual contributions. We need to honor our teams more, our aggressive leaders and maverick geniuses less."

Do businesses grow on the strengths of individuals of entrepreneurial ambition or on the strengths of team entrepreneurship (Stewart, 1989)? This conflict between individual and team leadership is central to the case study presented in this chapter. The company that I studied was led by a powerful, charismatic leader, but that leader worked within an entire support system, both internally with the other founders and executives of the company, and externally, with a university program geared to launching start-up companies. These types of programs are commonly referred to as business incubators, and they, too, enjoyed a boom in the 1980s.

Universities, Start-ups, and Incubators

The spawning grounds for many of these start-ups were a number of American universities that took steps to transfer to the private sector the technologies being studied and developed on campus. These universities created incubator centers and technology parks—places where the whiz kids and faculty could build commercial ventures and where organized programs could attract and funnel venture capital to the technological talent coming out of the universities. In step with the economic atmosphere of the times, many university administrators and venture capitalists of the early 1980s saw the university-as-incubator as a major boon to local economies. In a study of selected programs, Hisrich and Smilor (1988) analyzed the ingredients of successful university incubator programs: "In the university, successful technology transfer through entrepreneurial development results from effectively linking academic resources with technology-based entrepreneurs. For this to occur, four critical components—talented people, ideas, capital resources, and know how—must be brought together" (p. 15). Furthermore, the authors explain, incubators can help start-up companies in four key ways:

1. Credibility: By being associated with a known and respected institution through the institution's incubator program, a start-up gains a measure of credibility with potential investors, distributors, and/or customers.

2. Shortened learning curve: "If a high-technology company in an incubator is to grow and eventually be on its own, its entrepreneurial leader needs to learn how to run a young, developing organization. The learning process must extend his or her business skills—planning, management, marketing, accounting—which gain importance as the company develops. Through entrepreneurial education, the management of tenant companies can tap the know-how of more knowledgeable university faculty and more experienced business people" (p. 16).

3. Faster problem-solving: Because start-ups do not have much time to succeed or fail, they must solve problems quickly. Incubator programs can offer problem-solving expertise through the university and other sources of expertise that the program develops.

4. Access to entrepreneurial network: Start-ups must become a part of the web of social-business contacts that can lead to investment and other types of external resources needed to succeed. Incubator programs can be designed to help new companies enter into that type of network quickly.

Although a number of companies became quite successful through this process, the dreams of quick and widespread success of university incubators have not been realized. In the 1990s we are beginning to see headlines like the following from the *Chronicle of Higher Education*: "Wariness Dampens 1980's Craze for Building University-Sponsored Technology Parks" and "Pitfalls of Research Parks Lead Universities and States to Reassess Their Expectations" (Grassmuck 1990, Blumenstyk 1990). Headlines like these can be supported by recent research as well. Udell (1990), for example, reviews a number of empirical studies of business incubators and raises doubts about incubators' performances in stimulating the rate of new business formation, increasing the survival rate of new businesses, producing jobs for the locally unemployed, and enhancing the rate of industrial innovation (pp. 118–120). (Scherer and

McDonald 1988 provide another example of an analysis of the problems that afflict small start-ups in incubator programs.)

Even with a new and exciting market like the microcomputer market and even with the help of large institutions that attempt to bridge the gap between academically researched technologies and the marketplace, many companies that began with high hopes in the early 1980s did not succeed, nor have their incubating mothers done as well as expected. New companies can succeed or fail for many, many reasons; this chapter explores how several documents played a role in the rise and decline of a start-up. The documents that I will investigate were two business plans. These types of texts represent the genesis of new companies, especially ones involved in high-tech, incubator-sponsored programs.

Business Plans

Business plans are written primarily as a vehicle to raise investment in a potential business. Although a number of books have described how to write business plans (Williams and Manzo 1983; Brooks and Stevens 1987), Bell and McNamara argue that there are no absolute rules governing the contents of a business plan. Even so, they say all plans should contain the following sections: summary, market, product, people, and financial projections. And because the primary function of the plans is to attract money, their primary audiences are venture capitalists, the potential investors. This major function of business plans, notes Roberts (1991), is well known but little studied: "Formal business plans have taken on so large a role in financing that they deserve more explicit assessment. . . . Many 'how to' books have been written on the subject and most university entrepreneurship courses . . . are dominated by their preparation and evaluation. The business plan constitutes the entrepreneur's main line of attack on (or defense against?) the venture capitalist. Yet little objective analysis has been done on their contents or impact on investor decision making" (p. 16). Roberts goes on to analyze the failings of unfunded business plans by pointing out how many of them do not provide realistic projections of costs and projected earnings, enough analysis of the marketing issues or other subjects of fundamental importance. For example, "In only 30 percent of the cases had the companies developed a detailed sales (not marketing) plan, explaining who would sell the product, how they would be paid, and so on. Twenty percent of the plans implied a broad sales strategy but gave no details. Half of the cases contained no sales plan" (p. 17).

Yet capital raising may not be the only function of business plans. As the case study in this chapter will show, the rhetorical situations for business plans may be far more complex than merely an appeal to investors for money. Business plans may serve a number of functions. For example, Bell and McNamara argue that "the business plan serves many critical purposes. It is: a set of guidelines for operating the company, the standard of record against which the firm expects its results to be measured, a sales brochure directed at potential investors (although the downside and the risks the company faces must also be covered), [and] a place where the founders can describe their vision for the firm" (p. 35). The last point, say Bell and McNamara, is most significant: "The company's vision of its future is the most important part of the business plan. Without a dream, the firm is unlikely to excite either itself or potential investors" (p. 36). The case study in this chapter provides a glimpse of a young company with a business plan that expressed an exciting vision that motivated its employees and investors—a vision tied to the promise, in 1982, of a great economic explosion in the emerging microcomputer industry. It was within that atmosphere that the company, Microware, was founded by a group of people who had, like thousands of others, grand entrepreneurial dreams. This case study, however, is an analysis of the downside of those entrepreneurial dreams. But it is far more than that.

While many experts in the fields of technology transfer and university-industry collaboration are concerned with the contents of business plans—Does plan X contain all of the appropriate information? Does it present a compelling vision of the future of the company and its market?—few have looked at the social and organizational impact that the process of writing a plan has on a fledgling organization. Nor have many considered how the document plays a role in shaping reality for the participants in a start-up enterprise. The elements of these processes have as much to do with the success or failure of a new company as any balance sheet projection or technological breakthrough.

A Rhetorical Analysis

In the most general terms, my case study of Microware is an analysis of the constructive nature of texts. It explores how writing processes influenced the process of organizing a company. It is an analysis of the relationship of collaborative writing to the tensions between individual and team approaches to work, the kinds of problems that faulty texts can have on fledgling enterprises, and one aspect of the rhetorical nature of technology transfer. As such it is part of a small but growing body of work that focuses on the writing as social action (Odell 1985; Paradis, Dobrin, and Miller 1985; Debs 1986; Cross 1988; Spilka 1988; Kleimann 1989; Lutz 1989; Winsor 1990a; Herndl, Fennel, and Miller 1991; McCarthy 1991; Paradis 1991), a concept defined by Bazerman and Paradis (1991) in the following way: "Writing is more than socially embedded: it is socially constructive. Writing structures our relations with others and organizes our perceptions of the world. By studying texts within their contexts, we study as well the dynamics of context building. In particular, by understanding texts within the professions, we understand how the professions constitute themselves and carry out their work through texts" (p. 3).

This chapter explores how Microware's two business plans were socially embedded—influenced by the context within which they were written—but it also explores how those plans were constructive. Thus, it portrays a reciprocal relationship between writing and the organization: writing both reflects and shapes the social/organizational context.

The case study is the result of approximately one year's on-site observations and interviews. As a participant-observer, I spent one to eight hours a day, three to five days a week, at the company offices. I observed and tape-recorded meetings, took field notes on informal conversations and observations, and tape-recorded informal and formal interviews—both open-ended interviews focusing on a particular topic and discourse-based interviews (Odell et al 1983) focusing on particular passages of written texts. (For a fuller description of these methods, see Doheny-Farina and Odell 1985 and Doheny-Farina 1986.) All names are pseudonyms.

Case Study

Microware, Inc.

Creating a Business Plan/Creating a Start-up

In the fall of 1983, after less than two years as a corporation, Microware, Inc., was on the verge of bankruptcy. On October 13, the company's executives met to collaborate on the writing of a crucial document, a new business plan which they would send to potential investors with the hope of persuading them to invest at least $750,000 in the company. An analysis of that meeting will serve as the culmination of my analysis of the reciprocal relationship of writing to social action. To explore this relationship, this chapter will ultimately focus on two of the many rhetorical choices that the collaborators made during the October 13 meeting. These rhetorical choices were important because the debate over them forced the confrontation of two different views of how the company should operate and who should operate it. In short, this debate pitted two different views of reality against each other. More important, the collaborative process enabled these two realities to merge bringing a resolution to the conflict. Ultimately this chapter shows how the executives' collaborative writing process both reflected and shaped social reality.

In order to explain those two choices in at least some of the complexity that they involved, I first explore the events, ideas, arguments, projects, successes, and failures that led up to that climactic meeting. Then I analyze the meeting and its aftermath, concluding with a rhetorical analysis of this entrepreneurial enterprise.

The Start-up

Microware began when IBM entered the personal computer market. Its stated purpose was to produce and sell software for the IBM PC. While most high-tech start-up companies begin with less than $50,000, most of it from the pockets of the founders (Roberts 1991, p. 9), Microware was relatively well supported early on. From 1982 to 1986 it raised approximately $400,000 in investments and loans. While many microcomputer software companies of that time consisted of a few programmers and marketers, Microware, at its peak, employed approximately thirty-five programmers, engineers, managers, marketing specialists, and salespersons. The company became well equipped with a range of advanced microcomputers, peripherals, and printers, all housed in one of two offices, one in the center city area and the other in the office complex of the Northland State University Start-Up Project of which it was a member from 1982 to 1984. In addition, the company had attracted as principal financier and adviser Ted Wilson, a senior partner for one of the Metro region's most successful and respected law firms. By 1984 the company had produced Micromed, a business systems product designed to computerize a range of operations in hospitals. The product received a favorable review in a health care industry trade magazine and garnered approximately $340,000 in sales. Yet in 1986, the year that could be called the height of the 80s boom, the company went bankrupt.

The primary informants in this study were the following executives and key players in the company in 1983:

Bill Alexander, president, one of the original founders and an officer of the company, age 22. Bill's most notable feature was his manner of speaking. He talked fast, laughed easily, and was continually citing information and scenarios to support his point. Although Bill took an active interest in the design of the software, his primary activities were to promote the company, raise capital, and control the company's finances.

Greg Jerling, vice president of software development, a founder and officer, age 22. Greg first conceived the company with Bill and was one of the two people who headed the company's software programming. Specifically, Greg headed the programming of computer games and computer graphics products.

Dave Kruger, vice president of engineering, a founder and officer, age 23. Dave's duties varied the most of anyone in the company. One day he would be in construction work clothes building additions to the physical plant; another day he could be found editing computer documentation, while yet another day he would be taking a prospective investor to lunch.

Bob Hatlin, Ph.D., associate professor of business, member of the board of directors. After serving on the board, he temporarily served Microware as a consultant and as an interim comptroller. Both Bill and Greg had taken a course from him when he was a visiting professor at NSU.

Ted Wilson, lawyer for Microware. Ted's law firm was one of the best known and most highly repected in the Metro region. Besides providing legal services, he served as primary financier and adviser to the company.

Paul Pastore, treasurer, a founder and officer, age 22. Paul shared with Greg control over the company's software development. His primary responsibility was to head the production of the company's major business application software product, Micromed.

Liz Cates, marketing and sales, age 20. Although not a founder, she began working in the company the day it was incorporated, May 25, 1982.

Frank Ramis, vice president of sales, a founder and an officer, age 22. Frank headed the sales effort for Micromed and therefore traveled quite a bit to customers, medical conferences, and software conventions nationwide.

John Rinaldi, programmer for Micromed, a founder, age 22. John was a principal programmer for Micromed.

The Start-up Project as Renaissance

From 1982 until 1984 Microware was one of what became known as the NSU Start-up Project companies. One of the purposes of this project was to help generate small, new companies that could develop commercial applications of the technology being studied and researched at the university. If NSU aided high-tech industrial development, then the Metro region of central New England could develop a stronger, more diverse economy similar to that of California's Silicon Valley or Boston's Route 128 high technology region. Such a vision was held by Microware's lawyer and major outside supporter, Ted Wilson. Ted's vision expressed the lucrative dream of the Start-Up Project: technological incubation can breed financial success. This hope was buoyed by the early performance of one of the first NSU start-up firms, Macro Technologies, which was founded in March 1981.

To a few of the people who would later be instrumental in creating Microware, Macro served as a model of the high-tech dream of financial success and rapid growth. Not only did the company produce and sell a product within its first year, but it also attracted a major venture capital group to invest a large amount of money in the company. By December 1981 the company had received a $1 million venture capital investment.

Yet this success was a double-edged sword for those who saw the Start-up Project as a source of economic rebirth for the region. With Macro, the dream worked too well: the company grew too fast for the Metro region to contain it and in 1982 moved its operations to the Boston area. Nevertheless, an exciting possibility had been established: a firm could actually grow out of its start-up stage and successfully move into the business world.

Ted Wilson was a senior partner in the law firm Wilson, Smith, and Lloyd, which had Macro Technologies as a client. Through his dealings with Macro Technologies, Ted decided that he wanted to become involved with another viable start-up coming out of NSU. Microware became that start-up. During Microware's first two years of existence, Ted was responsible for keeping the company afloat during some difficult times. He played this role because he was taken by the attractive possibility of an economic renaissance for the Metro region through the Start-up Project. He was motivated specifically by Macro's success and the entrepreneurial ambition of Bill Alexander.

On August 31, 1983, in his law office Wilson talked to me about the success of Macro and his dream of a renewed prosperity for his home city:

Macro got themselves positioned . . . to get a million dollar commitment from VenCap, a New York City venture capital group. . . . VenCap insisted on a consultant coming on board, a business advisor. He came from Boston. He was competent, and he served the company well. But he picked up the whole operation when it got going and brought it over to Rte. 128. Now that was a heartbreaker. A young man came in from Dale and Darwin, a Boston law firm, and picked up the file from us one day and the client was gone. It wasn't so much the loss of a client that I minded. Clients come and go and we are always afforded with work here.

But I'm a third-generation resident on my father's side. And my progenitors lived to ripe old ages, so I'm going back to the middle of the last century. And I am very concerned about this city. It was the heart and soul of the industrial revolution. And during my lifetime—I'm now 70 years of age—I've seen it go downhill. It's stabilized somewhat at the moment. But it's not the vibrant and creative driving force that it once was in our national economy. It's been in the backwater. I had seen the possibility of its reemergence as a driving economic force in the American economy in the new high technology communications revolution with an unending stream of talent coming out of NSU, particularly in the computer science field. . . . I know of the university's efforts to develop that synergism between industry and university that has been spawned around Boston and out in Silicon

Valley, and I want very much to play a role in developing that industrial complex for the new age.

He went on to point out that there were three ingredients needed for the resurgence of industry in the region: venture capital, entrepreneurs, and managerial talent.

In many ways the story of Microware's first two years is based on the interaction of these three ingredients. This story consists of a search for venture capital, as well as a search for the right mix of managerial talent. The entrepreneurial ingredient, Bill Alexander, was provided from the start. Ted stated that when he met Bill, he realized that Bill had the ambition and skill necessary to head a successful high-tech firm: "Did he sell me? He certainly did. He is a consumate entrepreneur. . . . He is entrepreneur from head to toe, and as I told him early on . . . I bet on people. He impressed me. I knew he'd provide the entrepreneurial spirit, the driving force to get things done." One of the primary ways that Bill would sell his vision to others was to illustrate a credible or intriguing hypothetical scenario promoting this vision of the future.

It was Bill's gift for promotion that made him powerful. It is also a key element in two interrelated themes that this case study will follow: the major theme of the opposition of promotion versus production and its subtheme of entrepreneurial control versus committee management. These oppositions are devices that enable me to structure an argument holding that although Microware was a tangible enterprise—comprised of employees, machines, buildings, products, financial statements, bank accounts, meetings, telephone calls, marketing systems, production systems—it was in many key ways a rhetorical enterprise. And by understanding it in that sense, we can better understand some of the dynamics of creating and maintaining a new organization in a new industry.

Promotion

The Nature of Promotion in Microware   On September 20, 1983, I recorded a meeting in which Bill promoted his vision of the future of entertainment software to Dave Kruger, one of the company's top managers. Bill wanted to convince Dave that his vision, which required purchasing an expensive computer graphics device, was the direction that Microware must go in during the next year.

Bill began by showing Dave some pictures of a new and revolutionary video game, Dungeon Trek, which had recently been a big success in video arcades. This game did not feature the graphics of the typical computer video game; instead, the graphics were animated. The animation, according to Bill, looked nearly as well drawn as a Disney cartoon. Although displaying a film in an arcade game was not new, the revolutionary aspect of this game was that the player could still control the actions of the characters on the screen. In other words, the game was designed so that the player could participate in this Disney-like adventure film on the screen.

This innovation was the result of the marriage of computer and laserdisc technology. The major problem for companies attempting to develop laserdisc computer games was the cost of animation. The first successful commercial game, Dungeon Trek, cost several million dollars because it was drawn by animators. Bill's argument to Dave was that the games were too costly to create in this traditional way. Instead, Bill claimed a state-of-the-art computerized animation system produced by Graphics Systems Corporation (GSC) was the profitable way to go. Bill wanted to convince Dave to purchase this system.

Dave was impressed with the animation. "That's Walt Disney quality," he said. Bill replied,

Yes, that's what I'm saying, that's what I'm saying. [With a microcomputer alone] you'll never be able to generate that kind of quality, but [in conjunction with a laserdisc] you can always call up that image from a laserdisc. That's all you're doing; you're accessing a frame, calling that frame up and loading it into the screen. You're not ever generating that kind of graphic [through the computer alone]. But what is going to generate that graphic? Traditional [animation] techniques that cost $2 million and take nine months? No. You've got to turn these around in two or three months, and they've got to be a few hundred thousand dollars maximum [in cost]. That's why I'm pushing for that GSC system. That can do this [the Disney-like image that Dave was looking at] and better. Very quick and very low cost. . . . That is where the megabucks, the megadollars are going to be. This one [Dungeon Trek] sold 3000 units, $18 million so far, in advance orders, in three months.

The key strategy in this argument lies in the statement that the GSC machine will do it all for the company. Bill did not say that the workers at Microware will produce Disney-quality animation; instead, employing a hypothetical sequence, he painted an exciting picture that says, that the GSC machine will quickly produce high quality graphics at low cost, thus generating a profit.

Bill also explored other hypothetical possibilities of the laserdisc system, continually emphasizing the outcomes of buying the GSC system—for example, "You know what I want to do with this whole thing, this laserdisc thing? You know what's going to be big in the future? Mass merchandising of products in big malls of stores, using laserdiscs to flash up items. . . . It'll show you every product, or you could point to the type of product you wanna see. And it'll show you the product, the price, the whole thing."

Bill emphasized the applications and outcomes of the GSC system but never the work involved. His hypothetical sequence stated the immediate goal that he wanted to achieve and any number of future outcomes of that goal—none of them the sequence of steps that the production people would need to consider to reach any of these future outcomes.

The discussion illustrates internal promotion. Similarly, sales pitches to prospective investors on the great production potential of the company—external promotion—purposefully glossed over production details because the company's production effort was consistently weak. It was not producing marketable software, but the heads of the company had to convince investors that the company was quite able to do so. In other words, external promotion often involved deception.

Sean LaMountain, who joined the company as a marketer shortly after it incorporated only to quit four months later, stated in 1983. "My bit was to get up and make some presentations over a fictional [product]. You know, we had all these gadgets and whiz kids with unfinished toys and we're snow-jobbing." One of LaMountain's major objections to this type of work centered on Bill's and others' relentless drive to promote the company regardless of what it produced: "With this missionary zeal, everything falls second to getting [their] goal achieved." Ultimately, LaMountain realized that he had a very different view of reality from some of the other heads of the company. His attitude toward Bill and some of the others was that "you don't think like I think about what is real and what's not real, what's kidding yourself, what's a waste of time." According to LaMountain, the other promoters at Microware did not know "what is real and what ain't. . . . They think that what is, is what you can convince somebody else it is, or what you can convince yourself it is, or what you can convince the bank to keep paying [for] to promote what it is."

Thus, there existed in Microware a view of the world, a promotional reality, whose participants accepted this belief: if we say it persuasively, it is perceived as being real. This belief caused many problems for the company because often the promoters persuaded people to believe that Microware could produce software that it later could not produce. By predicting unrealistic accomplishments and forcing programmers to try to match these predictions, the company could not turn out money-generating products. This failed outcome required still more promotion to convince potential investors to support the company, since the company could not generate money from product sales. Thus, promotion raised money for the company and simultaneously helped to deter the creation of money-generating products.

Central to this promotion-vs.-production scenario was the fact that the principal promoter, Bill, was also the entrepreneur who initiated and controlled the company largely on his own. For much of its first two years, Microware was a reflection of its principal entrepreneur. With Bill in control the company became promotion-oriented.

Promotion as a Reflection of the Entrepreneur   From the beginning of the company, Bill saw himself not as a technical expert who could produce innovative and profitable products but as a leader for others who would build such products. This self-perception can be traced to the origins of the company in an independent study project at NSU. These origins go back to a snowy night in December 1981 when he and Greg Jerling were hanging around the fraternity house talking about creating a course project that could also be a money-making computer software business. Since both needed to take an elective course for the next semester, they agreed that it would be best to design a course of their own, a course that could evolve into the software company that they wanted to start. Greg was a computer science major and had experience in writing graphics software. According to Bill, Greg asked him that night what Bill could offer such a project. Bill said that he had "enough leadership potential" to get the company going. In other words, Bill had no specific technical ability that would help them design and construct products; what he apparently did have was an ability to lead, to motivate, and to supply the entrepreneurial spirit to sell themselves and their products.

The course they designed reflected Bill's personality. Bill wanted it to be an independent study because he believed that he worked better in an independent atmosphere. He could set his own guidelines and time frames and choose whom he wanted to involve in the project. In short, Bill could be the creator and controller of such a project and the business that it spawned. He could be an entrepreneur.

Bill's control was quickly manifested in the type of market that the course/company would try to enter. He wanted to create software for the mass market rather than a more specialized segment of the computer market. This reflected Bill's personal goal to get into the microcomputer business which was just beginning to become a mass market product. Originally Bill and Greg had considered trying to sell the idea for an independent study course/company to the Chemistry Department because Greg and another friend had designed a computer graphics product for chemists during the previous year. Bill and Greg discovered that the Chemistry Department was not interested in expanding what Greg had already done for them. Also, according to Greg, Bill recognized that big money was to be made not in software for the chemists but for the mass market, especially in games for microcomputers. With the growing success of video arcade games, the microcomputer market seemed to have the potential to become a true mass market. Therefore, they chose their goal based not on their proved ability to write mass market microcomputer software but on Bill's vision of the lucrative possibilities of that market.

Bill's independent study course was designed to reflect his abilities in that he suggested that they try to do the independent study through the Management Department at NSU [Bill was majoring in Management] rather than through a specific product-related discipline, such as chemistry, or even a technically oriented discipline like computer science. Instead, by creating a technical project within the Management Department, the emphasis could be put less on technical production and more on those who manage and promote technical production.

When Bill tried to initiate the course, he promoted a credible hypothetical sequence of events to Management Professor Edward Murphy. The first stage of this sequence had recently occurred: IBM had begun selling a microcomputer, and it was quickly becoming successful in terms of sales. There was at that time, however, little software produced for it. The rest of Bill's proposed sequence of future events was up to the students who joined the independent study course. Bill, Greg, and the others were going to produce programs for this machine, filling a much-needed void in the marketplace and laying the groundwork for a successful company that would sell mainly game programs. Although Murphy was somewhat skeptical about how well games would sell for a machine designed primarily for business use, he told Bill that he would teach the independent study.

Just as the independent study course reflected Bill's vision, the company that evolved out of the course was also reflective of Bill's vision. And during the course, Bill's vision of what the company should become grew more detailed. This occurred as Bill wrote the company's first business plan. This plan was ostensibly written to raise investment capital, but the writing of this first plan was Bill's act of creating the company. It began organizing the students as a company, eventually enabling them to join the Start-up Project provisionally, and later gain permanent start-up status. Bill recounted how important his business plan was: "It was everything. Without a product, without money, without furniture, without machines, without anything, the business plan is it. That's your whole case for existence. That's what attracted money. That's what kept us in the [start-up] program. That's what got most of the board members into it. That's what got a lot of the employees into it. It did a lot of things."

Microware's First Business Plan   A number of people were persuaded to support Bill's vision as it was constructed in the 1982 business plan. In particular, three people were persuaded who were among the most essential to the establishment of the company: Ted Wilson, Ed Murphy, and Paulo Abruzzi [one of the NSU administrators who advised members and potential members of the Start-up Project]. Bill attracted each of these individuals with differing types of arguments and in doing so attracted money, employees, and institutional support from NSU.

The first argument was based on a generic form for business plans presented to applicants to the Start-up Project by Abruzzi. This form required that the applicants develop a document that served as "a road map," as Abruzzi said. It must give specific direction to the fledgling organization; in addition, it must attract supporters. The way one does this, according to the advice that Abruzzi gave Bill, was to build the plan based on a simple structure: delineate the product or service that will be provided, analyze the existing market, and lay out the strategies designed to achieve a share of that market. Bill did just that: Microware would produce three different types of microcomputer software for three potentially explosive markets by tapping the computing and management talent of NSU.

The second key argument in the plan related to one element in the simple formula of product-market-strategies—the market. Bill devoted approximately twenty-two of a total of forty-seven pages to describing the exciting and potentially lucrative market for microcomputer software. It was this market potential that first attracted Edward Murphy, who went on to play a key, early role in the development of the company, and a number of the early employees. The major premise of this simple but effective argument was that the total potential market for microcomputer software was extremely lucrative. The following excerpts give a bit of the flavor of Bill's characterization of this premise.

Advertising Age estimates that the gross revenues for video games in 1982 will top $6 billion, and will approach $20 billion by 1985. . . . Today's computer revolution has been growing at a pace of well over 50 percent annually for the past several years. This growth, along with the expectation of future growth, has prompted several venture capital firms and public companies to invest significant amounts of money in recognized industry leaders, and in new start-ups such as Microware. . . . Only 10 percent of American homes have video game systems, which leaves 90 percent still to be conquered. . . . In 1981, Americans spent 20 billion quarters on video games. . . . The release, in the summer of 1981, of IBM's new Personal Computer has brought significant attention to the microcomputer industry. . . . By the end of 1982, less than a year after initial release, IBM will have 250,000 to 300,000 personal computers installed. Estimates place the number of IBM personal computers [to be] sold in 1983 at 3 million machines.

The minor premise was that other companies, similar to Microware in that they were entrepreneurial start-up companies, have gained highly profitable shares of that potential market:

Atari, owned by Warner Communications, has been the leader in the video games market since its humble beginning back in 1971 when Nolan Bushnell and Joe Keenan founded Atari. Warner Communications bought out Atari in 1976 for $32 million, and in 1981 Atari had gross revenues of 1.23 billion. . . . Activision was founded on October 1, 1979 by its current President Jim Levy and 4 ex-Atari game designers. . . . in 1980 Activision's gross sales were $6 million.

The conclusion of the argument was that Microware was positioned to take a significant share of that market: "Microware's five year milestones include gross annual sales in 1987 of $100 million." The unstated premise—that Microware could produce the software—was largely hidden. Ultimately Murphy and some potential employees were persuaded that the market was ready for such a company.

The third major argument relates to Ted Wilson's point of view. Ted was attracted to three aspects of the Metro region—NSU—Microware mix: the possibility of revitalizing the region with high-technology start-ups, the technological and managerial talent coming out of NSU, and the quick success and sudden loss of Macro Technologies. All three of these issues were discussed in the business plan, and these were the key elements that attracted Ted Wilson. (For a detailed analysis of these arguments, see Doheny-Farina 1991.)

The 1982 business plan worked well as a promotional document; it was less successful as a road map, providing neither clear nor efficient guidelines to give direction to the company's production operation. A year after he had written the business plan, Bill noted that the biggest problem with it was that it created a company going in too many directions at once without indicating a common purpose for all directions: "I didn't build a synergy in. So when a reader reads it he is confused as to what our direction is—as to what takes priority over another. . . . They're [readers/venture capitalists] not sure what the hell we do. Are we trying to do everything? Are we trying to do nothing? . . . 'Cause in some cases I set my priorities wrong. In some cases I gave too much information on graphics and nowhere near enough on the hospital product (the business application product). . . . So when they read all the way through it, they were confused still."

Bill's admitted lack of focus in the plan carried over to the company's operation. During most of the company's first two years, its production effort was scattered and ineffectual; it could not produce three different types of software simultaneously. Although Bill claimed that the business plan gave the company guidance, what it did was provide goals without showing the steps necessary to meet those goals. The promotional hypothesis—since IBM sells lots of machines, we will sell lots of software—became bogged down when the technical people in the company tackled the details of production. Eventually a potentially effective production strategy arose within Microware but not before the company went through many production difficulties early in its development.

Production

The Macro Technologies' Model and Early Problems   Professor Murphy attributed the independent study group's production problems to Bill's emphasis on creating an organization and a business plan before the group produced marketable software. He felt that the students had scattered their effort by following the prescribed path of the business plan, when they should have been concentrating on production first, and then organizing the company around the products that they created. As Professor Murphy stated:

Murphy thought they should have followed the model of Macro Technologies. As he recounted, Macro built products, showed them at trade shows, and then went on to form a company. Murphy believed that Macro answered the two vital questions before becoming a company: Can we produce a product? Will the market accept it? The answers to both questions were yes. As a result, Macro eventually received major investment money and the company thrived. Microware, by contrast, put together not products but an organization and eventually tried to sell the organization's production potential to investors.

This organization arose through weekly meetings among Bill and the other student participants. Through these meetings, their ideas began to come together. They tried to answer some key questions: What type of products were they producing? What types of markets were they entering? Bill recalled that it was "a lot of brainstorming and a lot of the initial conceptualization and formal design of not only the software but [of what would later become] the company." The "company" that the students formed was a small, multifunction group with Bill as head. The group included games, business, and graphics programmers, a director of marketing, and a sales representative. Through this organization, the students claimed that they would produce a number of results by the end of the semester. The salesperson and marketer were to do research and market forecasting, and the programmers were to produce software. These claims were not met.

Dr. Murphy summed up their results: "It was a disappointment from an academic standpoint in that the people did not deliver all that well on their contracts." They did not produce many programs that ran. They were overly optimistic on how many programs they would be able to write. The only games that worked were ones that had been started before the course began. The market research on the business application system was disappointing. In some cases, Murphy added, what was planned was too complicated for them to do during the time allowed. While Bill later did admit that he overestimated how much they could accomplish, he did note that he faced two major production-deterring problems during the semester.

The first problem was a lack of commitment from most of the students in the course. Bill could not get a strong effort from every one of the eight students. According to Bill, many in the group worked on the project haphazardly, treating it as just another course, although Bill expected more. He tried to solve this problem through a bit of promotion: midway through the project he knew that he was going to incorporate and take the business beyond its academic stage. Bill said that he "surprised the hell out of the others" when he told them he was going to incorporate. Greg noted the effect that this had on some in the group. He recalled one day in March 1982, during the project, when Bill laid out his five-year milestones, which projected sales revenues in the millions over this period. One of the programmers, Mary Talbert, said "'Bill, don't you think those numbers are a little big?' and Bill blew up at her, and he said 'If you don't believe that we can do this, then you don't belong here, because I believe that we can do this. This is what I'm out for, and if you're thinking small time, then you might as well walk out now, and that goes for anybody else in the room.' And everybody stayed." Bill apparently reasoned that if the programmers, sales staff, and marketers looked at their work as being "small time," they would put a small effort into it. But if they believed Bill when he promoted his large-scale vision of an exciting and profitable future—the big time—then it was thought that they would put a big time effort into their work.

A second problem that hindered production was the lack of support from the school. At that time NSU had no IBM PCs for the independent study students' use, and the management school would not allow these students to use the Apple computers that it owned. Consequently, Murphy arranged for them to use his own Apple. He put it in one of the rooms in the management building, and the students were allowed to use it there. Thus, initially, they had only one machine for at least six programmers, and that machine was not the brand that they intended to build their business on. Also, later in the semester when the students as a company applied for start-up status, they ran into many problems with the school. An administrative memo stating that all dealings with the group should be done at arm's length had been sent to the faculty and administration members who were involved either with the students or with the Start-up Project. That is, if these students were to become a company, then faculty and administration must treat them not as students to be advised without payment but as business clients to whom services are provided under standard business conventions. Bill and Greg felt that the school was offering encouragement to begin school-related companies and then discouraging faculty involvement with these companies.

Nevertheless, months after the independent study ended and the company had incorporated, Microware was well equipped with strongly committed workers and numerous IBM PCs; they had the full support of the Start-up Project and they had access to the expert business advice from both the start-up committee and Ted Wilson's law firm. But the company was still not producing marketable software. Commitment, equipment, and advice were not the only elements needed to produce profitable software. Another major element that they still lacked was an organization that integrated all aspects of production in a detailed chronological sequence of steps culminating in the sale of products.

Nature of the Defective Production Organization   For well over a year after the independent study was over and the company had incorporated, Microware was beset by production problems: programmers had trouble writing programs that worked as expected; the managers had problems getting programmers to finish the programs on time; once products were complete, they were unacceptable for sale. Overall, Greg noted that most of these setbacks were the result of shortsightedness and poor planning. The need for crucial design changes in a product were sometimes discovered long after the products had been conceived, designed, and, in some cases, manufactured in large numbers. Often programmers who had been writing a product so that it would perform certain tasks were told midstream to stop and instead write programs that did something very different. There seemed to be little consistent company direction. Clearly one of the company's principal production problems centered on its production management.

For quite a while, there was little direction given to programmers from management because the company was not structured for this to happen. For example, in April 1983, nearly a year after the company incorporated, one of its programmers, Larry Williams, was asked if there was a system for deciding on production projects. "No, everyone just does what they want, what they have ideas on," he said. "Some games are developed totally by one person. It depends. Some people are very organization minded. Others are not." This freedom for product developers to do "what they want" resulted in chaotic production.

Games were the first products to be completed, but few, if any, had been designed with the competition in mind. The programmers were writing games not for a specific market audience but according to their own whims. Most of the games that were completed during the company's first year were not received well by potential buyers, especially software dealers and distributors, because they were too slow; that is, the apparent movement of the objects on the screen was not as fast, and therefore not as challenging, as other companies' games. The games were too slow because the programs were written in a "slow" computer language. Greg, the head of the games programming, believed that the way to remedy this problem was to rewrite those games in a "faster" language. Recognizing this problem and then remedying it took most of 1983. Nearly two years had passed from the start of the independent study that was to produce some marketable games to the time that any were complete.

One of the company's computer graphics products, a program called Graphware, needed to be rewritten in a different language after it had been completed. This rewrite was necessary because the original language took up too much memory space on the floppy disk and therefore limited the program capabilities. Some of these limitations made the product impossible to sell. For example, the product had been designed to be used by businesspersons who needed to represent numerical information in line charts, pie charts, or bar graphs. When the user fed in the numerical data, the program would produce the specific graphic representation of the data that the user wanted. But, the user could not include negative numbers in the data, so the charts could show only positive figures. Few businesspersons could use a chart maker that could not illustrate losses. For this and several other similar inadequacies, Graphware, like the games, was not completed until near the end of 1983.

Improved Production Organization and Committee Management   In contrast to the free-form production effort that Microware had been practicing, a more structured production system arose during the middle of 1983. This was a team management system in which each member of the team managed different stages in the chronological sequence of production stages. As this system became organized, most of the company's operations came within the team's control, thus creating a team, or committee, management system for the company as a whole.

In April 1983 the company was just beginning to evolve from what Greg called "one fluid mass" into a more departmentalized organization. It was the evolving marketing department that was to attempt to give some direction to the programmers. That is, the marketers were supposed to evaluate the kind of product that would be marketable and give that information to the software designers. This kind of system may appear to be simple, but it was a complex process that took a few months to develop.

Helping Microware to organize the marketing-programming system was a member of the company's board of directors, Bob Hatlin. Hatlin recognized that the basis for improved production lay in the interaction of the company's managers. He saw that some of the managers could embody most of the needed facets of a successful production operation: Greg and Paul, the technical managers who headed programming (which they called development); Frank and Liz, who headed marketing; and Dave, who headed manufacturing and quality control. From Hatlin's point of view there was no one to fill the financial budgeter's, or comptroller's, role. Eventually Hatlin himself would fill that role. In Hatlin's scheme, Bill would be simply a money raiser and overseer of the management team.

During July 1983 Hatlin helped each of these persons to gain a better idea of what their roles were to be. For example, Frank and Dave came to understand the relationship of their jobs to those of the others. Dave was particularly frustrated in his job, claiming that he had been doing so many different tasks that he really did not know what his job should be. Hatlin helped him focus in on his central duties. For example, Hatlin saw the need for one person in management to have the authority to decide when a product was actually finished. No one person had had the responsibility to proclaim that a prototype was truly ready for manufacturing.

Hatlin thought that this should not be decided by either a technical person or a sales person but instead by a manufacturing person. This, Hatlin felt, should be within Dave's authority.

When Frank was unsure of his role in the company's evolving marketing group and was becoming quite upset about it, Hatlin spent a couple of days helping him to sort out his optimum role in the company: concentrating on marketing the company's business applications system. Marketing games and graphics would be handled by Liz.

Overall, Hatlin had a profound influence on these people, taking individuals in a free-form environment and helping them to see their relation to each other. Greg and Hatlin became particularly close during this time. Greg noted in one of the staff meetings that he saw Hatlin as their teacher, leading them through some of the company's most perplexing production problems.

After defining roles in the system, Hatlin presented the production group with the ideal production process. He told them that they needed to see this process as a time sequence which consisted of four stages. The first was the project stage, when the overall concept of a product was decided upon. This concept should come from various sources. For example, on July 26 Hatlin helped the production group to organize the concept development system for a new product that had not yet been designed, Graphware 2.0. This system depended on a liaison person between the marketers and the technical designers who was to do research on the type of product that customers needed and tie that to the technical capabilities of the company's programmers, thus refining a product concept that could then be designed.

The second stage was planning or defining a set of activities to reach the goals of the project concept. In other words, once the concept was at least initially confirmed, the production managers would plan the steps needed to turn the concept into the product. For software production, this was the technical design stage.

The third stage in Hatlin's ideal production process was the budget stage. After the group had begun to set firm plans for production, they would need to reduce that plan to the resources needed to do the job. If the product was not affordable, they would have to go back to the planning stage, and possibly back to the project concept stage, and redesign at these levels.

The final stage was the control stage, when the group would monitor and adjust the process as it proceeded. This stage took the results of the previous stages through to the completion of the project, resulting in either a finished product or an aborted project.

Hatlin urged the company's top management to try to strike a balance in the overall system between planning (setting up a project to produce and sell software) and doing (designing, programming, manufacturing, marketing, and selling software). He told them that they could wind up planning 90 percent of the time and doing 10 percent, or vice versa, but that they should strive for something in the middle. He noted that the best way to ensure this balance was through the weekly management meeting with Greg, Paul, Dave, Frank, Liz, and Bill. In effect, Hatlin was urging them to form a committee management system.

Approximately a month later, on August 25, 1983, Frank, Liz, Greg, and Dave agreed on their version of a production system similar to Hatlin's ideal. This system was a sequential loop that began with the product concept stage, followed by the product design stage. The third level was the product development of the prototype stage, followed by the demonstration stage. The final point was the product distribution stage. At any one point in this process, the product could be rejected and sent back to the concept stage. Frank, Liz, Greg, and Dave each explained where his or her responsibility began and ended within this system.

Members of the management of the company had come to an understanding of the cooperative and timely effort needed to produce software. The strategy of the production team was that of a temporal sequence in which different steps were handled by different individuals. In helping them come to this understanding, Hatlin designed a committee management system that, if employed, would control most of the company's operation.

Eventually this production-team, committee-management system would stand in opposition to Bill's promotional, entrepreneurial control. Ironically, it was Bill who, at one point during the company's first two years, pointed out in a local magazine article the importance of timing and a synchronization between promotion and production. Companies need balance, noted Bill, or they become inefficient.

The Rhetorical Situation for the 1983 Business Plan

There thus arose two views of reality within the company: the promotion-entrepreneurial reality of Bill Alexander and the production=committee management reality of the production group (Dave, Greg, Frank, and Liz). The participants' perceptions of these opposing realities formed the social and organizational context within which they worked, influencing conflicting conceptions of the rhetorical situation for the 1983 business plan and conflicting views of how the participants should collaborate to write that document.

Exigence: The Money Shortage

During the last half of 1983, Microware faced a serious money shortage. This lack of financial resources was the exigence for writing a new business plan, since this plan was designed to function as a money-raising tool. Although there were different beliefs as to why this shortage occurred, all of management agreed that one of the principal reasons the company was going bankrupt was that it was not producing marketable software. From January 1982, when the independent study with Dr. Murphy began, until August 1983, Microware made little money from selling software. In fact, after that first year and a half it still had not completed its first product. Until August 1983, the company existed primarily by the grace of Ted Wilson.

Because Ted believed in Bill's promotional vision and his entrepreneurial drive, he was determined to help the company succeed. Consequently, Ted supported Microware in four ways: he afforded them hundreds of hours of legal advice without charge; he helped Bill sell between $50,000 and $100,000 worth of Microware stock; he rented to Microware some of the company's equipment and one of its offices and by the fall of 1983 had collected little of the rent owed to him; and, most important, he had cosigned and guaranteed a loan of $250,000 from the Northland Bank to Microware. The company received the first $110,000 during the summer of 1983. The rest of the loan was contingent on the bank's approval. If it was not satisfied with the use of the first installment, the bank could refuse to loan Microware the rest of this money. By July 1983, Microware existed not on the fruits of its production but on the fruits of Ted's confidence in Bill and the rest of the company.

The company was adept at promoting itself but not at producing software. Dr. Murphy said the managers had "done a very good job of presenting themselves to investors: in terms of their [original] business plan, how they look, how they articulate and present themselves. They have looked good at trade shows. They have looked good in the press." But he added that they had not made much money selling software: "Although there seems to be talented programmers working for the [company], they have not produced marketable programs." The heart of this incongruity between promotion and production stemmed from Bill's original business plan which created a company designed to produce three different types of software without showing how this diversity could be integrated.

This lack of focus was the topic of discussion during a July 12, 1983, meeting with Bill, Frank, Paul, and Greg. They agreed that Microware was trying to produce too many different kinds of software. (The next day Dave told me that he also agreed with the results of this meeting, although he was not in attendance that day.) They noted that all of the company's products were late because the production effort for each type of software disrupted the production effort of the rest of the software. Bill was especially afraid that games would "go down the tubes and pull the rest down."

The managers agreed that this problem could destroy the company financially. Pursuing three different types of software production had been very expensive. They had hired more and more employees during the company's first year and a half. When Microware had incorporated in May 1982, it had approximately eleven employees. Fourteen months later, it had approximately thirty employees, who cost the company $50,000 a month on payroll alone. In order for these employees to do their work, the company had purchased or rented thousands of dollars worth of computer equipment, office space, furniture, and supplies. They were in debt to Ted Wilson for some of these rentals, but they were also in debt to a number of companies that would not be as forgiving as Ted would.

Yet with all these expenses and after more than a year of work, the company did not have one finished product to be sold. By August 1983, it was beginning to sell an unfinished product: the Micromed business applications system, which was designed to computerize certain aspects of small to mid-sized hospitals, but these sales were not yet covering the costs of producing the system. By the end of August the $110,000 from the Northland Bank two months earlier was virtually gone.

During a meeting on August 25 attended by Ted, Bill, Dave, Greg, Paul, Frank, and Bob Hatlin, Ted noted how desperate their financial situation was: "You are really a defunct corporation. You are bleeding to death." He then mentioned Hughes Associates, a venture capital firm that Bill had claimed was interested in Microware. In late June, Bill had told Greg that Hughes Associates planned to invest $450,000 in Microware "tomorrow," but the venture capitalist firm never did. To make his point, Ted said, "As Hughes said [to me] you're not only looking at Chapter 11 [bankruptcy], you are there now." In addition Bill noted that his recent negotiations with Mark Whitney, the executive who arranged the first half of the $250,000 Northland Bank loan, led him to believe that Whitney might not approve the remainder of the loan. Apparently it appeared to Whitney that the company had not proved itself worthy of more money. Ted told management what they knew too well: their biggest problem was missing production deadlines; if they had been out to market by now they would not be in this trouble. But they were, and they needed to find a way out. One of the potential solutions was to write a new business plan. The participants seemed to share one view of the exigence for writing this new plan; that is, they agreed with Ted that their financial troubles stemmed from their inability to produce marketable software. Later their perception of exigence became significantly at odds with Bill's perception of it. But there were other aspects of the rhetorical situation that the participants agreed upon.

A Way to Save the Company: Hatlin's View

The organizational context of Microware began to shape the participants' conceptions of rhetorical situation and the collaborative writing process. These conceptions were influenced by Bob Hatlin's presentation of his view of the rhetorical situation and of the need for collaboration, which he presented to the rest of the participants during the August 25 meeting.

With little remaining investment money, meager income, and large expenses, the participants discussed two options for saving money: cut back on the company's operations with the intention of trimming expenses while making the operation more efficient or try to raise more investment capital by sending a new business plan to potential investors.

The first option, the one management termed the bailout scenario, was to drop the production of games and concentrate on finishing and selling Micromed. This product was by far their most sophisticated and most smoothly run operation, though it was, ironically, understaffed. Micromed had been well received by potential customers, and the company had already made a few sales, although the product had not been completed. The group tried to determine if, by cutting down drastically on their expenses and firing all games and most graphics programmers, the company could survive on income from Micromed sales alone. They concluded that it would be difficult because Micromed was not spectacularly profitable. It required a lot of customer support after the sale, and this meant that sales profits would be minimal. But the games market looked worse, and the company's production to date in graphics, represented by the company's only graphics product, Graphware, was weak.

Since the bailout scenario was problematic, Bob Hatlin urged the group to pursue the second option, basing survival not on what products were completed and sold but on how well Microware could present itself as a vehicle for potential profitable production. This time the accuracy of the company's self-portrayal needed to be more closely considered than in the past. During the August 25 meeting Hatlin stated: "My opinion: go after the venture capital funding. To do this take to Whitney and other venture capitalists a very carefully crafted business plan with no bullshit—including all doubts about games, no bullshit—including Micromed's potential—no bullshit. Put down how much it will cost, period. Lay this out on Whitney's or Bellow's desk [a venture capitalist] and they'll be impressed. They will then investigate it, and if you get good feedback [if Micromed customers rate Microware favorably] and if the valuation of the company is a good deal [if the price of the company's stock is reasonably priced], it's there." Hatlin made it clear why Whitney was their primary audience: if Whitney thought that other venture capitalists saw Microware as a worthwhile risk, Whitney would give Microware the rest of the $250,000 loan and then help the company secure a much larger venture capital investment.

Although Hatlin urged the entire management group to collaborate in writing the new business plan, he recognized the power that Bill held over the company's promotional activities. He noted his concern about Bill as their promoter while tactfully justifying Bill's past promotional behavior: "Let me be blunt. Everyone tells me, Bill, that you inflate everything. That's because (1) you want to promote and (2) you haven't had anything to really sell. Now you have to lay it all on the line." The time for inflated claims was over; the management group must present a credible ethos.

By August 25, 1983, the organizational context had begun to shape an important writing task by influencing conceptions of the exigence, purpose, audience, and ethos for the 1983 business plan:

Exigence: Because of the fuzzy and diverse goals of the original business plan, the company scattered its production efforts, producing no revenue-generating products, and, therefore, the company needed to raise more loan and investment money.

Purpose: The heads of the company needed to show that Microware was a good investment because the company was structured to produce profitable software.

Audience: The management group was to show Mark Whitney that venture capitalists would have a favorable reaction to the business plan; therefore, the audience was comprised of Mark Whitney and a group of venture capitalists, as Mark Whitney conceived of those venture capitalists.

Ethos: The management group was to write a proposal that did not inflate past accomplishments but explained current problems and present an accurate version of their products' current and future marketability.

In addition to influencing the rhetorical situation, the organizational context was beginning to influence the process of collaborative writing. Starting with the August 25 meeting, the participants began the direct phase of collaborative writing, which would be completed at the October 13 collaborative writing session. By urging management to write a new business plan, Hatlin was urging them to take collaborative action. "You make it or die together," he told them. Yet, he realized that this collaboration would center on Bill: "Bill is your voice."

Collaboration at this point did not mean that all of the participants would write parts of the business plan; it meant that the others would provide Bill with information that he would need to write the plan himself. The collaborative writing process as of August 25 reflected the company's current authority structure: Bill would be in control of the writing process because he still controlled the company.

The writing of the 1983 business plan was a group effort, and as they all learned more about their tasks, they began to see things that they had not seen before. Some of these things they agreed upon. For example, they all agreed on a more detailed perception of their purpose—to write a business plan that showed what the company produced, how the company was structured, how much money the company was seeking, and how much control the major investor would have by investing that amount—and their audiences—primarily Mark Whitney and each of approximately thirty venture capitalists, and secondarily all of the company's employees. The management group felt that the employees should know in what direction the company was headed.

Other aspects of their work were not so cooperative. After August 25 there arose some serious conflicts between Bill and the production group concerning the writing of the plan. These differences centered on two elements: exigence and ethos. Closely tied to these elements were the growing differences between Bill and the production group over the process of collaborative writing.

Different Rhetorical Situations

Exigence   There arose among management some differences about the nature of the company's financial status. Although the management group agreed that poor production was the principal cause of their financial troubles, Bill did not appear to think that this situation was unreasonable or unexpected. He stated repeatedly during the days after the meeting that the company had been nearly bankrupt several times before—a not unexpected problem for a company like theirs. Several times he recounted a story about the bleak financial outlook that Bryan Hilt, the president of Macro Technologies, had faced just before that company received major funding. Outwardly Bill was not overly concerned about the money shortage; he was confident that he could raise the money if he had the support of the other company managers. An ability to attract investment made Bill quite a powerful figure, and he appeared to enjoy the prospect of raising money.

Not everyone agreed with Bill. Dave, Paul, Greg, and Liz, all members of the production group, developed a different attitude about the exigence for writing the new business plan. They came to believe that there were reasons other than just lack of sales that caused the company to flirt with bankruptcy, in particular Bill's sole control over the company's finances.

First, the production group had discovered that Bill had spent significant amounts of money on expenses that he alone approved. Months before the August 25 meeting, Bill had decided that the company would hire a public relations firm, Spencer and Fairfax, to handle publicity. Liz, who was supposed to be the director of publicity at the time, had not been consulted. The benefits of this move had been small, and it cost the company dearly. A similar situation occurred when Bill hired a California personnel consulting firm, Taylor-Parrish, to help the company straighten out its personnel files and write job descriptions. The consultants did little more than provide a questionnaire and charged Microware several thousand dollars. Bill had hired another personnel consultant for $1000 a month after he discovered that Taylor-Parrish was not doing the job he had hoped for. That he had made these decisions without consulting anyone else led the production group to question his sole control over the company's money.

There was concern that the company would soon be late in paying its payroll taxes. Bill did not share this concern: "We'll pay it in time. Don't worry about it, guys. We've been in worse positions. . . . We've realized from the beginning that without investment we won't make it whether we're in debt $2,000 or $200,000." His attitude about the taxes drove a wedge between him and the others in management. When Bob Hatlin found out about this, he told the management group that if Mark Whitney were to know about this potential problem, he would not lend any more money and, in fact, would demand immediate repayment of the first $110,000 that Northland Bank had loaned Microware.

A third problem was that Greg and Dave had proclaimed passionately during a board meeting that they had lost all faith in Bill as their spokesman to investors. The production group was concerned with an exigence that included two types of problems: the production problems that deterred the creation of profit-generating products and Bill's control over the company's finances.

Ethos   During the August 25 meeting everyone, including Bill, agreed that they needed to write a credible business plan—one that expressed a credible ethos—and that the brunt of this responsibility would be shouldered by Bill. However, after August 25, it became apparent that there were different views among the participants concerning just what constituted a credible ethos. For the production group, projecting a credible ethos meant making sure that Bill did not overinflate or misrepresent the company's operations and developing a general strategy for the business plan in which any future claims about Microware would be based on its past accomplishments. For Bill, a credible ethos concerned portraying Microware as a fast-growing, innovative company that would attract investment.

From the August 25 meeting until the October 13 collaborative writing session, Bill's promotional personality was a major issue with the production group. There was concern that Bill's penchant for promotion would lead him to express an overly promotional ethos in the business plan, and within a week after the August meeting, these worries about Bill heightened. On August 31 Liz told me that she, Dave, Greg, and Paul had talked the night before about how Bill had overpromoted Microware in particular or the software business in general. They were worried that regardless of what was said at the August 25 meeting, Bill's tendency to promote would lead him to fill the new business plan with inflated claims. This fear, coupled with their concern about Bill's poor judgment in running the company's finances, led them to lose trust in Bill to lead and to be the principal writer of the business plan.

The second aspect of the production group's concept of ethos concerned the general strategy of the business plan. Dave and Bob Hatlin agreed that a credible ethos would be expressed in the plan if the company's projected actions were shown to be closely tied to its past actions. Arguing for future actions on the basis of the company's past record was different from the persuasive strategies that Bill had employed in past money-raising documents that he had written. According to both Ted Wilson and Dave, Bill had supported his claims in past proposals with a flood of information from computer trade magazines or computer industry forecasting services. Ted expected Bill to write a new business plan that is not just "full of quotes from Future Computing [a market forecasting service that makes projections about the computer business]."

Dave wanted the plan to show what Microware could do by showing what it had previously done, not by basing its argument on outsiders' projections about the computer industry. Such a strategy would provide a credible ethos because the company's capabilities would be the basis for its goals. But he did not trust Bill to do that.

On September 11, Dave complained to other managers that an early draft of the new business plan that Bill had written was inadequate: "There's too much hand-waving and no details. This is too much Future Computing. A business plan should be usable, practical." Dave wanted it to show a detailed, chronological sequence of steps for the company to follow over the next year and a half. After this, the plan could project more speculative actions. The next day Dave told me, "If you have thirty pages, twenty-eight should be specific plans of the first eighteen months, and the two [pages] of puffery." This was a production-oriented view of a business plan. Dave did not think that Bill understood this.

For Bill, ethos was based primarily on his concern for portraying the company as an exciting investment vehicle for a venture capitalist. This concern came out of a meeting that Bill and Ted had on September 8 with Mark Whitney. Whitney told them that venture capitalists wanted to see a glamour item in a business plan—a product or business that would show fast growth, something innovative and new. Bill thought that this could be a series of sophisticated computer graphics products and shortly after this meeting began promoting the glamour item: laserdisc and the GSC computer animation system. "This must be in the business plan," he said. For Bill it was extremely important that the business plan express a bold ethos. The overall strategy of the plan should be to state that the company would finish Micromed, finish the current consumer products, and then go into "big-time graphics."

The issues involved in the clash of these conceptions of ethos, particularly the question of the glamour item, would be the central battleground for the confrontation between Bill's promotion/entrepreneurial reality and the production group's production/committee management reality. The differing conceptions of exigence and ethos also split the participants in their views on who should write the business plan and were directly related to an impending struggle for control of the company. That struggle was directly tied to the process of collaborative writing.

The Collaborative Writing Process
During the August 25 meeting, the collaborative writing process reflected the structure of authority in Microware: Bill was to be the principal writ-

er just as he was the principal authority in the company. But the seeds of a more decentralized source of power had been sown in the form of the production group. This group, whose duties encompassed running nearly all of the company's operations, had just begun to function. Its members had drawn up some overall production plans that integrated programming, manufacturing, marketing, and sales, but the money crisis appeared to squelch most of these plans because the production of games and graphics appeared to have been eliminated. Moreover, collectively the group had no formally sanctioned power. And while Hatlin urged the management to collaborate on the new business plan, all of the participants acted as if Bill would do most of the writing himself, even though there was concern about Bill's ability to do the job like the production group believed it should be done.

Writing a new business plan was very much a process of recreating Microware, just as Bill had created it in 1982 by writing the original plan. This time there was more raw material to work with—a year and a half of development. Members of the production group wanted to make sure that the company that was created through the plan's projections of future company actions integrated the past and current company with the future one. There was concern that Bill would not do this on his own and also there was doubt as to how the plan could be collaboratively written. Dave, believing that Bill would be the primary writer, hoped that the production group could enter the process at least midway. He said to me, "I would like for Bill to write it, give it to us, we'll give our feedback, and then he can finish it." This simple, linear collaborative process—Bill writing an entire draft, the other managers responding to it, and Bill then completing it—was not how the writing process proceeded. Instead, spurred by a growing dissatisfaction with Bill as the sole source of authority, the production group seized control of the writing process, altering the company's authority structure. The process that evolved became a challenge to Bill's authority, the rhetorical context shaping the organization of the company's top management.

Challenging Bill's Control   The production group spent a week after the August 25 meeting writing the business plan without Bill. The group held meetings in which they discussed company issues that would have to be dealt with in the new plan. This process was characterized by a cooperative team effort in which each member of the team was primarily responsible for his or her area of expertise. Out of this team process came three challenges to Bill's authority, challenges that eventually led to an official dissipation of that authority.

This authority-challenging collaborative effort took place while Bill was out of town on a business trip arranging a deal to sell Micromed to a California health care franchising organization called HCA which had expressed interest in having Microware sell Micromed to some of its franchises. Having a contract in hand would greatly increase Microware's chances of getting the rest of the Northland Bank loan. During Bill's absence the production team became a formidable management committee challenging Bill's authority.

The first challenge concerned restructuring and integrating the games and graphics production system. Bill had unilaterally decided to eliminate these operations because they were costly and problematic. But on September 1, with Bill in California, Liz, Greg, and a games programmer/designer, Don Mathews, presented a plan to reinstitute games and graphics production in spite of Bill's decision. They presented a staged, chronologically sequenced plan to save these products without incurring the massive costs of a Christmas ad campaign that Bill had argued so strongly for in early August. The three managers believed that the company could set smaller sales goals while improving their production system and still keep Microware in the games and graphics markets. Liz, Greg, and Don tried to incorporate this new production system into one organized system, which Hatlin later called Consumer Products. Their assumption was that Whitney and venture capitalists would be interested in seeing a Consumer Products division in Microware. Greg, Liz, and Don presented this new Consumer Products plan to Ted Wilson, Bob Hatlin, Paul, and Dave, who chaired the meeting.

The second challenge to Bill's authority occurred during this same meeting when the group discussed ways to improve the organization of the Micromed production system. These reorganization discussions created a picture of a changing structure of Microware, with Paul heading the Micromed production team, and Greg, Liz, and Don handling the Consumer Products team. When Hatlin asked the production group what Bill's role was in all of this, Greg responded by stating a plan he had apparently discussed with Paul and Dave before the meeting. This plan proposed a new structure to control the entire company, with Dave as president and Paul and Greg as heads of the two divisions. Although the topic was dropped, it is clear that this period of reorganizing brought on by the writing of the new business plan was affecting the structure of authority in the company.

The third challenge came the next day, September 2, during another meeting of the production group. Once again Dave chaired the meeting, and a Micromed system programmer/designer, John Rinaldi, was in attendance. The purpose of the meeting was to clear up the intricate maze of debits and credits that the company had amassed, so that they could put together an accurate financial statement for the business plan. At the same time, the production group decided that they should track down the sources of the company's expenses so management could better see where the investment money was being spent. Each person at the meeting tried to identify and claim responsibility for any expenses that came within that person's realm of authority. By analyzing all of the company's debts, the production group hoped to be able to synthesize the debts into an integrated payment schedule and include that in the presentation to Whitney. During the process of disentangling the company's debts, the production group came to realize that Bill had been the source of some large, and highly questionable, expenses.

While the attitude toward Bill grew increasingly hostile, the production group seemed impressed by their own cooperative effort. Near the end of the meeting on the company's finances, Liz noted their unusually high level of productivity: "Look how many decisions we made here today." Dave replied, "This has been the most productive meeting ever—no huffing and puffing." Before long, however, the huffing and puffing resumed; Bill and Frank returned from California and entered the meeting, tired and irritable. The tone of the meeting quickly changed from one of cooperation to one of confrontation.

This confrontation led to an officially sanctioned change in the company's authority structure—a change that reflected the collaborative writing process that had arisen during the week of Bill's absence. Bill's entrepreneurial control was officially brought to an end after Ted and the production group discovered that Bill was nearly late in paying the payroll taxes. An executive committee was formed to control the company, with Bill's presidency integrated into it. Similarly, Bill would be integrated into the collaborative writing process that had begun during his absence.

Developing a New Authority Structure   The fact that Bill had committed some serious mistakes in the eyes of Ted, Bob Hatlin, and the other managers enabled them to sanction a collaborative decision-making structure to control the company. This would be similar to the structure exhibited by the production group when its members worked on the business plan in Bill's absence. As Ted and the others devised this structure, they also devised a way to integrate Bill into the decision-making process, and, thereby, into the process of writing the business plan.

On the evening of September 2 Dave, Greg, Paul, Bob Hatlin, and Ted met to decide what should be done about Bill and Microware. One possibility was for the board of directors to fire Bill, but they thought that Whitney might feel that a company that had fired the president was too unstable to invest money in. Moreover, Bill was the only member of the company who had had any dealings at all with Whitney. Ted suggested that Bill be kept as president but with diminished power. Ted thought Bill should remain as the company's promoter—Bill had, in fact, admitted to Ted that promotion was what he was best at—but Ted wanted Bill to be under the control of a group decision-making forum.

By the end of the meeting the company officers had accepted Ted's suggestion: Bill would remain as president, but his authority would be severely restricted. The decision-making forum would be an executive committee comprising the company's entire operation: Dave (manufacturing), Frank (marketing), Greg (programming, Consumer Products), Paul (programming, Business Systems), Bill (promotion), and a comptroller position temporarily filled by Bob Hatlin. They also appointed a chief administrative officer (CAO) to oversee daily operations. They agreed that Dave should fill this position, since he had done such a good job of administering the meetings in Bill's absence. On September 7 the executive committee was officially approved by the board of directors.

Ted proclaimed that the new structure was needed "so that we all will be working as a team. . . . The purpose is to put to an end the lack of communication and to structure so that information is dispersed and the team works together." By September 7, the company's structure reflected the collaborative process of the production group—a team approach with each member responsible for a certain part of the whole.

On September 11 the executive committee met to decide how to finish writing the new business plan. They had read Bill's draft but it was just a combination of sections of previous plans and proposals. Dave and Bob Hatlin agreed that it contained very little of what they thought the new business plan should contain. The committee members decided instead to discuss the following topics: what the plan should include, what order that information might be best presented in, and who should write each section. By the end of the meeting, they had parceled out all the writing duties for the entire plan: each person was to write his or her section and then give it to Bill, who would put them together into one plan, which they would then revise. The executive committee was attempting to fulfill the teamwork ideal, integrating Bill and the production group in a collaborative writing effort. Just as this collaborative writing process was tied to the management structure, this process would also test that structure.

The Writing Process: Challenging the New Authority Structure
Just as the production group's conception of ethos led them to challenge Bill's authority, Bill's conception of ethos led him to challenge the authority of the executive committee. During a meeting on September 13, some committee members questioned Bill's claim in the section of the plan that he was writing that the company was capable of fast growth—faster than others on the committee thought possible. He projected that the company could produce another business application product like Micromed before 1986. When Paul, Frank, and Dave disagreed, urging Bill not to set unrealistic goals, Bill became frustrated with their unwillingness to be bolder. This control on Bill's desire to promote brought his frustration about the control on his authority. During the meeting, Bill said, "I realize that I needed to give up responsibilities. [But] there is a problem here. You can't run the company by committee. I got frustrated yesterday because I don't have the power to do my job. Yesterday Liz told me that she was doing her financial statement according to Dave's and Hatlin's suggestions and it was wrong, and Liz did not listen to me. If I'm not going to be listened to, I won't feel like doing my job."

Greg did not sympathize with Bill's plight: "You've got to realize that you have lost a lot of credibility in the company. You have built a wall between yourself and the employees in this company. . . . You've got to realize that we put responsibility on Liz and believe in her ability. And your input should be heard, but you don't decide." Bill replied, "I'm saying that I get the shit for our failures, but now I don't have the control to affect these areas. I won't work in that case. . . . If I don't have control then I will leave." Greg held his ground: "If you are constantly being overruled by the executive committee, then you are not leading this company. In that case you should leave."

Bill tried to avoid a serious confrontation, but added that he should be able to do what he does best: "All I'm saying is that we should respect the strengths of each person." They eventually dropped the issue, but Bill made it clear that he was not sure that the new authority structure was the best solution.

Bill had been forced to change the plan in a way that did not reflect the ethos he wanted to portray and this led him to challenge the new authority structure. During the argument, Greg shared Bill's desire to portray the company as capable of fast growth but also shared the belief in the power of the executive committee to make such decisions. The latter belief took precedence over his desire to portray an exciting ethos. Greg would play a similar bridging role during a more volatile clash in October at the collaborative writing session. The need for Greg to play a mediating role indicated that Bill remained opposed to the new authority structure and to the team approach to writing the business plan. By September 20, Bill realized that the sections that Frank and Liz were to write needed to be changed quite a bit, and he complained that he could do little with their drafts. He told the executive committee, "I can crank out this stuff in four to six hours, but I need the authority to do it from you people. . . . I could have done it last week but you all said 'No, no, no! Let Liz and Frank do it.'" Paul pointed out that there was some good material in what Bill was given, but the executive committee agreed that Bill should do whatever he felt necessary to complete a draft and they would collaborate on revising it.

For approximately two weeks, Bill wrote the plan on his own. During that time, the daily operations of the company seemed to be proceeding much as they had before the new authority structure had been instituted. After taking over the task of writing again, Bill came to feel that little had really changed. He acted as if he was still the company's voice and that he had de facto control. On October 5, he was completing the plan, and he told me that the way this plan was being written was the same as all the others had been written in the past:

I have not changed the way I have put together the business plan. What has changed is the others' attitudes toward this process. Their input is minimal, but their conception of their input is maximal. The process hasn't changed; they just think it has changed. They have become more involved somewhat. The stuff they gave me was not very useful. When I was writing it by myself, they said, "No way." I said, "OK. Give me your input, and I'll include it verbatim." You should have seen what I got! It wasn't good enough to include without changes. They told me that my projections were bullshit. Theirs were even more bullshit than mine!

Bill recognized that when management got together and collaborated on revising the plan, he would have to convince them that his version was good, but he was not worried: "I'm still going to have to sell it to them. It was harder to do this in the past, because they didn't know enough and therefore weren't a part of its creation at all. Now they have more of a role, so it'll be easier to sell them."

Bill was sure that there would be no objections to any part of the business plan when management met to discuss it, and he appeared to be as much in control of the company at this point as he had before the financial crisis. On October 13, Bill discovered that this was not so.

The October 13 Collaborative Writing Session

On October 13 Microware management—Bill, Greg, Dave, Paul, and John Rinaldi—met to attempt to complete the business plan. (John, the primary Micromed system programmer and designer, was a replacement for Frank who was on a business trip. John delivered Frank's written comments on the plan as well as expressing his own opinions on the issues.) Each participant had read the entire draft, making notes where each thought changes should be made.

During the meeting the collaborators made dozens of rhetorical choices. Two of these choices, however, took up approximately thirty minutes of the meeting. The debate centered on a passage included as one of a list of statements under the heading "1984 Milestones." Before the passage was revised, it read:

• Purchase of sophisticated computer graphics production laboratory to generate graphic frames used in laserdisc/microcomputer consumer products (Graphics Systems Corporation's Image Animation System).

The revised passage read:

• Initial staged development of sophisticated computer graphics production lab to generate graphic frames used in laserdisc/microcomputer consumer products (contingent upon capital raising).

The original stated that the company would buy the entire graphics laboratory in 1984; the revised passage stated that the development of the laboratory would be done in stages and this development would depend on whether the company received enough money to do so. These changes may not seem significant, but the process of making these rhetorical choices involved complex social interactions. Bill wanted to implement the laboratory in 1984; the others, except for Greg, wanted to put it off or delete the idea entirely. Greg saw benefits to both arguments and eventually worked to mediate the conflict.

Ethos: Projecting the Right Image

In the debate over Bill's proposal to build a laserdisc graphics laboratory in 1984, both sides were deeply concerned with the image that they would project to others in the new business plan. Bill wanted to portray an image of himself as a leader in his field and the company as an exciting investment. Bill noted that he had foresight and knew where games and graphics would be going in the future. He wanted to project that image in the business plan. He touted his own expertise by saying that he had predicted the creation of a laserdisc/microcomputer game. And because the others expressed skepticism, Bill argued that Microware would soon become obsolete by not keeping up with the state-of-the-art technology in games and graphics.

His drive to lead the field of consumer products fueled his drive to portray the company as an exciting investment. Bill was convinced that the graphics laboratory proposal was a way to portray an innovative and ambitious image of the company in the business plan, and during the meeting, he tried to convince the others of this in two ways. First, he promoted Microware as a creative and opportunistic company. He told the others that laserdisc graphics for microcomputers could succeed with "a small company who's innovative and moves fast—[a company that] can get in and start something with it." Second, he indicated that it was his discussions with Mark Whitney that led him to propose building such a lab: "Northland Bank won't touch us without this graphics, I'll tell you right now." He was clearly arguing that his concern for presenting an ambitious ethos was the result of his superior knowledge of the audience for the business plan:

Bill: These are milestones, and they [venture capitalists] want to see you literally going for more than you can handle.

John: I don't know about that. I think they want you to be realistic.

Paul: I think so too.

Bill: I think this is pretty close.

Bill's proposal was both an image-building ploy to satisfy Mark Whitney—a proposal that the managers could choose not to follow through with after they received some investment capital—and an expression of Bill's desire to be a leader in his field. The opposition to the proposal from the others was an expression of their collective ethos.

The members of the production group wished to portray a credible ethos by basing their projections of future actions on its own past actions. They believed that making claims that the company would not keep was damaging to the company. This issue came up in the meeting. When Bill mentioned the company's poor production track record, Paul angrily argued that the company did not have a poor production track record because it was working within impossible time schedules that had been created by overly ambitious claims about the company's ability to produce.

The production group wanted to be sure that the company's abilities matched its projected actions, especially if those actions were to be taken within the next year. As John said to Bill, "You're not providing a realistic picture if we don't think we're going to get in it [building the lab], and we really don't think we are really going to get in it." Dave exclaimed to Bill that the company's employees would "laugh in our faces" if they read that the company was going to develop a graphics laboratory in 1984. At another point Dave contended that they would appear to be overly ambitious by trying to do too much at once in 1984. Bill countered that he was arguing not from the point of view of a conservative, production group but from that of potential investors. The source of authority that Bill was claiming was the source of money.

The Question of Money

Although the executive committee had agreed to try to raise $3 million to $4 million over several years, members of the production group doubted whether this amount of money could support all of the company's operations and build a graphics lab. Given their perceptions of Bill's performance as a financial manager, they were skeptical about Bill's claim that they could afford to build the laboratory in 1984. They were suspicious of Bill's judgment of how much the laboratory would cost to build and fearful of Bill's tendency to spend impulsively. When Dave questioned Bill's cost projection for the lab, Bill countered with a promotional strategy. He posited an implicit hypothetical sequence that was based not on Microware's record, but on the accomplishments of another company. The implied hypothesis was if that company had built a graphics laboratory for X amount of dollars, then Microware could do it for less. Moreover, the money for the laboratory would not come solely from the investment they were seeking; it would also come from money generated from the sales of other products. Dave disagreed, stating that profits from other areas of the company would be needed to support those areas: "I think we're wired on working capital. [We are] basically tying ourselves [to the working capital], pumping, regenerating that money into its own areas, in areas we're already involved in. I don't really foresee us having $1.5 million, even sitting here one year from this day, the middle of October."

The production group was wary of Bill's tendency to spend company money impulsively. Dave was worried that if Bill were given the go-ahead to purchase such a system, he would spend the money all at once. If they were to proceed on such a project, Dave wanted to be sure that the GSC graphics system was the best buy; he wanted to shop around. He was afraid that Bill would demand to run to GSC and buy the graphics system immediately.

This concern with Bill's impulsive spending was discussed by Greg in an interview two months after this meeting. Greg disagreed with Bill's attitude toward spending money on this project. He said that Bill believed that "you go out with a carte blanche, you buy whatever you need, and you stick it in the [graphics] laboratory and just start the operation." The production group's fear of Bill's spending habits attested to the power that they still perceived in Bill. They feared what Bill would do with the investment money even though the executive committee had official power over such actions. Dave wanted the spending controls to be explicitly stated.

The Question of Managerial Ability

Another reason the production group felt that Microware could not build and run the graphics laboratory in 1984 was that they feared they could not manage its operation, a concern closely tied to their poor past record as managers and their inability to set clear company objectives and stick to them. Bill's answer was to base his argument not on the actions of those in Microware but on the actions of those outside the company. He did not cite another company's performance but instead conjured up a hypothetical sequence based on the ideal of the experienced manager—a "professional" whom they would hire. "I am not saying, at all, that we have people on board to manage this graphics products. . . I'm saying that we may have to go out and get somebody. So that's fine. You go out and get one or two very key people to manage this project, and go out and get six or seven people to run it."

Even if the company hired experts, Dave was still concerned that the production operation for the laboratory would require the top management to be in control of that operation. And, in stating this, he reminded Bill of a mistake that management had made in giving responsibility to an ex-employee named Tim Hamner: "Five of us, or six of us, or whatever the hell's running this company has to pull the strings on their puppet no matter how fantastic of a wonderful guy he is, and tell him what he's gonna do with that [lab]. If you just tell him, hey, come on in, have a good time, here you go Tim Hamner, you know." He then argued by using Bill's strategy. Dave's hypothetical sequence concerned actions that the management group themselves would need to perform. Unlike Bill, Dave projected Microware's future from Microware's past experience—a key strategy that the production group wanted to employ to project a credible ethos.

Dave: I'm just saying, even if you get a very experienced person, if you do not dictate to him and clearly define your objectives . . . . That's part of the problem we're having right now with Liz [there had been some recent confusion as to exactly how she was to go about selling certain products], that we did not for a while clearly define what [she] was supposed to have done week by week, month by month.

Bill: Professional businesspeople who have several years of experience don't need that handholding.

Paul: They need a certain amount.

Bill: Fine.

Dave: They need a company direction.

Several times during 1983 top management agreed that they had not been able to provide a consistent company direction since the company had begun; thus, the production group based its opposition to the graphics lab proposal on past performance. The promotion argument was based on a predicted outcome from the work of someone from outside the company.

The Question of Technical Knowledge
The production group also lacked sufficient technical knowledge to build and run the graphics laboratory in 1984. Paul and John, both programmers, were especially concerned about the company's technical ability to tackle the laserdisc project. Greg and Bill argued that they had already done the technical research, but others argued that it was the technicians who needed to do the research to discover what type of products they could produce with the system. Research information derived solely from magazines was inadequate.

Paul: Are we going to do the research?

Bill: We've already done research.

Paul: To what extent, reading an article?

Dave: Yeah.

Bill: I have a thirty page report to Graphics Systems Corporation which mainly deals with interfacing laserdisc with an IBM PC Peanut, so I've done a fair amount of research.

Greg: We did do research over the summer on the whole process . . .

John: But what I think we really need, when you say research, you've got to have the damn thing in here and screw around with it.

Greg: That's not true.

Bill: That's not true.

Paul: I think you have to have somebody devoted to doing the research and writing out a plan. I think what you did was that you got an overall view of what it would entail.

Later Paul pointed out that it was not Bill who needed to know the appropriate technology; it was the production people, those who would be running the project. The production group posited that based on the company's past performance, it lacked the ability to undertake such a large and complex project. Dave recalled that Bill had wanted to buy such a lab a year earlier, and Dave assured Bill that if they had already had done so, they would have wasted it. Bill argued that he knew the system and they would not have wasted it. Paul countered that it did not matter if Bill knew it; it was the production people who would need to know the system:

Dave: Bill, come on, we couldn't even handle the things that we thought we knew, let alone something that's totally tertiary to our knowledge.

Bill: Oh, its tertiary to maybe your knowledge; but I've been doing a lot of research about it.

Paul: But you're not going to be running it. It's not tertiary to your knowledge, it's tertiary to all of ours.

Paul's last statement was an admission that Bill was not considered part of the production team. Greg, however, was a programmer and one of the production management group. Later in the debate, he brought the two sides together, but that did not happen until the debate reached a complete deadlock, one that threatened the authority structure of the company.

Deadlock: Promotion versus Production
The two sides were unable to reach agreement because they were arguing from two different foundations. This uncompromising clash of realities

kept them from achieving a collaborative rhetorical choice and kept top management from operating as a team—both before and after the establishment of the executive committee. The clash of these realities threatened the authority structure of the company during this meeting, just as it had several times in the past.

Three of the production managers, Dave, Paul, and John were adamantly opposed to Bill's milestone statement. After approximately twenty minutes of intense debate, these three aggressively held to their objections to the passage. Bill was equally tenacious, arguing that 1984 was the only time the company could get into this technology. If they waited too long, large electronics/computer companies would enter the laserdisc market and squeeze out the little companies like Microware.

This, the most impassioned part of the debate, was triggered by Dave's fear that Bill's proposal would project a foolish ethos to some readers of the business plan. The entire issue, as Bill exclaimed at the end of the following passage, came down to one version of reality versus another reality: promotion versus production:

Dave: I mean you are going to show this to every single . . . employee. We promised them that, and I do not want to . . .

Bill: I promised them a cut-down version of this.

Dave: Bill, you've got to. . . I mean if you can't give them this [the "Milestones" section], then there's no sense in giving them the whole plan.

Bill: I'm saying that certain parts of this thing will not be given to them including some of the financial information.

Dave: True, but I mean Milestones? Hell, every employee should know where the hell you're headed.

Bill: Hey, I hope, and I wish, and I will make sure that every employee knows that's [the graphics laboratory] one of our goals.

Dave: Bill, I think we're fooling ourselves in thinking we're seriously having that in there next year!

Bill: All it says is that we're looking at purchasing it in the last quarter of 1984.

Dave: You're splitting hairs.

Bill: I think you're splitting hairs goddammit! You're saying, "Push it to '85 I'll be happy." I'm saying "put it in '84 or don't bother with it!"

Dave: OK, then don't bother with it!

Bill: Then don't bother with Consumer Products!

Dave: OK, don't bother with it!

Bill: Let's just drop it right now!

Dave: Fine!

Bill: Can the advertising, can everything else, because I'm not going to go any further unless we have something we can really make [unintelligible].

Dave: Fine.

John: If that's the way you feel, then we should have done that!

Bill: The way I feel is, let's keep this going, let it work for itself, and let it move on to something that's going to make some money.

Dave: You are showing this to fifty, or to thirty employees, and they're going to laugh in our faces!

Bill: They are only going to laugh when guys like you, Dave, will say it's a joke and it's not worth it, and . . .

Dave: Bill, it's not going to happen!

Paul: If it's not going to happen, then it is a joke!

Dave: It is not! I mean I do not think it is going to happen!

Bill: Fine! You don't!

Dave: John doesn't! Paul doesn't! and Frank doesn't! That's six of us! I don't know how Greg and you feel!

Bill: Then let's drop Consumer Products right now!

Dave: Bill, Jesus!

Bill: I'm serious, David!

Dave: I know we have to . . . if you really . . . I agree with you we have to get involved in this but we do not . . . We are fooling ourselves thinking in the next twelve months we are going to spend $1.5 million, hire the people and get this up and running in the next year, because we are fooling ourselves!

Bill: Fine. It's your idea of realism versus mine, or versus Greg's or versus anybody else's!

When the debate came down to this standoff between the two competing realities, the central issue became the control of the company: entrepreneurial control versus committee management. Immediately after Bill said that it was his reality versus theirs, Dave asserted the ideal of committee management: the group must come to an agreement that satisfied each of them. Bill countered with his one last source of entrepreneurial power—his connection with Mark Whitney:

Dave: I mean we all have to believe in this 100 percent, and I don't believe in this.

Bill: But we also don't have to have every decision to be a compromise so that everybody has to agree, otherwise it doesn't even get put down on paper. That's what it's been up to this point, and I'm getting tired of it!!!

Dave: Well, Bill, I'm sorry to say, but based on past performance, that's the way it's going to be for awhile.

Bill: Well, we'll see about that.

Dave: That's the way it's going to be.

Bill: We'll see about that.

Dave: Bill, you can argue about it as much as you want.

Bill: And I'll say I'll walk out that door right now and you can finish the business plan. Raise the rest of the money among yourselves! See if Northland Bank gets involved!

Regardless of the official sanctioning of the executive committee's authority, as long as that group of managers included individuals separated by such different points of view as that separating Bill from the production group, the teamwork ideal of Ted Wilson and Bob Hatlin would not be achieved. But just as the process of writing the business plan brought this confrontation to the surface, the writing process was also the means by which these realities were merged. The compromise that led to an agreement on the graphics laboratory passage served as an instance of the cooperative teamwork that the executive committee was designed to achieve.

Compromise: Setting a Promotion Goal Through a Production Strategy
Although the debate was at a standstill, the two sides did agree on one important thing: without something like the laserdisc technology, the company's long-term projections looked dim. Everyone agreed—some reluctantly—that Micromed, although their best product to date, had only a limited future:

Bill: We could be put out of the (Micromed system) market so fast by a competitor. One of our major competitors, and we're starting to get a lot of them now, Health Systems is on the IBM PC or will be in the next six months. What if one of us goes to a major health care supplier, and they start pushing it nationwide? There's only 70,000 hospitals out there total, meaning 40,000 to 50,000 that are going to automate.

John: Only 70,000. That's a lot.

Bill: Only 70,000; well you got forty other competitors who are fighting for that 70,000 and [some] even bigger than us.

Dave: It [the potential market] is cutting down.

They were also concerned that their other products would quickly become obsolete. The relevant technology would continually evolve, rendering the current technology inadequate in a few years:

Bill: You ain't going to [make lots of money in 1986] with our current round of products, nor any future round of products like we have; it's got to be something totally revolutionary, unique.

Dave: True, so you think . . .

Bill: I think laserdisc games, interfaced . . . do I have to, again . . . I said this nine months ago that this is going to happen and people said, "You're crazy, you're joking" . . .

Dave: OK, no, I agree with you that it's going to happen.

If the hospital software business was not a long-term money maker and their current games and graphics technology would soon become obsolete, a new venture, like the laserdisc project, would be necessary. The participants all agreed to this. The major stumbling block was time: when would they be prepared to do it? As Paul said immediately after Bill played his Mark Whitney trump card to gain more control of the company's decision-making process, "We're not saying don't do it! We're saying do it in a realistic time frame!" But when would it be too late to do it? As Bill said in reply to Paul, "I'm saying if you push it to 1985 it is unrealistic because there's no chance of us being in the market."

In the face of this impasse, there were the seeds of resolution. The general agreement about the inevitability of developing innovative applications of new technologies was the basis for that resolution. Everyone at that meeting believed that start-ups had to indicate that they were, to use the cliche, "cutting edge." What was needed was a compromise that merged the promotion and production realities.

Greg merged these realities; he held a significant middle ground between the promotion-versus-production debate. He shared Bill's a vision that stemmed back to their precorporation days of Microware as a success in the field of computer graphics, the field on which he had originally wanted to base the company. But Greg was a disciple of Bob Hatlin and a part of the production team that Hatlin helped to develop during the summer. Greg was in a position to merge the promotion and production realities. He did this by arguing for the graphics laboratory project by using the production strategy: he presented the project in terms of a temporal sequence that would integrate various members of the production team. By describing the graphics laboratory project in terms of the past action of the Micromed production group, he demonstrated that the project could succeed. He thus addressed the three production questions of money, managerial ability, and technical knowledge.

The first part of Greg's compromise introduced the conservative beginnings that the project would have if implemented:

Greg: OK, a compromise. The compromise is as follows: First of all, you've got to understand that you can bring this operation up in staged manner. The way the staged manner goes is that peripheral to the main system is the introductory system, which can be delivered in thirty days. It can bring up an operation by starting to enter images one at a time and then finishing those images later on. OK, so if we got the money, if we got a little bit of money, we could get those systems on lease for—what was the figure?

Bill: $7,000 to $8,000 a month.

Greg: At $7,000 to $8,000 a month just to begin to bring it up, so first of all we don't need the whole dollar amount. That's the first thing.

Dave: OK.

Greg: So, it's not, boom, you set up the whole . . . it's not, boom, you go out and buy a building, buy a room, outfit the room, and put in a million dollars worth of equipment. But you start with one piece of equipment and one or two people, and you build it up from there. It takes some time to do.

Dave: Right.

Greg was beginning to illustrate the sequential steps necessary to build the graphics lab. This sequence led Bill to suggest revising the original passage:

Greg: That's number one. Number two, if you state that it is a staged approach, and number two that the staged approach won't begin until the capital raising begins, then you build in a contingency. I think we ought to start this in the first quarter of '84 just for the fact that we've got a lot of learning to do.

Dave: Oh, right, but, I mean, going out and spending $1.5 million.

Greg: We won't spend it all; we might want to say that we begin building a lab . . .

Bill: Why don't we say "staged purchase"?

Not only did Greg begin to portray the sequence of events necessary to develop the technical side of the project, but he also integrated the financial aspect of the proposal in the sequence. A few minutes later, Greg based the entire production sequence on one of Microware's most successful past accomplishments and in doing so discussed the problem of managing the project:

Greg: I want to make an analogy to the growth of the Micromed group. I mean when we started, you two guys [John and Paul] were it, with Frank helping you out a little bit in the marketing end and he was also trying to handle everything else at that point in time. Look at what happened. You two guys busted your butts for the longest period of time, slowly built up your operation. Added programmers and . . .

Dave: And they're about fifty people short.

Paul: Yeah.

Greg: OK. Then you added your marketing staff; then you added your sales staff; then we started to get production and engineering. The same thing is going to happen with any division that we start, OK? We're going to start a graphics division, and you've got to assume that we're going to start it small with a couple of key people, not necessarily on the vice-presidential level—maybe only a manager with a couple of key employees and a systems operator beneath him, and a computer, a PDP 11. And that's going to build, and there'll be a second PDP 11, and that'll build on top of that, we'll get the operation staff for the VAX.

The argument to start the project in 1984 became a production argument through Greg's presentation of the proposal by means of the production strategy. When this was done, the production group agreed to the proposal. Dave then wanted one other part of the original passage altered—the financial statement—to reflect the production strategy: "I can agree on starting [in '84], but when it says 'purchase of sophisticated . . .' I can picture you [Bill] . . . wanting to go down and spend $1.5 million and buying this whole package of goods and come back." Paul also was concerned that the financial statement in the sentence still indicated an unrealistic promotional action. Bill proposed one more revision that included the issue of finances:

Paul: OK, yeah . . . I agree with Dave where we're just not going to have the time to start it up all at once in '84.

Bill: I'm not saying start it all up.

Dave: "Staged approach."

Bill: I'm saying start it.

Dave: "Staged approach" I have no problems with, but the way this is stated here, it's cut and dried; we are going to blow all our money . . .

Bill: "Staged development?" and then in parentheses "contingent upon capital investment"?

Dave: That's great!

John: "Dependent on capital investment"? That what we got?

Paul: Yeah.

With this point, the two sides agreed on the revisions to the passage. The original passage read:

• Purchase of sophisticated computer graphics production lab to generate graphic frames used in laserdisc/microcomputer consumer products (Graphics Systems Corporation's Image Animation System).

The revised passage read:

• Initial staged development of sophisticated computer graphics production lab to generate graphic frames used in laserdisc/microcomputer consumer products (contingent upon capital raising).

Two collaborative rhetorical choices were made. The process of making these choices consisted of two phases. The first its origins in the company's beginnings and proceeded up to August 25 when the exigence for writing a new business plan became known to the participants. The second phase, which began on August 25, was the period of direct collaboration that ended during the meeting when the participants wrote the final version of the graphics laboratory proposal.

After the 1983 business plan was completed, Microware received the rest of its loan and continued to raise money through investment and through increasing sales of Micromed. But it was unable to escape from the debt it incurred in its first two years and went bankrupt in 1986.

Writing and the Organization: A Reciprocal Relationship

This study, like those of Paradis, Dobrin, and Miller (1985) and McCarthy (1991), illustrates some ways that writing processes and written products can shape the collective work of individuals tied to a common enterprise. It thus posits a reciprocal relationship among writing processes, products, and the social and organizational contexts within which those processes and products are enacted. In this relationship, elements of the organizational context influence writers, writing processes, and texts, and, conversely, writers, writing processes, and texts shape the organization. As Harrison (1987) states, "Communities of thought render rhetoric comprehensible and meaningful. Conversely, however, rhetorical activity builds communities that subsequently give meaning to rhetorical action" (p. 9).

The participants' perceptions of the computer market, the local economy, NSU and the Start-Up Project, advisers, consultants, and bankers all influenced and made comprehensible and meaningful the rhetorical activities in Microware. At the same time, the community-building aspect of those rhetorical activities was particularly evident in the Microware environment because the organization, as well as the microcomputer software industry, was new and unstable.

The Influence of Social and Organizational Contexts

In its simplest form, two points of view dominated Microware's rhetorical activity: the promotion point of view, embodied by Bill Alexander, and the production point of view espoused by the company's other managers. The managers who formed the production group came together on the basis of shared attitudes and shared awareness of past experiences. These group-forming and group-binding experiences formed the basis of their view of reality, which influenced their rhetorical activity.

The conflict between the promotion and production realities centered on control over predicting the company's future. When it was necessary to predict the future to raise money or to plan the company's work, these opposing viewpoints clashed over the best way to do so. When the participants perceived a disorder in their community, which they attempted to solve rhetorically—that is, when they conceived of the rhetorical situation for writing the 1983 business plan—there arose differing views of the rhetorical situation. In particular, there arose differing views of ethos, the image of the company that readers would perceive in the business plan, and audience, the characterization of the needs and desires of those to whom the plan was written. Among the collaborators there was a continual tension between conceiving of their readers as embodying the glamour-seeking characteristics that Bill described, or conceiving of the audience as embodying the conservative characteristics that the production group expressed as their own point of view.

This conflict is echoed in Bell and McNamara's (1991) analysis of the purposes of business plans. A business plan should serve as "a sales brochure directed at potential investors" and "a place where the founders can describe their vision for the firm" but also as "a set of guidelines for operating the company" and "the standard of record against which the firm expects its results to be measured" (p. 34). At Microware, these two sets of goals were not easily reconciled. Can one document both sell an image and represent a clear production plan that will guide the course of the company? Can it present a vision that is at once exciting and feasible, compelling and practical? Which of these purposes better serves the intended audiences? While trying to serve all of these purposes, which should be emphasized? The social and organizational environment at Microware made the answers to these questions quite difficult to answer.

While the social and organizational context influenced conflicting views of audience and ethos, the authority structure of the company shaped the collaborative writing process. On August 25, when the direct phase of collaboration began, Bill was still very much the entrepreneurial leader of the company and the collaborative process reflected this structure of authority: Bill was planning to write the business plan and use the other participants as his sources of information.

By September 7, the company's authority structure had changed from entrepreneurial control to committee control. The collaborative writing process mirrored this change by proceeding along the lines of the production group's team/committee approach to decision making. In this approach to running the company, the decision-making authority was consensual; decisions were discussed, and no one person had the ultimate authority to make a decision. Individual expertise, however, was respected; each member of the group was responsible for his or her areas of expertise. Writing the plan was a process of allowing each person to write the parts of the plan that covered his or her areas of responsibility or expertise. The president's role was also integrated into this committee approach to collaboration. On September 11, when the newly sanctioned executive committee met for the first time to write the plan, Bill, like each member of the production group, was assigned certain sections to write that covered his areas of responsibility or expertise.

From September 11 until October 13, the relative authority of the executive committee and the president was unsettled, and so was the collaborative writing process. The authority to run the company that had officially been given to the executive committee had effectively reduced the authority of the president to that of the other officers and vice-presidents. In practice, this structure was problematic. Because of their differing views of reality, the president and the members of the production group were not yet integrated into a committee that worked as a team.

Nor was the writing process proceeding as a team process. The committee approach to writing the plan had only been moderately successful. Not everyone wrote his or her sections to the satisfaction of the others, and thus the executive committee gave Bill the authority to finish the plan on his own. After completing a late draft of the entire plan, Bill believed that little had changed and that his decision-making control remained intact.

By the October 13 collaborative writing session, the authority structure of the company was still in question, and the writing process reflected this uncertainty. These uncertainties reached a climax when the graphics lab debate was deadlocked. Simultaneously the company's authority structure and the collaborative writing process were threatened: the collaborators could not agree on a rhetorical choice, and Bill threatened a power struggle for control of the company. The company's authority structure was split by the clash of opposing realities. As a result, crucial rhetorical choices concerning the graphics lab could not be agreed upon. The process of collaboration reflected the relative authority of the collaborators.

The Influence of Rhetorical Action
Writing processes can help plan and coordinate the activities of the individual and the organization and serve as a primary means of bringing the activities of different groups and individuals into phase with one another. At Microware, the process of writing the business plan brought the participants' activities into phase with one another by forcing them to clarify the relative authority of each of the participants over the running of the company. The collaborative writing process played a significant role in the reapportionment of authority among the participants by providing a means to challenge the president's authority and by providing an opportunity to resolve the power struggle between the president and the other members of the executive committee. The collaborative process first served as a challenge to Bill's authority when the production group began to collaborate on writing the business plan. This challenge occurred in two ways: while collaborating, the production group made decisions about the company's future and evaluated some of Bill's past decisions. These evaluations led the group to question Bill's judgment as the company's primary decision maker. The process of writing the plan enabled the production group to make decisions about the company that reflected

their production-committee management view of reality and thus chal-
lenged Bill's promotional-entrepreneurial control of the company.

Second, the process of collaborating served as a means of resolving the
climactic impasse of the promotion versus production conflict. By employing the strategy of the production ethos to rewrite a proposal that
was primarily an expression of a promotional ethos, the participants integrated opposing realities. The collaborative writing process thus
achieved a balance that was necessary for the committee management
structure to function as it was intended—as a team. The writing process
helped to resolve the power struggle, shaping the social reality of the top
management of the company.

Matching Entrepreneurs and Venture Capital: A Rhetorical Enterprise

In the conclusion to my previous analysis (Doheny-Farina 1991) of the
company's first business plan, I summarized one of my primary arguments about that plan. I had argued that the document shaped the company in a defective way and that flawed beginning eventually led to the
company's demise. But this reasoning, I went on to say, was quite simplistic. The business plan could not be the only influence that shaped the
company:

Although it is tempting to paint the 1982 business plan as an extremely powerful
document, it may seem quite implausible to place the company's failure squarely
on the deficiencies of that plan. I have done this largely by presenting an uncritical
depiction of Bill's and Abruzzi's claims that a business plan must serve as the complete "road map" for a company's operation and development. An alternate view
indicates that the failure of Microware demonstrates not just the deficiencies of
Bill's plan, but the failure of Bill and Abruzzi (and others) to understand the limitations of business plans. This interpretation suggests that the business plan as a
genre is insufficient to serve the function that Bill and Abruzzi claimed it could
serve.

Supporting this view is the seemingly obvious assumption that even a startup
company cannot be solely constituted by discourse but must be composed of significant nondiscursive reality as well. Clearly, in this case, those nondiscursive elements—the technical means to produce software—were deficient and no matter
how exacting the business plan, those deficiencies could not be overcome. This
view, while suggesting a generic limitation of business plans, does not undercut
their potentially constructive power. Indeed, this case shows how an entrepreneurial vision expressed in a business plan drew the attention of, ironically, experts in
the assessment of technology away from the problematic technology of the company. Thus, while it may have been a mistake to assume that such a document
could give direction to an entire organization, in this case the organization was

left with little else to give it that direction. Therefore, we are left with a picture of a text that played a very important but not exclusive role in the rise and decline of a new organization. (pp. 330–331)

The problem with believing in the generic form for a business plan is that that form must operate in a volatile environment. Business plans are not simply containers of information; they are transactions and part of a process. How can one establish or accept a set of conventions for a transaction that has few rules to guide it? The answer is that business plan conventions are tenuous at best and simplistic at worse.

Much advice about writing business plans is based on the components that the plans should include. Looking at the writing of business plans as a process of including components (product, market, strategy, management, financial projections) is initially a useful but ultimately a limited view of business plans. This supply-the-components approach is based on a container metaphor of written communication that assumes that the key to writing an effective document is to fill it with the right mix of elements. This is a limited way to look at the communication that goes on in the process of attracting venture capital and employee support to entrepreneurial enterprises. This container approach also assumes that we can identify the generic argument (the claims and support that the entrepreneur puts forth) of business plans.

The flaw in this assumption is that start-up enterprises are often operating in unstable environments characterized by new technologies, new applications, and new markets. Think back for a moment to the exciting but fast-changing environment of the fledgling microcomputer market in 1982. Not only were the technological applications new; the whole industry was new, and many questions were unanswered: What do microcomputer software companies do? Do they produce a range of product types or only concentrate on one? What is the nature of the market? Who has, wants, needs microcomputers? Are they truly personal or home products? Is this really a mass market? The possible answers were as many as they were unclear. Add to that uncertainty the variable nature of the entrepreneur's primary audience: the venture capitalists who may invest in the enterprise. Citing his own research and the research of others, Roberts (1991) argues that it is difficult to characterize the readers of business plans. Venture capitalists are a diverse group and their criteria for judging plans are neither rule-bound nor are they predictable. Even when venture capitalists state their own preferences in business plans, their actions may undermine some of the criteria they claim to follow. The foundation for generic business plans is problematic.

Although those who advise start-ups can recommend that they develop business plans containing certain sections and certain types of information, written in a clear style (or a glamorous style, or an understated style or some other style), that is only a partial view of the communicative situation for starting a company and raising money. A more complex view sees business plans as highly rhetorical actions. The difficult nature of these actions lies both in the instability of new technologies and markets and also in the indeterminancies of the potential audiences. A business plan is based on a shifting, imperfect mix of what you can do and what you say you can do, what you want your employees to think that you do, what world (market, technology, business environment) you want to construct, and what elements of that world you want to emphasize to potential investors.

As in this case, business plans are central to the transfer of technology from universities to the marketplace. The act of writing a plan is not merely an attempt to communicate such enterprises; it is an attempt to create them. Similarly, interpreting and accepting or rejecting business plans are also highly constructive acts. Entrepreneurs and venture capitalists are continually involved in negotiating the shape of their worlds; they are powerful rhetoricians.

3
From Lab to Market: The Role of Instructional Texts in the Transfer of Biomedical Technology

In an age of global competition, the nation's industries must continually improve the ways that new technologies are adapted to the marketplace. Indeed, experts from government, business, and academe are calling for improvements in the commercialization of new technologies and their applications. For example, Robert Reich (1989) argues that the United States needs to improve the ways that new technologies are turned into competitive commercial products. One of the ways that this increased competitiveness must come about, says Reich, is through improvements in the ways that new technologies are adapted to users. Certainly the technical communicator must play a central and effective role in these processes.

Reich is not alone in recognizing that crucial connection between technological advances and commercially viable applications. Robert Breuder (1988) has also identified the importance of making technology more available and more usable: "The American technology 'factory' needs to provide customer support that trains users, helps them navigate the maze of available options, solves their problems, and modifies the product to fit their particular requirements. A nation that develops new technology but neither rapidly distributes this technology to users nor supports these users as they change their methods will not survive in an increasingly competitive marketplace" (p. 31).

Technical communicators play a key role in this process of tailoring innovations to the market. In fact, technical writers often see themselves as the customers' advocates in new product development projects and as liaisons between the innovations and the potential users of those innovations. This task of bridging that gap is fraught with difficulties. Often the writers may cause or experience obstacles in their path. Indeed, when we begin to look at the large issue of technology transfer through the narrow focus of communication research, we can start to see some of the significant *rhetorical* barriers to successful technology transfer.

Rhetorical Barriers to Technology Transfer

In order to understand these barriers, it is useful to examine what assumptions we bring to the term *technology transfer*. Roland Schmitt, the president of Rensselaer Polytechnic Institute, indicates that it is tempting to see technology transfer as a process of moving a piece of technology from distinct point to distinct point along a route that begins in R&D and ends at the customer: "Technology transfer is a misnomer. It has the implication of being a handoff process—that you have knowledge, a discovery, or a better understanding of something, and then you simply transfer it to someone else. That isn't the way it works" (Schmitt in Maguire 1988, p. 14). The ideal instead, Schmitt notes, is for knowledge to move from labs to factories to markets in a continuous, seamless way, characterized by frequent communications across disciplines, hierarchies, and stages. It must be a reciprocal process—moving forward with help from those from earlier stages. Those who are downstream—the people who will turn the new technology into a product—should influence those who develop the technology. Conversely, those downstream who are bringing a technology to market later need to interact with the developers even as the technology moves closer to its commercial application.

An ideal of continous, seamless movement must operate on the fundamental assumption that everyone at all places in the transfer has similar conceptions of the nature of the technology, the purpose of the technology, the purpose of the application, and the means to bring the technology from its origins to the market. Unfortunately, such an assumption may rarely be validated in practice. Indeed, the differences in these conceptions represent the central barrier to successful, seamless technology transfer. As Carolyn Miller (1989) argues in her critique of the buzzword *technology transfer*, we commonly see the term as meaning something neutral and value free, a perception that often masks significantly differing ideas of what is being transferred and how that transfer is taking place:

Since these kinds of transfer transactions are usually motivated on both ends— both supplier and recipient believe they benefit, one from the sale and one from the product. The problems are located in *what* is transferred and the location to which it is transferred. That location is not a simple place; it is complex, and differentiated. . . . And what is being transferred may not be understood in the same way by supplier and recipient. The technology transferred involves not only a product but a set of practices, and many times the practices embedded in the technology are deeply incompatible with the practices indigenous to the transfer destination. (p. 10)

Sometimes a new technology is inappropriate for a new site or new culture; sometimes it is disruptive, ineffective, or wasteful. Sometimes it could be useful but it is not being adapted effectively for those who will benefit by its use. The process of adapting technology from its origins to the marketplace must involve technical communicators. They must be at the center of the transfer process. Yet even skilled communicators will face difficult hurdles as they attempt to make such transfers. To gain insight into the ways that industries can improve the transition innovations from research lab to the marketplace, it may be useful to understand some of the rhetorical barriers that hinder these transitions. In this chapter, I will present a case study that explores some of those obstacles. From the outset, this case describes a *highly successful, highly cooperative* transfer. Yet it *still* was fraught with barriers that had to be overcome in order to bring an advanced technological innovation to the marketplace successfully.

This case study of a company that attempted to bring a highly sophisticated, experimental, electromechanical device to market provides a glimpse of the innovative technology involved in this new product, as well as the three different institutions involved in its development. More important, it provides a detailed analysis of the role that certain technical texts played in this process and the problems and successes that occurred along the way. Ultimately this case focuses on the rhetorical barriers involving rhetorical actions in the transfer of technology and the ways those barriers were crossed. This journey begins with a story.

An Attack in the Night

Let us imagine that it is 7:30 on a cold winter evening, and you are sitting at home reading a comment draft of a manual that you wrote at work. You must do this because you are caught up in some tight deadlines in your job as technical writer and you have been feeling a tremendous amount of stress for weeks. The comments from editors and engineers are particularly biting, and you are unhappy with their unenlightened responses to your work. As you page through the report, your tense stomach gurgles, and you get a faint taste of what for you was a typical evening meal: something fried with some greasy sidedish and some fat-laden dessert, which you did not really enjoy because your mind is on your job and its impossible deadlines. You light up your thirtieth cigarette of the day and reach for your after-dinner drink. For the moment, you are completely unaware that blood is coursing through your body, oxygenated by your lungs and pumped by your heart. You are becoming aware, however, that your arm is feeling numb. Suddenly you clutch at a sharp pain in your chest. You are having a heart attack. What you will learn over the course of the next weeks is that the oxygenated blood that was reaching other parts of your body was severely restricted to the pump itself: your heart has not been receiving that blood because the arteries that carry blood to your heart are clogged. That lack of blood has damaged your heart.

Now let us jump ahead a few days. You are on the table in the operating room of a hospital. You are anesthetized, and a team of surgeons, nurses, and medical technicians is performing surgery designed to replace those clogged arteries with veins from your leg—veins that are clear, potentially effective vessels that will enable more blood to flow to your heart. In order to graft these vessels to your heart, the surgeons must open your chest and stop your heart from beating. They lower your heart's temperature and flood the heart with a chemical solution that will stop its beating. But the surgeons also must use some means to continue pumping blood throughout your body. Part of your surgery involves attaching you to a heart-lung machine, a device that enables your blood circulation system to bypass your heart, allowing the surgeons an unobstructed operating area. Your unoxygenated blood leaves your body through a tube, flows through the device where it is oxygenated, and then returns through a tube back into your system. Your blood is pumped through those tubes by what is known as a roller pump; the tube that contains your blood is placed against a wheellike set of rollers. That wheel spins, and each roller presses against the tube and for a moment pushes the contents of the tube in one direction. The effect of rollers' continually hitting the tube, rolling, and then leaving the tube creates a pulsation, pumping your blood. This extremely valuable technology that enables your surgery to be performed has one particularly serious limitation. Because of the way that the heart-lung machine pumps fluid—it squeezes some of the blood every time the roller hits the tube—the pump damages some of the blood that it pumps. So that your blood does not become damaged to a significant extent, the device can be used only for two or three hours.

Over the course of these two hours, the veins from your leg have been grafted to the proper points without difficulty. Now the surgeons are trying to wean you from the heart-lung machine and revive your heart. Unfortunately, your heart is very weak, and the surgeons are concerned that it will not be able to pump blood effectively without some support. But time is running out on the usefulness of the heart-lung machine. In order to remove the heart-lung machine from your circulatory system, your surgeons make two decisions: they apply some drugs to your system to help the heart increase its ability to pump, and they insert a balloon pump into your aorta. The balloon pump is designed to slip into the aorta and expand and contract in concert with the natural pumping of your heart. With this help and the application of drugs, the surgeons hope that your heart will recover to the point where it pumps sufficiently on its own. A medical technician is called to run the balloon pump after it is inserted into your system. That technician wheels into place near the operation area a console the size of a small desk. When the pumping is started, the technician reads a screen that provides a visual indication of the beating of your heart and the pulsations of the balloon. The technician watches the screen and slides an adjusting bar across a scale on the console in order to adjust the machine so that its pulses and your heart's pulses are aligned properly. As the technician moves the bar, the pulsation indicators move on the screen. All the technician needs to do is match those two pulsations by moving the pumps so that it matches your heart's pulsations accordingly.

Your heart is not responding well to this strategy. You are nearing the end of the potential options that will save your life. Your years of dietary excess, work stress, and physical inactivity have led you to an advanced stage of heart disease, and your chances of survival are quickly diminishing. Your surgeons decide that there is only one more option left to save you. You had been told of this option the day before your surgery, and you agreed that, if necessary, you would be willing to participate in this experimental procedure. What you had learned was that this hospital is a participant in an experimental program to develop and test a new type of cardiovascular support system, a new pump. This system has been used on a number of patients in a limited setting and now is being tested on a wider scale. Within a couple of years, the developers of the pump hope that it will be widely used by hospitals nationwide. But in order to reach that goal, it must be approved by the federal government. It must go through a series of clinical trials, actual-use tests in hospitals that will make the system part of its cardiac care services.

The surgeons have decided to use the experimental device. They will hook you up to the experimental pump so that either your heart will have more time to recover or your surgeons will have more time to replace your heart with a healthy donor heart. This third pump is what the popular press calls an artificial heart, but unlike some of the celebrated experiments with artificial hearts in which a patient's heart is removed and replaced with the electromechanical heart itself, this pump will serve only as a bridge to one of two options: natural heart recovery or transplantation. Therefore, this pump is referred to as an assist pump.

This assist pump is clearly needed if you are to survive. During your surgery, there were some crucial moments for you and some tense moments for the new assist pump team. Because the new pump is not used until all other options have been explored, the surgeons cannot predict when the team must be assembled to do the appropriate surgery. A small group of potential team members must be trained so that there are team members on duty around the clock. In your case, this part of your surgery began in the evening, and some of the team members were from the night staff. All of these individuals had been trained, but some of them had not participated in this surgery before. During the process of attaching the assist pump to you and setting it up to pump, the surgeon worked with one of the night staff technicians whose responsibility was to operate the pump's drive unit, the file cabinet–sized device that contained all of the controls needed to run and adjust the pump during its use. This operation was the first assist pump operation for this technician.

Several times during that phase of the surgery the technician had to make crucial decisions based on interpretations of the condition of your heart and the capabilities of the assist pump. Shortly after the surgeon gave the go-ahead to start the assist pump, the surgeon indicated that you were not responding well. You were at a crucial juncture: the assist pump needed to perform more efficiently to keep you alive. The surgeon turned to the technician and said, "I'm not getting enough output. What can you do to increase the output of the pump?" You were lying on the table with tubelike cannulas connecting the atria in your chest to the pump; your heart was pumping weakly. Your cardiovascular system, and with it your life, was threatened. At that moment, the technician could have made one or more of several adjustments to the device. These adjustments each could increase the output of the pump, but they would also have a physiological effect on you. A poorly chosen adjustment may hurt your condition, which at this point is tenuous at best. Which adjustment or combination of adjustments should the technician make? Fortunately, the technician made some good decisions at that point and other equally crucial points in the procedure, and the entire assist pump staff handled the device well throughout its use.

Over the course of a week, you survived as this pump, attached to your chest but sitting outside your body, kept your circulatory system running so that your heart eventually recovered. By the week's end, you were weaned from the assist pump, and your natural heart was strong enough to take over on its own. We will leave you as you lie in your hospital bed, munching on a celery stalk and contemplating a new, far less stressful career.

What is missing from this story is the long, difficult process that brought that technology out of a research lab and adapted it to the marketplace. A case study of this process is the focus of this chapter. Although there have been many academic and industrial case studies written about technology transfers and the processes of taking innovations to the marketplace, this one is a bit different because it focuses in general on the role of technical communication and in particular on the role of certain types of technical documentation in that transfer process. In presenting an analysis of this type of transfer, I explore the answer to one question that relates to the story I have just told. The question is not, What did the users do to implement the technology effectively? Instead, it is "How did the users learn how to make those decisions and operate that technology effectively? The answer reveals not only the important role that technical writers played in this process but also the daunting problems inherent in transferring an innovative technology from use by experts in a research and development lab to use by nonexperts in the marketplace. The following case study explores the significant but often overlooked function that technical writing can play in technology transfers and reveals the ever-contingent nature of not only the instructional materials associated with the new technology but also of the new technology itself.

Case Study

Documenting the Art of Science

At a university medical school, a team of scientists, engineers, and surgeons have spent ten years developing an artificial heart system designed to assist a patient's heart to survive bypass surgery or to serve as a bridge between the removal of a patient's heart and the transplantation of a donor heart. Over these years of bench testing and clinical trials, project participants have not only built these machines but have also learned how to manipulate them in differing and sometimes novel situations that demand interpretation and creative decisions.

During the process of developing the technology, these engineers, scientists, and surgeons have become skilled at the art of interpretation. They have learned this art by working in the lab with the technology and with other experts. This learn-by-doing process raises a key question for technical writers: how does a technical writer design an operation manual for new users of these devices—those who are completely unconnected to the original researchers and cannot go through the same lab apprenticeship? This was the task of several technical writers and engineers who were involved in the transfer of the artificial heart technology from the university research medical school to the hospital marketplace. But there were four rhetorical barriers to this transfer:

Barrier 1: Difficulty in discovering and communicating key knowledge from technical developers. The novices at the R&D site learned how to operate the device partially through an informal quasi-apprenticeship. In addition to the fact that the device was the central focus of their research work, the novices became experts through experimenting with the device in the lab and in actual patient use. Through this learn-by-doing approach, much of the detailed learning process was never formally recorded and eventually became internalized as tacit knowledge by those experts. When the technical writers from the corporation try to understand what the experts need to know in order to operate the devices, many of the details that have become internalized by the experts are difficult for the technical writers to discover and communicate in the instruction manuals.

Barrier 2: Difficulty in establishing ideal examples based on users' experiences. Because no combination of patient, hospital protocol, users' knowledge and abilities is what can be portrayed as *typical*, writing complex instructions is problematic. It is difficult to say, for example, that a normal adjustment is X and variations on that normality are A, B, and C. In a new technology—especially one with as many crucial variables as appear in this biomedical application—the norm often encompasses a wide range of possibilities.

Barrier 3: Difficulty in establishing an effective level of detail. How much information should a manual provide? Should the writer minimize the amount of information in order to create usable documents or elaborate in order to provide informationally complete documents? When and how should these two approaches be mixed?

Barrier 4: Disparity of technologies and users across the transfer. The customer-users have experience with other heart-assist technologies, but certain fundamental principles that underlie those technologies and influence decisions in their use are different in a few key ways. Users cannot rely on their experiences with other similar technologies. Furthermore, at the R&D end, the users are highly educated, highly experienced experts; at the customers' end, the users do not have advanced degrees in biomedical engineering and are relatively inexperienced with key aspects of this technology.

Methods, Organizations, and Participants

This case study, which was funded in part through a research grant from the Society for Technical Communication, was developed through a variety of qualitative data-gathering procedures, which I employed over two and a half years. I visited and observed work at three sites, conducted numerous interviews with the participants, collected documents, and observed and tape-recorded selected meetings and training sessions. All of the names of the participants, organizations, products, and certain medical processes are *pseudonyms*. One of my most fruitful techniques was the discourse-based interview (Odell, Goswami, Herrington, and Quick 1983) in which I would present the interviewee with the passages of a document that had been changed from one draft to another. By posing these oppositions to the interviewee, I attempted to break through the interviewees' tacit knowledge in order to probe the meanings that the participants attributed to the events, actions, and texts of their jobs.

The participants in this study span three organizations: Research Medical School (RMS), a large university research institution where the technology was developed; Biomed Corporation, a biomedical products company that purchased the rights to develop and sell the technology for large-scale markets; and Central Hospital, one of the first hospitals that will use the Biomed device in an experimental clinical trials phase of the product's development cycle.

I began by visiting and interviewing participants at the research lab at RMS, a large, multidimensional hospital and medical university. It is at this facility where the surgeons and engineers designed, built, and used prototypes of this device. The assist pump team at RMS has been working on the technology since the early 1980s and has used the device on more than 50 patients over that time. At RMS my primary sources of information were two biomedical engineers, Reza Said and Morris Lodge, who were principal members of the research team as well as users of the device. They not only have worked to design and build the assist pump and driver but are also the principal operators of the drive unit when the device is used at RMS. Reza holds a master's degree in biomedical engineering and is a doctoral candidate in the biomedical engineering program at RMS; he has worked as an engineer at RMS since the early 1980s. Morris holds a Ph.D. in biomedical engineering and has worked on the assist pump development program at RMS for approximately ten years. In addition to the interviews I conducted with Reza and Morris, I recorded a meeting that included their manager, Tom Neuman.

Biomed Corporation, the company that contracted with RMS to develop the assist pump for the marketplace, usually initiates new products in-house. It has developed a number of highly successful biomedical devices, some of which use blood pumping technologies. Biomed is a subsidiary of a major high technology–based company, and some of Biomed's laboratory research on this project was conducted at one of its parent corporation's facilities.

My central source of information was Rob Florio, the original technical writer on this project. Rob is the coordinator of regulatory affairs and clinical research on the assist pump project. These two functions require that he oversees Biomed's application to the federal regulatory agency (the Food and Drug Administration) that regulates projects such as this and the initial experimental uses of the device in selected hospitals. The latter is known as the *clinical trials phase*, and it is on this phase that my study focuses. Rob began this project as a technical writer in the mid-1980s. He wrote early versions of manuals before being promoted to the clinical trials coordinator. As coordinator, he designs and implements the clinical user training program and is still deeply involved with all aspects of the instructional texts. In fact, he is the principal reviewer of all drafts of the manuals. He conducts training for potential users of the assist pump drive system and arranges training sessions for potential surgical staff—the doctors and nurses at clinical research sites who will use the device. In addition, I briefly interviewed Bradley Fenton, the manager who heads the assist pump project at Biomed; Brian Bell, a technical writer who contributed to Rob's drafts of the assist pump manuals; and Tracey Kernan, an engineer who reviews the legal liability issues for new products.

One of the first customers for the Biomed device is Central Hospital, a large, modern hospital. Unlike many other potential customers, Central Hospital is not a heart transplant center; it will use the assist pump solely as a means to help patients recover normal functioning of their own hearts. Like RMS, Central is a busy, diverse institution that offers a comprehensive range of hospital services, and the heart assist is one of the newest. The hospital personnel who will operate the pump drive unit during and after surgery include the hospital's respiratory therapists. In most institutions the perfusionists would be the principal operators of the device; at Central, the drive operator team will consist of respiratory therapists and a small group of perfusionists.

My principal informant at Central was Mark Ivers, the head of training for the respiratory therapists at the hospital. He organizes training for all technologies that the therapists use. In this capacity, he has served as the liaison between the future drive operators and Rob Florio of Biomed. A second major informant was Arie Fagan. She has been a respiratory therapist for a year and has moved into a supervisory position among the therapists. She has an associate's degree in medical technology from a lo-cal community college and works with a number of biomedical technol-ogies. She does pulmonary function tests in which a patient's lung volume and air flow is tested in order to assess the patient's lungs before an oper-ation, operates devices such as ventilators and balloon pumps, and has been trained as a technician in blood oxygenation (BOX), a procedure that involves blood pumping during surgery. Training and experience in this procedure was a prerequisite for inclusion in the Central heart assist operators team.

The Corporation, the University, and the Challenges of Technology Transfer

Long before the heart assist pump was introduced into the Central Hos-pital repertoire of services, Biomed and RMS had developed a working relationship designed to bring the laboratory prototype to the market. Be-cause the device had largely been designed by RMS, it would not be a typ-ical new product for Biomed. Not only would it not be initiated in-house, it had already been used dozens of time with patients. Nonetheless, the Biomed group that took over the project decided to make a number of al-terations to the prototype. Some of these changes altered the way certain features worked, some improved the feasibility of manufacturing the de-vice, and some made the device easier to use. Integrated with this work was the development of full documentation for the new product.

The project was run at Biomed through a business development unit that consisted of about five top and middle management people. Al-though the design changes and the development of documentation was a large task, it was a medium-sized project in comparison to the develop-ment of other Biomed electromechanical products. In a typical project there would be a couple of engineers and one person for each facet of it, with a total of ten or so people. The typical small electromechanical project would involve about a year and a half to two man-years of work. But the company's standard product line does not require the amount of federal government regulatory work that this one did. Before the project entered the clinical trial phase, Rob noted the inordinate length of time the project had taken: "We have been involved with this project for four years and probably have been six to eight man-years of effort into it already and we still haven't done our first clinical case."

This issue of time is crucial but problematic in this product development project. According to Rob, this assist system is generally considered to be the best available for the applications that Biomed will sell it for, although this could change because of rapid developments in the field. As Biomed was planning to move into the clinical trials phase, the system was state of the art, but a few years later, it could be passed by another corporation's product. Because of lengthy government regulatory reviews, the product could not be sold while it was still clearly ahead of the competition. And by the time it gets FDA approval, it may no longer be as attractive a product. This problem is not unusual; such products take a while "to get out into the medical community and be reviewed," notes Rob. The length of time that it has taken this product to reach the market is due in part to the demands of government regulatory approval, but also, said Rob, it takes a while for the medical community at large to approve of this type of product. Any competitors would most likely face similar delays with comparable products.

The head of the project, Bradley Fenton, noted the complexity of the endeavor: "A project of this magnitude is multifaceted. It has to do with product development. It has to do with the clinical trial. It has to do with the interface of manufacturing and marketing, and everything else." As the top manager, he tried to make sure that those doing the engineering, testing, technical writing, and regulatory work were doing their jobs with the needs of the market foremost in their minds. In addition, he had to make sure that the ongoing relationship with RMS was fruitful.

The Industry-University Relationship

Fenton believes that the combination of Biomed and RMS makes for a good team on this project because it "involves a wide range of technologies, both in the physical and biological sciences. And it is impossible to have all that together in one place at one time." Although RMS is an academic institution with its own needs and motivating factors and Biomed is a commercial organization, they have been able to collaborate well. In an academic institution, there is great pressure to publish, and research is judged on the quality of the resultant publication. In industry there is a need to maintain confidentiality about research until the product gets out to the market. According to Fenton, Biomed does ask RMS if their publications can be reviewed with respect to confidentiality, and they respect that. At the same time, Biomed understands RMS's need to publish their results.

Because of the nature of the institutions, says Fenton, Biomed's goals are different from RMS's. But the goals are compatible, and that is the advantage to having a separation between the organizations. Some of the academic research goals may "be inconsistent with getting a product to market and making the devices available to patients on a large-scale basis. They may have more fundamental questions relative to device performance [than us]. [But] they can continue to pursue those goals independent of what we're doing." One of the major inconsistencies between corporate and university goals is related to the university-driven need to publish research results. Fenton notes the double-edged sword of academic publishing in an industry-university collaboration: "We have to be a little bit careful in that you don't want to publicize negative results, but if negative results are going to help other investigators to learn and cause them to not do what caused the original negative results, then that's to everybody's benefit too." Over the years that Biomed has worked with RMS, there has never been a conflict between the desire to publish and the need for coporate confidentiality.

Academic publication of research results helps Biomed to produce a better product in another way as well. Biomed provides far more than just the assist pump and drive system. It provides much customer support through training documentation. But Biomed cannot possibly teach the customers everything they need to know in order to operate the device; the customers must already have some knowledge base upon which to build and some desire to learn. Part of the documentation that informs the training are research reports written by other investigators using other similar experimental devices. Publications such as these help to build a community of knowledgeable peers within the medical community. That is why the academic need to publish can be a help to the corporation's project because it serves to make for a more ready market. This holds for publications from other research centers and corporations that make differing but competing devices.

So even with all of the potential difficulties that could arise in such a relationship, Fenton believes that this particular collaboration is ultimately beneficial to both organizations. RMS, he says, is more "research-oriented than we are, and that's good. They certainly have done much of the initial work on these devices. And then we are serving as the potential commercial outlet of this research. They are doing some excellent research, but one of their motivating factors is to eventually see these devices being made available to patients. And they see we are an avenue to that; it's something that they can't do. And so they take things up to a point and then turn it over to us, which they did in the case of this assist device."

One of the keys to this relationship is the extent to which the two groups can communicate with each other on a number of levels. As the Biomed engineers worked on altering the design of the prototype, they communicated formally and informally with the engineers at RMS. The formal communication included detailed documentation—drawings of parts and the specifications of those parts. Because some of the design changes would alter the way the device worked, the RMS engineers did not always agree with the proposed alterations. But when they saw the alternatives, they could recognize the validity of those changes. The key in this process was the informal communication among the two organizations engineers. Reza Said, an RMS engineer, noted that either group can try to document formally the technology but cannot easily document all of the thinking that underlies that technology. That kind of communication usually moves through informal channels.

Bradley Fenton agrees that communication is a central issue in the working relationships of the different organizations. A constant question that he has to answer as the head of the project is, How do you keep everybody informed and let them participate in decision making? That question was complicated in this project because RMS is quite a distance away from Biomed. Within Biomed, much gets communicated informally—at lunchtime discussions, chance meetings over coffee, and the like—and it is difficult to facilitate that kind of informal communication when dealing with RMS and parent company. The Biomed personnel continually tried to overcome this problem of proximity by telephone, fax, overnight mail, and face-to-face meetings.

Yet, although he believes that a key to successful transfer is informal communication among personnel from collaborating but distant organizations, he also believes that the lack of proximity can also be advantageous for all involved. It can help the process at certain points, if the differing groups have some distance and independence. If the groups can communicate about key issues effectively, they inevitably reach a point when both groups need to withdraw and work out those issues, free to experiment without answering to the other group during the process of that experimentation. This pattern of communicate and then pull back can serve as a general description of the way that Biomed's technical writers developed much of instructional material for the assist pump system.

The Work of the Technical Writers

One of the major tasks of the Biomed development team was to prepare complete engineering documentation: drawings, schematics, quality control procedures, assembly procedures, and instructional manuals. This documentation was part of the package of information sent to the FDA to gain approval to proceed with the clinical trials. In addition, the documentation is part of the product that goes to users in those trials. The most important part of the user documentation is the instructional materials: the user manuals and other materials used to support training. Biomed produced a manual that was meant primarily for surgical staff and one that was meant primarily for technicians who would operate the system. According to Rob Florio, the latter was the more difficult documentation project. With other products, the user manuals were sketched out in a draft by the technical writer, who continually revises selected reviews from others until he or she developed a draft ready for formal review by a small group of in-house experts on the project: the marketing person, the technical person, the legal person, the government regulatory person, and the clinical person. This occurred as late as possible in the product development cycle because typically the new products were being altered throughout the cycle. Those experts met to hash out the issues that each of them saw in the manual. Eventually, when all issues were resolved, the group gave its approval, and the revised draft was ready to be adopted and used.

One of the most crucial facets of the manuals that must be resolved centers on the issue of legal liability exposure caused by the new product. The device and its end user documentation must go through a review by the label review committee to ensure that the proper warnings and cautions have been included as part of the product. The FDA considers any printed material that accompanies the device to be a label—whether it is a sticker on the device, an instructional manual, or even advertising literature. According to Tracey Kernan, a Biomed engineer who specializes in issues of legal liability exposure, the label review process is designed to establish that the claims that the labels make are accurate and that the warnings and cautions are potentially effective and legally sufficient.

All labeling is done by the technical writing group. The writers must know how a product functions and how it is to be used by customers. The writers also must learn the types of precautions (messages intended to protect the user) and warnings (intended to protect the patient) that need to be included. The label review committee's work is reviewed by an attorney. According to Kernan, there may be differences of opinion between the attorneys and the label review committee members. The attorneys typically want to include warnings about use and misuse that clinical personnel already know about; the label review committee might not include a warning because the members know that the users do not need to be told about that issue. For example, if air enters a certain blood pumping line, a patient could be seriously affected—possibly killed. Cardiac surgery personnel know this well. In the past Biomed did not include a related warning in their manuals; now they do in order to provide "a more comprehensive" document. This change has been incorporated because the legal climate is such that Biomed must increase its warnings in order to attempt to avoid failure-to-warn lawsuits. Biomed will include more warnings rather than fewer even if some of them seem obvious to the users. "Failure to warn and failure to provide adequate instructions is a common charge in the medical device industry," says Kernan. "It is part of doing business."

Although the manuals carry the important burden of limiting certain types of legal liability exposure, most people involved in a new product development project do not like to think about or deal with user manuals, according to Rob Florio. But when they do focus on the manuals, they realize that they must commit to a particular view of the product. Sometimes those views may clash among experts, and the manual review process forces the group to come to some decision on such issues. The manual review process poses for one last important time some fundamental questions: What is the product? What does it do? How does it do it? The manual review process for the assist drive system brought to the fore some fundamental questions about the nature of the product and its users.

The heart assist manuals were written over approximately two years. Originally Rob Florio had collected information and done early drafts of instructional manuals. Later, a technical writer, Brian Bell, visited RMS to observe the system in experimental use. He spent a few days at RMS, asked a lot of questions, and then returned to Biomed to produce a new draft. Several months later, the Bell/Florio drafts were sent to RMS for review. The engineers at RMS saw some significant problems with those drafts. Eventually the problems confronted Rob Florio in his capacity as coordinator of the clinical trials. Given the positive working relationship between the groups, Rob and the RMS engineers were confident that those problems could be worked out, and eventually they were. An analysis of the problems and the complexity of the task needed to overcome those problems provides insight into the challenging task of adapting new technologies to new users.

The Development and Use of the Manuals

Rob Florio began the information gathering process, and Brian Bell continued that process by visiting RMS, observing the system in experimental use, and subsequently writing drafts of the two instructional manuals that would support the system. One manual focused on the assist pump and was written primarily for the surgical staff, although it would later be distributed to the technical staff as well. The second manual focused on the drive unit—the console on wheels that controls the pump's operation.

After these drafts were completed, copies were sent to RMS, where they were reviewed by the head surgeon of the assist pump project and by engineers, Reza Said and Morris Lodge. All three readers made marginal comments in both manuals. The engineers made extensive comments. At one particularly problematic passage, Morris appended a two-page rewrite of the section in question. Morris and Reza wrote a brief memo summarizing their most significant concerns about the drafts and sent the manuals back to Rob Florio. Some of the suggested changes that the engineers made were incorporated into the next draft of each manual; some were not.

Meanwhile, Biomed was beginning to set up the first clinical trials of their device at Central Hospital. Rob Florio had begun working with Mark Ivers of Central to initiate training sessions for the potential operators of the drive unit. Mark took on this duty because he was responsible for the training and retraining of the respiratory therapists, and part of his expertise involved training technicians in the blood oxygenation procedures that involve artificial means of blood pumping during surgery. As an early step in Mark's education, Rob sent him a copy of the manuals and some other supporting documentation which included technical papers written by medical researchers who were working with a competitor's system. The plan from this point on would be fairly straightforward: Mark would learn how to use the system by studying the documentation, by visiting the Biomed site and observing the pump's use, and by working with the unit that Biomed was going to provide Central Hospital. Mark would then train the technicians, who would also study the appropriate documentation, visit Biomed, and operate the in-house device after it was delivered.

These events occurred as planned. Mark studied the documents and visited Biomed, as did the entire surgical and technical staff; a unit was delivered to Central and was set up in what is called a mock loop (the pump and driver are made operational and the system pumps water through the pump). Mark practiced on the mock loop himself and arranged for the therapists to do the same. At this point, the transfer of technology appeared to be going smoothly from RMS through Biomed and on to the customer/users.

The Role of the Manuals in Training

Before the training phase began for the Central Hospital clinical trials, Florio predicted that the manuals would be read carefully by the trainees because the assist pump is a new, and innovative product. Many other new products are actually variations of an already familiar technology. This one is significantly different from anything that the users had seen, and they would need all of the information that they could get, whether from the manuals or the training sessions. As the training began, it was clear that Rob was right. In fact, Mark Ivers compared the real need to read the assist pump manuals to the unnecessary documentation for the balloon pump. As far as he knew, no one ever consulted the instructional

materials for the most recent version of balloon pump that the hospital
had purchased; that technology had been learned over the years through
a variety of different machines, and the fundamental principles of its use
became widely known among medical technicians and those who educate
those technicians. In contrast, the assist pump and drive manuals would
play a significant role in this case.

Before his hands-on training sessions at Biomed, Mark reviewed the
manuals and found them to be very useful. He used the drive manual in
particular as a basis for exploring the machine and the technology: "It
was really the first time I got a grasp of the theoretical function of the machine as well as practical aspects of it. . . . I felt strongly enough about the
manual that I distributed it to all the therapists who are involved and
asked them to review it, and then I plan on using the manual as a resource
in terms of setting up our own check-off system for use of the pump. We
really have to check off the proficiency of our therapists before we allow
them to operate this pump." (A check-off involves a written test on the
device and its parts, as well as a hands-on test where the users demonstrate what they can do with the device.) The need for effective training
was crucial especially because this type of procedure would be an inter-
mittent one. It would not be done on a regular basis because the assist
pump is a last-resort attempt to save the patient. Therefore, operators will
not develop an expertise from constant, repetitive use over a period of
months. At Central Hospital, the heart group expected to begin by doing
approximately six assists during the first year, and because the manuals
would not be made available during the actual use of the device, the technicians needed to develop their expertise during training. "I don't think
that the manuals will be used at bedside," says Mark. "That isn't our pattern on any of the technologies that we use. The therapists should know
enough about the technology so they won't need the reference right there.
But the manuals will be a ready resource. They will be with the [assist
pump] department if we have any questions about operation."

Although Mark saw the manuals as a means for becoming introduced
to the technology, he did not plan to use them as the primary instructional
texts during training. Instead, he would follow a standard Central Hospital strategy and produce his own version of the documentation—one
stripped of everything but what he saw as necessary to train the therapists. His sources for the in-house version were the Biomed manuals, the

academic journal articles about artificial heart pumping procedures that Biomed had provided, and his own experiences with the device at the Biomed site. "I took material out the Biomed manual," said Mark, "and put it in a form that I thought was a little bit easier for them to follow." In doing so, he tried to anticipate the Central Hospital version of the procedure:

What I tried to do in my training here, tried as best as I can because we have never done it here [before], is go over exactly what the scenario would be from our O/R [operating room], to getting the patient settled down in Surgical Intensive Care Unit, and exactly what we would be doing in terms of responding to the physician to cranking the pumping rate up, what we would be doing for the transport, what we would be doing when we actually arrived at SICU in terms of changing modes, etc. So I followed the Biomed manual, but I tried to present it in such a manner so that they could relate to exactly what would be happening in our institution here.

Although his in-house manual was faithful to the Biomed manual, it turned out to be a source of some problems in this transfer.

Training the Users

The prospective trainees, chosen on the basis of their experience, included a few perfusionists, technicians whose jobs centered on blood pumping technologies, and a group of respiratory therapists, who had other sorts of cardiac support experience, such as balloon and BOX pumping. Once chosen, the group members went through a five-phase training period.

Phase one: They visited Biomed for a Biomed-led introduction to the device. Each participant saw the device to get an idea of the basic components and the technology and each was given the Biomed instructional manuals.

Phase two: Next, Biomed delivered an assist pump and drive system which was set up in a mock loop. Mark gave each team member a copy of his in-house version of the manuals. He began the training with a one-hour classroom session in which he used the device to provide an overview of the basic components of the pump and the drive. He reviewed the different modes of operation and talked about the physiological requirements for a patient to become a candidate for the device, some details of the operation to attach and detach the device, and potential complications during these operations and normal use of the device. He pointed to sections of his manual to explain or illustrate some general theoretical issues and then some practical do's and don'ts. At this session, he introduced a few key aspects of the technician's job—in particular, the task of adjusting the controls of the device once it is attached to the patient. This phase of the operation includes some of the most crucial and variable decisions that the user must make. Finally, he reviewed the safety warnings that Biomed had provided.

The trainees had not been able to preview any of the material before the class, so he lectured and there was discussion. The team members had had previous introductory experience with the machine, so they had a basic understanding. At the end of this session, Mark quickly went over all of the dials and connections and pointed out everything on the machine itself that he could. He showed how to start it up and how to turn on the tanks and get it cranking in the mock loop. He then made the machine available to them. Between this first training session and the next, he gave them a test on the in-house documentation to make sure they had read the information and had some knowledge of it.

Phase three: This phase encompassed classroom sessions designed to focus on specific techniques, strategies, and issues involved in running the pump—from starting the pump to weaning the patient from it. These sessions were based on his in-house version of the Biomed documentation and combined lecture and discussion.

Phase four: The culmination of the training occurred in one-on-one sessions with Mark and a trainee in a room with the assist pump and driver set up in a mock loop. Mark began each session by asking a series of questions in which the trainee had to identify parts of the device. He then posed a scenario that described a call coming in from the heart bypass surgeon telling the heart assist group that they were going to use the device on a patient. The trainee described step by step what she or he would need to do from the moment the call came in to the actual operation of the device after it had been attached to the patient. Mark listened and checked off steps that he had listed on a check-off sheet, a stripped-down list adapted from his in-house version of the manual (itself a stripped-down version). When the trainee had trouble remembering a step, Mark prompted the trainee with a question or two to try to get her or him on track. Each member of the team went through this process once to practice and then once officially as a test.

Phase five: Before Mark and the trainees had completed phase four, Mark envisioned the final training phase to occur during and just after the early uses of the device: "We're in a situation here where we have a piece of technology that no one has actually run before. When we put this on our first customer, the people here will never have operated it on anyone alive before, so what I plan on doing as a fifth step is to spend time on every shift making sure that the operator feels comfortable and again reviewing protocols with that person, reviewing the technology with that person on every shift. At least give myself the peace of mind that they know what they are doing."

The Challenge for the Team

Overall, Mark saw the project as a major challenge. "It will be exciting and scary at first," he said, "then hopefully just exciting, then later on routine." One of the challenges would be to keep the personnel prepared for irregular use. Because of the relatively low patient load expected, Mark predicted that the team would probably have to have quarterly training updates.

Those in charge of the drive operator facet of this project were the hospital's perfusionists. Having the most expertise in pumping technology, the perfusionists made the major technical decisions about how to do this entire procedure. Even so, it would not be the perfusionists who would do the bulk of the work as operators of the assist pump drive unit. "In fact," Mark predicted, "the way it will work out, though, it is the respiratory therapists who will be managing the device in the SICU and assisting with the initiation of this service in the O/R and who will probably have the most on-board time and actually assume the most responsibility."

One of the therapists who expected to have among the most experience was Arie Fagan. For Arie, this project was unique although the training process was similar to BOX. She had balloon pump experience, but she said, "this goes beyond that." It was different from the BOX technology too. In fact, the assist pump combined different aspects of both of the other technologies that she has worked with. In the oxygenation procedure, the heart is bypassed, and the pump moves all of the patient's blood; it is a complete support system in order to rest the heart. The balloon pump assists the heart's pumping of the blood. The Biomed device assists the heart but also pumps blood. It is more invasive than the balloon pump, but the heart still pumps also.

As she prepared for her role on the team during training, Arie described the responsibilities of the drive operators: "Our role will be to manipulate the assist device, to take total control of it and work with nursing and patient care, sitting there watching the drive unit readouts and doing all the hemodynamic [blood flow] monitoring for it. We will go over to the operating room and be with the pump while the surgeons are inserting it and hooking it up. We'll be at the other end of the controls of the assist pump. And then we'll assist with the transport from the O/R over to the Surgical Intensive Care Unit and then just stay with it from then on."

The User's View of the Manuals

As a dedicated member of the team, Arie dutifully read and studied the manuals through her training: "We started out with the Biomed manual, and I kept reading through that, picking out certain things that I think that I would be doing versus what the thoracic surgeon would be doing. And then with Mark's version I just go through and kind of say, 'Yeah, when I turn it on I have to do this and this, and when we do this, these are the steps I follow.' We have used the manuals as a study guide and a review." Arie preferred Mark's version of the manual; she found it more concise with less information to digest. All of the team members had to fit their studying and training sessions into their already busy daily work schedules. For example, a trainee may have been on duty throughout the night and then would have to attend a training session. Or a trainee may have been in the middle of a training session when his or her beeper would go off, calling the trainee to some other task. The environment within which these team members worked was crowded and tiring, and this project was just one—albeit an important one—of their many daily tasks.

Mark's in-house training materials may have been quite useful for the trainees, but the content of those manuals would later reveal some problems, problems whose source was the original Biomed manuals. An analysis of these problems illustrates some fundamental challenges in adapting a prototype to the marketplace.

The Heart and the Assist Pump

The heart is the pump for the cardiovascular system, the system of vessels through which oxygenated blood flows from the heart and lungs throughout the body and then returns lower in oxygen back to the heart. For our purposes, we need to understand only how a few parts of this system work. The system has two subsystems: one contains vessels that carry oxygenated blood from the heart throughout the body and then return that deoxygenated blood to the heart. The other contains vessels that carry blood from the heart to the lungs and then back to the heart. These two subsystems correspond to the two sides of the heart—the right and the left. Each of these sides is a pump in itself, and each consist of two chambers—an upper called the atrium, and a lower called the ventricle. The deoxygenated blood returning to the heart enters the heart through the right atrium and then is pumped by the right ventricle to the lungs, where it is oxygenated again. From the lungs, the reoxygenated blood enters the heart in the left atrium and is pumped by the left ventricle out into the aorta and to the rest of the cardiovascular system. The assist pump technology is designed to support either or both of the two sides of the heart.

The goal of left-assist pumping is to capture all of the blood entering the left atrium (the left side, upper chamber) and pump that blood into the aorta so that the left ventricle (lower chamber) can be bypassed; a tube (cannula) is inserted and attached to the left atrium to capture the blood flow, and another cannula is inserted and attached to the aorta to serve as the outlet from the assist pump back into the cardiovascular system. When this is complete, the left ventricle has been bypassed. This bypass does not happen until the drive unit operator turns the assist pump on and brings it up to a certain pumping rate. When the pump is turned on, it begins to take over the function of the patient's left ventricle and starts to divert blood from that ventricle. The pump operator starts the pump slowly so that the surgeons can look for leaks around the cannulas in and out of the chest. When the surgeons are satisfied that the assist pump cannulas are secure and tight, the operator starts to speed up the pump by turning the appropriate dial on the drive unit. At some point the device captures the output—it diverts all of the blood from the left ventricle.

The assist pump is a clear, hard-shelled chamber with a flexible sac inside. That sac fills with blood and empties during pumping; therefore, the sac is connected to the tubes that carry blood out of the patient's atrium (upper chamber) and back to the aorta. Another tube enters that hard-shelled outer casing of the pump. But this tube, called the drive line, is sealed off from the blood flow. This tube applies vacuum and pressure to pull and push the flexible blood sac back and forth. This action causes the device to pump blood.

It is important to understand what occurs when a heart, natural or artificial, pumps. Each pump stroke (what we commonly call a heartbeat) has two parts, filling (diastole) and emptying (systole). These two parts can be read by the drive operator as the assist device is pumping. The drive unit has a computer screen that shows a continual readout of the pumping. This readout is represented by a wave signal, which shows a certain kind of blip when the blood sac is full and another kind of blip when the sac is empty. The drive unit fills the pump and empties it by changing the pressure on the blood sac. When filling the pump—taking blood from the atrium—the drive unit applies a vacuum to the flexible blood sac. The vacuum creates a pressure differential that brings blood out of the atrium and into the plastic sac. When the blood sac is full, the operator sees a "sac-is-full" signal, Typically, when the sac is full, the vacuum ends, and, through the drive-line, pressure is applied on the blood sac. At this point blood is ejected out of the blood sac and into the aorta. When the pump is completely emptied, the operator sees the "sac-is-empty" signal in the wave form. At that point the pump stroke starts anew.

The drive operator can control this process in a variety of ways. First, the pump operator can choose one of three operating modes each of which sets up the system to repeat the pump strokes in a different way:

1. Heart-synchronous mode: The pump is matched to the heartbeat rate of the patient automatically pumping at the same rate as the patient's heart.

2. Fill-sensing mode: The pump automatically begins to empty when it is filled completely. The resulting beat rate of the assist pump may not match the rate of the patient; if it takes a long time to fill the pump, the rate may be relatively slow.

3. Asynchronous mode: The pump rate is set by the drive operator. Like the fill-sensing mode, the pump may not match the patient's heart rate. The operator could run the pump at, say, ten beats per minute (far too

slow to sustain the patient) or eighty beats per minute. This mode is used when starting the pump for the first time. The operator starts pumping very slowly (e.g., ten beats per minute) so that the implanted cannulas can be checked for leaks and the setup of the pump and drive can be checked. At the request of the surgeon, the drive operator, still operating the pump in asynchronous mode, increases the beat rate so that it can "capture the output" and divert the blood pumping from the left ventricle. And when the patient is being weaned from the pump, the drive operator gradually slows the rate to a point where the patient's heart can take over pumping fully.

To complicate the adjustment options a bit further, the operator, by turning different types of dials on the drive unit, can adjust the following four variables which affect the way the device pumps:

1. Manual rate: By adjusting this variable, the operator can vary the number of beats per minute of the assist pump. This variable is in effect only in the asynchronous (manual) mode, because in the other two modes, the pump's beat rate is automatically set. This control is particularly crucial when starting the pump—the beat rate must begin slowly as the device and patient are checked out by the surgeon and the operator—and when weaning the patient from the pump.

2. Systolic duration: With this adjustment, the operator can alter the length of time to empty the pump of blood. This adjustment controls the time it takes for the blood to be pumped out of the assist pump and into the patient's aorta. The adjustments are in milliseconds (msec).

3. Systolic pressure: The operator can adjust the amount of pressure applied to the blood sac to eject the blood during pump emptying. The operator can determine how much force is applied to the sac to pump the blood out of the sac and into the aorta with this adjustment. The units are in millimeters of mercury (mm Hg).

4. Diastolic pressure: This adjustment is the vacuum that can be applied to the assist pump in order to pull blood out of the patient's atrium and into the pump's blood sac. Like the systolic pressure, this variable is adjusted in millimeters of mercury and the range of vacuum settings can fall between zero vacuum and –140 mm Hg (the strongest vacuum possible with this device).

Although the use of the assist pump can lead to a number of complications with both the patient's condition and the performance of the device, two very different but important ones should be noted here to illustrate some of the dynamics of the pumping situation. The first complication is related to one of the cardinal rules of blood pumping. Because of the deadly danger of pumping air into the patient's cardiovascular system, the assist pump operator must never apply vacuum to the pump when the patient's chest is open to the air. Air in the blood could cause an embolism, which could kill the patient. Therefore, one of the most important warnings that must be communicated to the operator is never to apply a vacuum when the chest is open. This potential complication is clear and absolute, allowing trainers and technical writers to state it unequivocally in a warning.

The second complication is a bit more subtle but still crucial. It is important to ensure that the patient's blood does not sit still for too long because it may clot causing a serious problem for the patient. When the assist pump is full of blood, the blood is swirling around in the blood sac and is less likely to clot; when the pump is empty, the blood is not moving and is susceptible to clotting. Therefore, the drive operator must try not to let the pump sit empty for any length of time.

These complications represent just two of the numerous difficulties that could face the surgical and technical staffs during the use of the device. In addition to these physiological and technical challenges, several of the participants faced some significant *rhetorical* challenges in trying to complete this technology transfer.

Manuals, Reviewers, and Problems

As Biomed and Central Hospital prepared for the clinical trials, two things occurred approximately at the same time that made the training process somewhat problematical. The first involved the engineers, Reza and Morris, at RMS. They were concerned about the revised manuals sent to Central. They believed that the manuals contained some inaccuracies, and, more important, some sections that might mislead users about certain fundamental principles on which the technology was based. The engineers believed that an operator who did not understand these principles might not be able to interpret effectively some potential situations during the actual use of the device.

All of these concerns had been expressed in one way or another in the comments that the RMS engineers had sent to Rob Florio some months earlier. The changes made in response to those comments did not satisfy the engineers' concerns. But the actual use of the device at Central Hospital was not imminent; the clinical trials were expected to begin several months in the future. And because of the excellent working relationship between both organizations, Rob Florio and the RMS engineers felt confident that any differing interpretations of the manuals could be worked out. The second occurrence was Mark Ivers' in-house versions of the manuals, which further complicated the problematic passages in the Biomed draft.

The clinical trials team received the Biomed pump manual and drive manual. At Central Hospital, Mark Ivers wrote the Central Hospital in-house manual on the basis of these two documents and an academic paper about nursing care in assist pumping written by a heart assist team from a university hospital other than RMS. The in-house manual contained two parts: a theoretical overview of assist pumping, nearly all of which was lifted directly out of the Biomed manuals and the nursing care paper, and a detailed set of instructions showing trainees how to operate the drive unit before, during, and after surgery. This latter section was taken directly from the Biomed manuals; however, Mark made three types of changes to the original manuals: he made his manual far more concise by stripping down most steps so that they described only the actions that the user should take; he changed the order of some of these actions, so that they matched the hospital's protocol more closely; and because a few parts of the surgery and operation of the assist pump would be changed to match certain hospital requirements, he rewrote certain passages entirely. For example, because the hospital planned to use a different brand computer screen with the drive unit, Mark rewrote a section describing how to set up the screen.

The Biomed pump manual contained information primarily for the surgical staff—for example, describing how to prepare the patient for surgery and attach the cannulas to the patient. These sections provided verbal and graphic explanations of surgical techniques and were written for the nurses and surgeons who would do these tasks. Even so, because this manual also contained information about the drive unit, it was deemed appropriate for the trainee drive operators to read and study as well. In fact, this manual contained a brief passage about adjusting the controls on the drive unit in order to run the pump. This section and the corresponding sections in the drive manual were of major importance to the potential drive operators.

The pump manual provided an overview of the entire surgical process; the Biomed drive manual focused on the particulars —running the drive unit before, during, and after surgery. The manual contained four major types of information:

1. Introductory and supplemental information describing the device and its use in general terms. It contained technical specifications, maintenance information, certain disclaimers, and a list of the safety warnings and precautions which were repeated where appropriate throughout the rest of the manual.

2. Controls and displays glossary defining the physical features (dials, lights, gauges, valves) accompanied by drawings, and differing operating modes.

3. Preparation instructions describing how to set up the drive unit for use (adjusting the wheels, checking the power sources, starting the system power, connecting all auxiliary equipment, calibrating the monitoring devices, making the initial settings of the controls).

4. Operation instructions explaining how to use the drive unit in detail. Subsections explained how to start the pump in manual mode, monitor the system and the patient, transport the patient from the operating room to the intensive care unit, adjust the controls of the device during and after surgery, use the fill-sensing mode, use the heart-synchronous mode, use the manual (asynchronous) mode, and set up and use the backup unit (in case of a system failure). The actions described in this section represent the central work of the drive unit operator.

When Reza and Morris read the in-house version of the documentation, they recognized that Biomed did not effectively capture all of the important issues regarding the pump and its use. Accordingly, Rob Florio wanted to make sure that Biomed covered as many of these issues as possible before the trials were to begin. Nonetheless, the manuals were written and the training was underway when the research engineers raised significant questions about the basis of the training. At that point, I had the opportunity to examine this conflict in terms of the three-part relationship of lab, manufacturer, and customer. Probing conflict enables field researchers to learn tacit meanings; that is, the meanings that people attribute to their actions. In this case, I faced a conflict that involved all three parts of the technology transfer in an issue bound by technical communication but involving a wide variety of aspects of the transfer. I conducted interviews, a think-aloud protocol, and site visits to all three institutions, including a visit to RMS to observe two days of meetings with Rob and the RMS engineers to negotiate solutions to the problems with the documentation.

This meeting took place in a hospital conference room and centered on problems in the Biomed manuals. During the first day of this meeting, Rob and the RMS engineers discussed and resolved issues that the engineers raised about the manuals. That evening Rob rewrote certain sections of the Biomed manual. The next day began with discussions of his revisions. Within a few weeks after this meeting, Rob produced a revised version of the Biomed manuals and sent copies back to RMS. After making a few minor changes at the suggestion of the RMS people, he sent the new draft to Mark Ivers. I was able to get Mark to do a read-aloud protocol about certain key sections of the manual during his initial reading of the new version. My analysis of all of the data that I collected reveals the central rhetorical barriers to a successful technology transfer in this case.

Rhetorical Barriers to Successful Technology Transfer

Rob's goal in this transfer was to get the future users to become experts—or at least to get them safely on the road to expertise. He and all of the others involved in this project achieved that goal; however, they had to overcome some daunting barriers on the way. The barriers had to do with Rob's dealings with the sources of the technology (discussed in barriers 1 and 2 below), the representations of that technology in the texts (barriers 2 and 3), and the learning processes of the users (barriers 3 and 4). My analyses of each barrier show how the users went from little knowledge to the indications of a developing expertise. It is this development that shows that the rhetorical barriers to the transfer were eventually overcome.

Barrier 1: Difficulty in Discovering and Communicating Key Knowledge from Technical Developers

In most product development cycles at Biomed, the R&D phase occurred in-house, enabling documentation and training specialists earlier involvement in the cycle than they had with the assist pump. Since the product was virtually whole when Biomed began its phase of the project, the documentation and training specialist had no choice but to enter the product development cycle in its latter stages. This at-the-end role is the tradition-al one for writers and trainers throughout industry (Chisholm 1988, Haselkorn 1988, Killingsworth and Jones 1989).

Yet as American corporations realize that they must develop products that better meet the needs of customers, some companies are enabling their experts in the customers' needs, including the documentation and training specialists, to enter the product development cycle earlier. For example, AT&T's Data Systems Group uses a learning-support system for customers: "A learning support system goes beyond the traditional customer documentation and training. The phrase 'learning support' focuses on a key element that must be present in a product's documentation and training: *support* of the customers' effort to *learn* to use correctly and effectively the products they buy. The object is not to overwhelm a customer with technical information about a product, but rather to help the customer learn how to use the product to meet his or her needs" (Cobb 1990, p. 36). In order to develop such a system efficiently and effectively, a company must allow its documentation and training specialists early involvement in the product development cycle: "The most important requirement is that planning and development of the system begin concurrently with planning and development of the product" (p. 36). If both facets can begin in concert, Cobb notes, the technical developers and the support developers can work from the same source of information about both the new product and the customers' needs.

Without this shared database of information, the support specialists will continually be trying to catch up to the technical developers or, worse, will have to play archeologist to uncover and recreate a past that is long gone. Late involvement places a heavy research load on technical writers. They must learn about both the products and the customers. In situations such as these, technical writers play the role of boundary spanner—they bridge divisions within or between organizations. In a discussion of the boundary spanning role of technical writers, Harrison and Debs (1988) draw on recent studies and argue for the early involvement of writers in the product development cycle. They describe the multiple sources and the massive amounts of information that technical writers develop, as well as the key role that writers must play in the product development cycle: "When scientists and engineers develop a solution or design a product, in a very real way, they construct something that did not exist before; they often develop codes, inventing and using language in particular ways to convey the sense of this new design, to be able to talk about it among themselves. Writers then reverse this sequence and use language, not only to convey, but also to construct the product's existence—to make real its potential for use both within and outside the organization" (p. 14). When this role occurs late in the development cycle, it can be fraught with difficulties. If the writer is constructing the technology through language, he or she must develop an understanding that is very close to that of the technical developers. To do so late in the development cycle is a challenge.

This was the problem inherent in the transfer of the assist pump technology: Rob Florio and others were faced with an archeological challenge. Although Rob knew something about assist pumping when he started the project, he was still a relative novice with the technology. But unlike Rob and the novices who would later need training at Central Hospital, those in the RMS R&D lab had learned how to use the technology in a far different manner from any later trainees—through an informal, quasi-apprenticeship. In addition to the fact that the device was the central focus of their research work, they became experts through experimenting with it in the lab and in actual use. Through this learn-by-doing approach, much of the detailed learning process was never formally recorded and eventually became internalized as tacit knowledge by those experts. When the technical writers from the corporation had to uncover what the experts knew in order to operate the pump and drive unit, many of the details had become internalized by the experts and were difficult for the technical writers to discover and communicate through the instructional manuals. Tom Neuman, the head of engineering at RMS, said, "We could have developed training materials here because we know it. But we didn't need to do that. We teach each other."

Bradley Fenton, the manager who headed this project for Biomed, saw the quasi-apprenticeship way of learning as one of the difficult obstacles that the Biomed writers had to overcome. As the company was preparing for the clinical trials, he discussed the difficulty of developing the product from a prototype that the RMS people had been developing and using for a number of years:

They were very comfortable with it. For many of them, they had been doing it for all of their careers there. They really didn't write down what they were doing, and they just did it. I think that there were many subtle things which we saw were important to communicate to any new investigators [users] that were not originally captured in their formal documentation. They just did it. Anything from the use and installation of the device to the care of patients to whatever, there is just a tremendous learning curve. And we are talking now about relatively new, relatively naive institutions and personnel, naive in the sense that they haven't had to deal with anything like this in the past. And we're trying to make sure that we capture everything that RMS just does automatically without even thinking about it. That's probably been the toughest thing. An important part of the clinical investigation will be to be sure that we have captured all these things.

As Rob Florio noted, the RMS engineers sometimes did not realize how much they knew about the device. Sometimes, he mused, it seemed as if they had forgotten more about it than most others knew about it. And both Reza and Morris admitted that maybe they had not communicated all of the important issues in enough detail when the Biomed people were collecting information about the device and its uses. For example, Reza was concerned about one passage in both the Biomed manual and the Central in-house version. In the Biomed version, the user was instructed: "Set the desired pressure and adjust the systolic duration [the time it takes to eject blood from the heart] to obtain complete emptying at the end of the systolic duration period." In an earlier version, the same passage had said just the opposite: "Set the desired systolic duration and adjust the pressure." In Mark's in-house version, this message was stated both ways at different times. Although neither statement was inherently incorrect, neither was completely explanatory and Reza was concerned that neither the Biomed nor the Central Hospital staff understood this passage. He admitted, "originally we may have said it the way Biomed said it, but we knew the underlying principle." The Biomed writers may not have understood the extent of that principle when they learned this step, and, admits Reza, by not explaining the principle to them, the RMS engineers may have misled them to think that the statement was not only accurate but complete.

Overcoming the Barrier

Ultimately, difficulties such as these were resolved through constructive negotiations between Rob Florio and the RMS engineers during two days of meetings. The RMS engineers felt a responsibility to help Biomed clear up these problems and made an effort to do so; Biomed enabled the RMS engineers to review their documentation *in the draft stage* so that significant changes could be made before the manuals were deemed finished. (The clinical investigators also were able to have drafts of the manuals and that fact complicated the process a bit. But resolving difficulties like these *was the purpose of the clinical trials*. It is to both Biomed's and RMS' credit that they were concerned with ironing out all of the problems before the trials began.) Therefore, without the benefit of early involvement in the design phase of the product, it is important for:

• Technical developers to be brought into the review phase of the the documentation and training materials.
• Technical developers to take responsibility for the quality of that information, just as the writers must take responsibility for its quality.
• Writers to develop systematic empirical research abilities since much of their work involves collecting data.
• Writers to devote themselves fully to learning the technologies at hand since much of their work involves interpreting data.

Barrier 2. Difficulty in Establishing Ideal Examples Based on Users' Experiences

Documentation and training specialists should be part of the design phase of a product because they can serve as customer advocates; that is, they should know the customer's needs and abilities well so that the product can be tailored to meet those requirements. Corporations must "become obsessed with listening" to customers, according to Tom Peters (1987), who has preached this message to business leaders across the country. Of all of Peters's prescriptions, he says that this is paramount: "First among equals is listening to customers, with an ear to their practical, application-oriented needs" (p. 178). Traditional market research is not enough; beyond the sophisticated, quantitative customer surveys that have traditionally informed product development, Peters calls for a new kind of qualitative, naturalistic research accomplished by observing actual customers in their natural settings: "To begin with, good listeners get out from behind the desk to where the customers are." In addition, he urges corporations not to dominate those customer visits: "good listeners construct settings so as to maximize 'naive' listening, the undistorted sort" (p. 182).

While it is a myth that any observer—even the expert ethnographer—can collect data in the field that are "undistorted," qualitative and naturalistic research can offer a different, complementary type of data that is no more or less biased than any other type. Gould and I (1988) have provided an overview of qualitative, naturalistic techniques that may be applied to the development of technical documentation. We argue that technical writers and trainers must observe customers carefully, systematically, and, to the extent that it is possible, unobtrusively. Although this suggestion seems to make common sense, it is unclear just what the effects of such practices would be. Janice Redish (1989) notes that if one is a technical writer working in a large company, "and you are working with people who are developing a product, their focus is on that product. The fact that salespeople are selling that product to other people out in the world who are going to use it is something that the [technical] developers don't really understand. Connecting those writers, or developers who end up writing, to their audience is something that needs further research, because we really have not solved this problem" (p. 94). This case study provides some insight into the effects of doing customer research. We find, surprisingly, that a strong connection between the Biomed writers and certain users of the assist pump led to some difficulties in the transfer of the assist pump technology.

Although the Biomed documentation and training people were not able to participate in the design phase of the assist pump, they were well connected to both experienced and novice users of the technology. The technical developers at RMS were also, in effect, part of the first group of customers of the device because those engineers also served as drive unit operators in the hospital affiliated with RMS. Reza and Morris and others served not only as technical developers but also as users. At the same time, Rob Florio had much contact with the future customers—Mark Ivers and the drive unit operator team at Central Hospital. But it was during the customer visits to RMS when the difficulties arose.

According to the Reza and Morris, the problems with the Biomed drafts began with data gathering. The Biomed employees visited RMS and observed the device in an operation in which the pump was installed in a patient. They recorded the decisions and actions of the surgeons and technicians and wrote certain passages as if those decisions and actions were universal. In fact, according to the engineers, those decisions were highly situational interpretations that may not apply to other patients in other conditions. This becomes a problem when the writers offer specific examples in order to illustrate larger principles; the examples are highly situational, but when they are presented in the manual, they appear to be far too generalizable.

Nevertheless, examples are important in instructional materials. A variety of usability researchers (Carter 1985) indicate that effective instructional materials contain examples, specifically exemplary scenarios, that enable readers to learn concepts. Flower, Hayes, and Swarts (1983) have written that documents that people read in order to take certain actions must describe those actions in concrete, grounded terms. The scenario principle suggests that writers of these documents "create a human-centered network of information focused on human agents and their actions" (p. 53). Accordingly, Gould and I (1988) point out that naturalistic research can help technical writers develop these scenarios because the research can help them learn scenarios of actual use. This strategy faced problems in the complex world of assist pumping.

Because no combination of patient, hospital protocol, users' knowledge, and abilities can be portrayed as *typical*, it was difficult to employ the scenario principle in the assist pump instructional manuals. It was difficult to say, for example, that a "normal" adjustment is X and variations on that normality are A, B, and C. In a new technology, especially one with as many crucial variables as appear in this biomedical application, the norm could involve a range of possibilities too numerous to document. In addition, the suggested actions based on a so-called typical scenario could be misleading.

When Rob Florio met with the RMS engineers to negotiate the problems with the manuals, the issue of defining a normal scenario presented that group with one of its most difficult hurdles. This issue was particularly relevant in the section that described how to adjust the controls of the drive unit before, during and after the operation. Reza and Morris had objected to the way that this section was presented in the Biomed and Central Hospital manuals. When Rob sat down with the RMS engineers to discuss how to improve the manual, the most important questions that they asked were: How do we best teach the readers to adjust the controls? How do we teach them so that they understand what they can and must do with the device? How do we teach them so that they can both interpret and act creatively? One of the answers to these questions was to present some scenarios that grounded these uses and interpretations in human actions.

The decisions that the drive operator must make involve the ways that the assist pump fills and then empties during each stroke of the pump. The drive operator can make these decisions based on a visual readout of the pump stroke that appears on a computer screen. By reading the waveform on the screen, the drive operator can identify each segment of the pumping, the filling, and emptying and certain subparts of each. The version that Reza and Morris objected to contained some drawings of sample waveforms in which the explanations were inaccurate and confusing. That version presented some waveforms that were meant to be typical in different situations; then it presented some waveforms that were distorted and stated the procedures needed to turn those distorted waveforms into correct-looking ones. The problem was that the waveform scenarios that were supposed to be typical were not necessarily so, and the instructions on how to fix the problem scenarios were too simplistic to be useful. In other words, the scenarios presented in terms of human actions were reductionist, presenting a highly contingent procedure that may involve a variety of responses depending on other variables into a simplified, concrete step.

To revise this section, Rob and the engineers wondered whether Rob should fix the inaccuracies and then add many more scenarios in order for it to be more complete. When Rob asked them to delineate a variety of scenarios about adjusting the controls, he quickly realized that the potential variations were far too numerous. When faced with the myriad of possibilities and special cases, Rob joked that what Biomed really needed to do was simply ship one of the RMS engineers along with each assist pump unit. Later, when they were all having trouble characterizing the best course of action, Rob sighed and said that all he needed to do at this point in the document was to tell the user to call RMS for help.

In order to understand how difficult this problem was to resolve, it is useful to continue to look at RMS as a two-sided resource of information for Biomed: the technical developers who had a wealth of technical expertise that was sometimes difficult to tap into, and users of the device with knowledge grounded in the particulars of their experiences. How could Rob interpret all of this so that his text could effectively teach future users whose experiences, abilities, and environments might differ? How could he generalize from the advice of the RMS engineers?

Overcoming the Barrier

After much discussion during their negotiations, Rob and the engineers agreed that the manual needed to provide a base scenario that purported to be typical. The new version of the section on adjusting the controls contained a drawing of what Rob called "the classical" wave signal ("Figure 15 shows a *typical* stroke volume trace with complete filling and emptying.") followed by a lengthy discussion identifying and defining each part of the scenario. From this base, Rob went on to classify sets of variations from that scenario. In fact, that basic, typical scenario was *largely a fiction*. It was, in effect, a description of the device as it ran on a mock loop. It was a fiction because as soon as an actual patient entered into the scenario, variations would occur. As Reza said, "They [the readers/users] may never see this [scenario] because it's too perfect, but at least they'll know what to call things [in other scenarios]." After building this scenario that the readers may never see, Rob was able to present drawings and explanations that showed variations in the ideal and then an explanation why that occurred, rather than a simple procedure on what to do to get rid of it. The key here is that even the variations are merely illustrative examples; a given user may never see them in practice. The key to the success of this strategy lies in the fact that within the fictional scenario, all of the components of pump stroke are present in an easily definable state (e.g., blip A is an ideal picture of the fill signal). Actual variations—say, a photograph of an actual patient's waveform—may be incomplete or quite distorted, but the reader can develop a representation of the ideal scenario, compare that to a possible distortion, and understand that there might be a range of variations.

Overall these issues indicate that technical writers can learn much about the customers by watching them do their jobs with the technologies in question, but the writers must be judicious in their uses of that information. Situational applications of a technology may need to be integrated into a theoretical explanation of the technology, so that the situational applications can be seen as potential variations rather than universal principles. Specific examples that are not tied to a theoretical overview may be misleading. Writers must go out to the marketplace to learn how users act and what users think is useful, but that is not a panacea to answer all documentation problems. Yet for a long time, developers and writers were kept from users, as Mary Beth Debs (1988) writes: "Few technical writers have the luxury of finding a user reading over their shoulders. In fact, many companies actually screen their writers from the product's eventual user, sometimes out of necessity or a peculiar notion of resource allocation. A company may keep the audience unknown and at a distance by not allowing writers to spend exploration and evaluation time with customers" (p. 11). A study of military instructional manuals (Duffy, Post, and Smith 1987) concludes that although the U.S. Department of Defense has funded a massive amount of usability research, military manuals are often ineffective, in part because the manual writers rarely observe the intended users doing the work at issue. In contrast, Carroll, Smith-Kerker et al. (1988) point out that the development of an experimental manual must be developed in an iterative manner; that is, a version of the manual is written and then it is tried by users, returned, and revised as many times as necessary to discover what information is appropriate and what errors the users typically make. (See Redish 1988 for a further discussion of this approach.) With the assist pump case, I want to argue for writers to have much contact with users, but the results of that contact must be tempered. Therefore, writers should:

• Have access to users so that writers can learn from observing specific, situational uses of a product.

• Have access to developers to learn the theoretical knowledge of the technical developers whose conceptions of the product may span specific users applications.

• Attempt to ground theoretical concepts with specific scenarios that involve applications of the technology.

• Illustrate how situtational specifics represent possible variations on the ideal in order to teach the readers to learn how to interpret other potential variations not discussed.

Barrier 3: Difficulty in Establishing an Effective Level of Detail

The struggle to develop useful scenarios in the Biomed manuals is central to a larger issue that Rob and the RMS engineers faced: the optimum level of detail for the intended users. For many years, usability studies have attempted to break down users into certain categories, the most obvious being novice and expert. The future users of the assist pump were clearly not experts in assist pumping, but neither were they total novices. Instead, they can be described as "another kind of novice. . . . This individual is an expert in the broad domain in which the technology is applied, but is a novice with regard to the particular equipment of application (Duffy, Post, and Smith 1987, p. 371). The future users at Central Hospital (and most likely at other future clinical testing sites) were largely experts in employing treatments and devices to support cardiac bypass patients but novices with this form of assist pumping. Given this not-quite-novice, not-expert status, the question arises, What level of detail should one employ to instruct such users? Duffy, Post, and Smith recommend a kind of middle route: "Detailed procedures that assume zero knowledge, such as those required for the technological novice, are inappropriate. However, the old approach to documentation, cryptic reference data, is also inadequate. Some intermediate level of functional or task-oriented documentation is required" (p. 371). Ironically, when lamenting the problems with the Biomed manual that had been raised by the RMS engineers, Rob pointed out that the manual was neither fully elaborated nor fully concise. It contained a middling amount of detail and that, according to the RMS engineers, caused major problems.

The issue of the optimal level of detail is in one sense a way of describing the age-old question of what the appropriate message is. In an attempt to break down classical conceptions of propriety to terms that can inform technical discourse, Killingsworth, Gilbertson, and Chew (1989) use both Cicero and Aristotle as their sources for a discussion of the relative merits of amplification versus diminution, or elaboration versus conciseness. The authors define the classical concept of amplification as "the set of rhetorical techniques by which a discourse is elaborated and extended to enhance its appeal and information value," and they argue that "even in the manual, long considered the most laconic of the genres of technical communication, amplification has its place" (p. 13). But exactly what place it should have is problematic. As Buehler (1986) shows, elaboration and conciseness can be seen as competing rules for technical writers. The writer, according to Buehler, should always strive to be complete for ethical reasons but concise for practical reasons. Buehler concludes that the ethical takes precedence over the practical, and therefore elaboration takes precedence over conciseness.

This principle assumes that elaborations are somehow inherently more effective ways to communicate. If we say that in a crucial passage of a document we must take all measures to ensure that messages are effective (well adapted to readers), the Buehler argument would assume that an elaborated communication would be more appropriate than a truncated one. Recent usability research has thrown such assumptions into doubt. The work of John Carroll and his associates has questioned the effectiveness of saying more rather than saying less in instructional materials. Promoting what they call the minimal manual, Carroll, Smith-Kerker et al. (1988) argue that novice users of computers can easily be overwhelmed with information while having the desire to act, to test out possibilities. In response, the researchers decided to "slash the verbiage" normally found in fully elaborated instructional manuals, create instructional materials that focused on key tasks that the novice both recognizes and needs to master to learn how to use the new device, and include procedures that explain how to recover from errors. Using the minimal manual as a self-instruction manual, Carrroll and his colleagues report that users learned faster, made fewer errors, and were better able to transfer learning to other tasks than the users of traditional commercial manuals.

The minimalist approach has been supported in part by others (Redish 1988) and questioned in part by some, notably Charney, Reder, and Wells (1988), who have provided an overview of the debate between the expounders versus the minimalists (p. 50). These researchers admit that studies have shown that "students learn the main ideas better from summaries of textbook chapters than from reading the chapters themselves" (p. 63), but their own work indicates that elaborations are useful if used judiciously. They conclude, for example, that elaborations are useful if they are in the form of "well-chosen situational examples" (p. 63). The key here is well chosen. It was quite difficult to create an effective example for the assist pump manuals. In fact, the RMS engineers raised serious concerns about the reductionist nature of such examples. The examples were accompanied by procedures that seemed to indicate that the procedures applied to a wide range of situations—far more than the procedures actually could be applied to. Subsequently Rob and the engineers struggled to structure examples within a framework that made those examples to appear to be nothing more than situational possibilities.

Overall, the major dilemma for Rob Florio and the Biomed documentation and training people centered on the extent of elaboration versus conciseness in the text of the manuals. This problem was crucial in the sections that covered actions based on interpretations of the status of the patient, surgical procedures, and the assist pump itself. The most important of these actions, adjusting the controls as the device is in use, requires much active interpretation by the drive operator. The key problem for the writer of those sections is this: How much information do users need? Does one try to provide as much information about all possible scenarios of interpretation that one can—or merely note that interpretation and adjustment must be done and leave the details unstated, forcing users to find out what to do through other means? Should the instructions be elaborated or minimized?

This issue can be illuminated by understanding the key role that the drive unit operator can play in interpreting the variables and acting during the operation. In order to do that, we return to our story of you on the operating table. This time we look more closely at one crucial moment: your bypass surgery has been completed, but your heart is not recovering. The balloon pump has been inserted to help your heart recover, and the surgeons decide that you need to go on the assist pump or you will die. You are in the operating room, and the assist pump cannulas have been inserted into your chest and attached. The surgeon is ready to begin switching you over from the balloon pump to the assist pump. The surgical team has been supplemented by the assist pump drive unit operator. Standing by the drive unit, the operator has started the device, and it is slowly pumping. In a few moments, the surgeon gives the go-ahead for the operator to increase the pumping rate, and a few moments later, the assist pump takes over pumping blood through your cardiovascular system. The immediate goal that the drive unit operator and the surgeon are hoping to achieve is for the device to pump an adequate output—an adequate rate of blood flow. When the output is less than adequate, certain members of the surgical team must take actions to increase that output. One person who will take an active role in this decision-making process is the drive unit operator.

In your case, the pump is not achieving an adequate output. Something must be done to increase it or you will die. The team members check their alternatives quickly and make adjustments accordingly. These adjustments could be to the controls of the assist pump—and therefore would be made by the drive unit operator—or they may be adjustments of a physiological nature—maybe you need to have certain drugs applied, or maybe the cannulas into your chest are leaking. Whatever the problem, the issue of adequate output is of primary concern to the drive unit operator. As Reza describes it from his experience at the RMS hospital, the drive unit operator must understand why problems occur:

Let's say you are in the operating room. You think everything is OK, and you are pumping, and you're not able to achieve the acceptable output. The surgeon will say, "Well, is there a pumping problem? How is it pumping?" At that point the operator is definitely involved in finding out what is the problem . . . The operator, in our case, definitely has a part in deciding what the problem is, and then it's the surgeon's decision what to do about it. If it is a problem with the cannula position, he'll adjust them, and then there is a real interaction back and forth. He'll say, "Is that any better?" And the operator will say, "no, that's worse" or "that's better." You see, it's better if the operator has a good sense of what is going on at that point, because that is one of their most important jobs in this whole thing is sorting out physiologic problems from pump problems. They have to recognize what kind of pump problems can occur.

The operator reads the situation by monitoring the pump's settings and the wave signal readouts on the drive unit computer screen, and, according to Reza, the operator must be wary of adjustments at several times during the entire use of the assist pump:

This process of looking at what's going on on the screen, looking at the pump settings, and—invariably the surgeon is going to come over say, "Well, how's he pumping?" and you've got to look at it and say, "well, it's good, it's bad, you know, we have a problem with it filling, etc." This comes up in the operating room when they are first trying to wean the patient from the heart-lung bypass. It comes up when they get back to the critical care unit. Invariably, every time they move these patients, everything changes.

Some of the key knowledge that the drive unit operator must have is unique to this form of assist pumping, according to Reza: "It is often not clear to people doing this for the first time what makes these patients different [from other cardiac patients not on the assist pump] and in what ways they are not different." The drive unit operators must have a fairly sophisticated level of knowledge to run the assist pump. But according to Reza and Morris, the drafts of the Biomed and the Central Hospital in-house manuals did not present some of these issues completely or effectively: "Since this involves the pump operators, to me it would be good that they would have a clear understanding of what are the potential problems and how to recognize them. That's what you're training these people to do: not only to plug it in and dial in the numbers; you want them to recognize difficulties and recommend to whoever is responsible ways of solving them. And that information is not all that clear here." *Everyone* involved with this aspect of the user's training agreed that explaining and teaching these things through both the manuals and in training sessions were the most difficult tasks of all. And although there were moments in the transfer when those who had written manuals had not understood or written these issues effectively, they eventually did overcome the inadequacies that Reza noted, and they did it well before the actual clinical trials were set to begin. In order to reach that resolution, Rob and the engineers had to wrestle with a number of tough questions. One of most important involved some differing conceptions of how the drive unit operators could control output of the pump.

Recall that the drive unit operator can control the filling (diastole) and the emptying (systole) of the pump. The flexible blood sac within the pump's shell casing fills with blood, and then the drive unit applies air pressure to the outside of that blood sac and pushes the blood out of the sac and back into the patient's cardiovascular system. To achieve complete emptying, there are two variables that can be adjusted: the amount of air pressure that the drive unit applies to the assist pump's flexible blood sac and the length of time allowed for emptying, known as the systolic duration.

A procedure to control the emptying of the pump was the first adjustment stated in the Biomed manual. Under the heading "Adjusting the drive system controls," the Biomed manual stated, "1. Set the desired Pressure and adjust the Systolic Duration (ejection period) to obtain complete emptying." This means that the drive operator should choose a fixed pressure that will be applied to the blood sac and then adjust the time of the emptying phase until the assist pump achieves complete emptying of the blood sac. In an earlier version of the manual, this same passage read just the opposite: "Set the desired Systolic Duration and adjust the Pressure"—meaning, fix the emptying time and adjust the amount of pressure needed to achieve complete emptying. In Mark Ivers's Central Hospital version, he wrote it one way in one section and the other in a following section.

Reza and Morris noted that neither version was incorrect, but neither version was complete or potentially effective. As Reza said, both versions miss the key point:

A lot of the confusion of this section comes from not explaining what is the underlying thing that you are doing here. There are two adjustments in the systolic part; one is the pressure, and the other is the systolic duration. If you increase either one of those, you make the pump empty more. But if you increase one and decrease the other, you don't really change the emptying. . . . What was done in the Biomed book was to say set the pressure—have a fixed pressure—and adjust the duration. In [the Central Hospital] manual, he [Mark] says, set the duration and adjust the pressure. While either way of doing this is possible, what is missing is an explanation of the differences in adjusting the two variables.

One could, for example, double one variable and halve the other and get complete emptying, or vice versa. Both procedures would have different effects on the patient. In one situation, the operator would want to empty the pump one way, and in another patient situation he or she would want to empty the pump in another way. "And that is not really talked about," said Reza.

In order to explain this issue, we go back to your operating table again. It took a while for the pump to produce an output that the surgeon deemed satisfactory. The drive operator had to make a number of adjustments to improve the ways that the pump filled and emptied in order to achieve that output and keep you alive. Also, during your most crucial moments in the O/R, you were bleeding at the cannulas in your chest, and your blood pressure was extremely high. The drive unit operator had to adjust for that. This type of scenario is one that Reza pointed to when he objected to the Biomed and Central Hospital drafts:

If you empty the pump in a very short time with a high pressure, you are pushing all of the blood out of the pump quickly. The patient's blood pressure pulse would be steep—a high pulse but short. If you went the other way and emptied the pump more slowly, you'd have a low pressure pulse in the patient. In some cases, if you have a patient who already has a high pressure and bleeding problems, you don't want to be dumping blood into their arterial system at real high pulse pressures. So there have been cases with patients that we've had where the surgeon will ask, "can you lower the patient's blood pressure pulse and still pump the same rate?" *And the way you do that is trade off: you put in more duration and less pressure. And once you know that, it doesn't matter if one is fixed or the other is variable. You know, you sort of play around with the two of them together.*

Furthermore, noted Reza and Morris, there may be a number of other scenarios that arise. For example, they pointed out an instance when one of them could not get the pump to empty, and he raised the pressure and duration without improving the emptying. What he soon discovered was that the outlet line was kinked. Thus, the operator must be able to discern if emptying difficulties are due to normal physiological issues or abnormal issues. To do this, the operators must develop a basic understanding of the variables and their effects.

At this point in this transfer of technology, Reza wondered whether those who were being trained at Central Hospital were achieving this basic understanding. He and Morris recognized that most of the Biomed manuals were quite well done (their major objections centered on the passages that described the operator's actions during the highly interpretive functions of the device) and that the manuals represented only part of the overall Biomed training package. But Reza was concerned that the Biomed manuals would be the only long-term source of information for future users. Long after the device was in the marketplace, Reza speculated, the manuals might take on an even more authoritative role in the use of the device. Reza also noted that one of the initial trainees, Mark Ivers, did not reconstruct the "Adjusting the Controls" section any better than did Biomed—and Mark had not only gone through the training sessions but had designed some sessions himself. Furthermore, Mark's version not only confused the two issues, but it said even less about them than did the Biomed version. That is, the messages of Mark's manual had been minimized but not clarified.

The problems with the manuals cannot be attributed to concision only. The elaborations were also problematic. The waveform scenarios combined with minimal procedures were seen by Reza and Morris to be reductionist. For example, in a passage that described a potential variation to the "normal" operating procedure, the Biomed manual showed a drawing of a "abnormal" waveform and presented a procedure to fix it: "If the sac-is-empty signal appears well before the end of the period, the Systolic Duration period is too long; decrease the Systolic Duration so that the pump doesn't sit empty." Said Reza, "You just can't make those single sentence—you know, 'if this occurs, then do this.' It is usually 'if this and this and this or this, then,'—it's more that kind of reasoning." Morris pointed out that they do not think of adjusting the controls as ⁓⁓⁓hat⁓⁓⁓setting the controls in certain ways: "None of us think of these settings as 'you set it to this number.' You set it according to what is required. You want the pump to fill, and you want the pump to empty, and you want sufficient cardiac output." The situation may demand different responses.

What was the best route to follow? Reza seemed to think that it was to both elaborate *and* minimize: "Sometimes it's better to explain the underlying principle [elaborate] and give a normal range of adjustments and not say which one to adjust [minimize]. For example, they may want to say 'Adjust the mixture of duration and pressure to achieve complete emptying.'" Reza wanted Rob to include more elaborations of theory: "My feeling is that in the Biomed manual, there should be a higher level of explanation. As it is, they are sort of halfway into it." While he also wanted to minimize the procedures:

We've been through this with training people here. First of all, what level of detail do you want to provide, and how clear do you want to be about all possible situations? Sometimes it's better just not to say anything because you'll really have people overly confused or overloaded with options that are all written down. They look at it, and they can never figure out which one they should be looking at. . . . From our experience, when you try to explain every step, it gets complicated. It gets redundant, and people never really come away knowing anything that well. And if you change anything, then you've really thrown them for a loop. It is better to know the underlying reasons and then they are better able to make their own judgments with a different set of circumstances that you may never have thought of.

The task that faces readers who "never really come away knowing anything" can be placed in a category of what Redish (1988) calls "reading to learn to do." When readers who must read to learn to do are forced to "just follow procedural steps without understanding *why* they are doing them, they may succeed in completing the tutorial [the training task] and then be unable to recall the procedures later or transfer them to other situations" (p. 227).

Although the RMS engineers had learned from experience, they never documented how they actually trained their technical staff, nor did they produce any detailed manuals for the drive unit operators. One of the Biomed managers pointed out that RMS did not document how they did their jobs; "they just did it." Thus, when the RMS engineers raised these red flags about the Biomed and Central Hospital manuals, Rob Florio came to visit to work out the problems.

Overcoming the Barrier

Although during the course of the discussions with Rob and the RMS engineers, they often found themselves suggesting specific procedures for the readers of the manual, they eventually agreed that the procedures should be minimized and the underlying principles that guide procedural decisions should be elaborated. Most of these principles were not fundamental physical principles but the applied principles of operation of this particular device.

The revised version "Adjusting the Controls" began with a statement of the goals for the drive unit operator: "The goal of assist pumping is to maintain flowrates and pressures while running the pump within appropriate operating limits. The major control variables are pressure and duration in the systolic phase [emptying the pump], vacuum and fill time in the diastolic phase [filling the pump]. The computer screen displays the stroke volume trace and provides a visible analogue of the pump systolic and diastolic phases for control purposes." This was followed by the so-called typical scenario, which allowed Rob to define all of the phases of the pump stroke without having to qualify anything as it would be in any actual use.

After defining the ideal pump stroke, the rest of the section was split into two parts: discussions of the systolic phase and the diastolic phase. Each part began with an overview of the phase. In the following example, for the systolic phase there are no procedural steps, nor are there any throughout this section:

Pressure and duration are generally interdependent: higher pressure will empty the pump faster, allowing a shorter duration; longer duration provides time for emptying when a lower pressure is used. Pressure and systolic duration should be adjusted so that the sac-is-empty signal is just visible in the stroke volume trace [the readout of the wave signal], as shown in the figure above. Figure 16 shows a pressure trace with no sac-is-empty signal: systolic duration is too short, or pressure too low. The pump is not emptying completely on each stroke, so output is reduced.

The remaining sections on the systolic phase are similarly structured discussions of potential problems (duration too long or too short) and some considerations (e.g., "lower pressures may reduce bleeding at grafts, reduce stress at sutures"). The discussion ends with a very open-ended, user-decides bit of advice: "If pressure and duration reach maximum limits and pump function is still not optimal . . . the patient management regimen may have to be adjusted to accommodate low pump output." In other words, an operator who understands how the pump works and what it can do must decide how to act in extreme circumstances.

The only procedure-like information in the entire section was a listing of broad ranges within which the variables can be set (e.g., "Pressure, left—220 to 250 mm Hg" or "Rate—30 to 90 beats/min"). The manufacturer suggests approximate safe operating limits that allow for a wide range of adjustments. The manual provides the limits of adjustment, the means of adjustment, and what the adjustments will do, so the operator can figure out what adjustments should be made when.

This approach can compare with two different types of manual-training strategies described by Charney, Reder, and Wells (1988). One approach they call discovery learning, which they equate to the guided explorations described by Carroll, Mack et al. (1988). This type of learning occurs when learners are given minimal information in manuals about the tools they have to use and are then encouraged to use those tools, within limits, to experiment. This approach assumes that people learn best when allowed to engage in "active, hands-on involvement [that] is superior to passively reading a text and examples, or even to obediently following tutorial exercises" (Charney, Reder, and Wells 1988, p. 58). The other approach that the revised Biomed manual can be compared to is what Charney, Reder, and Wells call the "working exercises" approach (p. 59). The difference between this approach and discovery learning is that instead of the learner's having complete freedom to decide what tasks to undertake with the tools at hand, the writer of the manual sets certain tasks for the learner to undertake. For the users of the assist pump technology, the task already exists, and the revised introduction to "Adjusting the Controls" reminds the users of it in the introduction to that section: it says to operate the pump in order to "maintain flowrates and pressures while running the pump within appropriate operating limits." The revised strategy is consistent with the active learning approach which is supported by recent research on the usability of instructional materials (Carroll, Smith-Kerker et al. 1988; Carroll, Mack et al. 1988; Charney, Reder, and Wells 1988).

This approach was effective. This version of the debate between the expounders versus the minimalists suggests that when faced with the job of documenting a task that has an indeterminate amount of variations, the writer should:

• Use procedural language only to establish the parameters within which the users' tasks should be done.

• Describe the principles that will guide the users' decisions.

• Describe the tools that users have to make those decisions.

• Make it clear that the users will have to experiment with the tools within the parameters in order to learn how the use the product effectively.

Barrier 4: Disparity of Technologies and Users across the Transfer
Where do I get the authority to say that the revisions made to the Biomed manuals were effective? I make that claim based on the responses of the readers of the manual—the users of the technology. An analysis of how the users' knowledge and abilities grew through their reading and training is the most important evidence to support my claim. In making this analysis, I explore the barriers that had to be overcome in order for that growth to occur.

Even when all parties expect to benefit, technology transfers can still be hindered by the differences among the people and the cultures across the transfers. Those cultural differences directly relate to the development and uses of technical documentation. Schriver (1989) points out, "Understanding the historical, ideological, and cultural forces in organizations, societies, and cultures can help us better anticipate the assumptions, motivations, and reasons that people read and write as they do" (p. 318). Accordingly, some research has explored the reciprocal relationship of written communication to its organizational contexts (Paradis, Dobrin, and Miller 1985; Doheny-Farina 1986; Barabas 1990, p. 56–91). Writing as discussed in these studies has the capacity both to reflect and shape the organization. Harrison (1987) believes "it is important to recognize that the relationship between rhetoric and the community in which it occurs is reciprocal. Communities of thought render rhetoric comprehensible and meaningful. Conversely, however, rhetorical activity builds communities that subsequently give meaning to rhetorical action (p. 9)."

This concept of communities of thought—what I equate to the term *discourse communities*—is the key to understanding most significant rhetorical barriers to a successful technology transfer. In the assist pump case, the role of discourse communities in the transfer becomes clear when we realize that the most important thing transferred was expertise. Developing expertise in the future users was the goal of Biomed in general and Rob Florio in particular. Rob wanted to ensure that the users in the clinical trials were at least beginning to develop expertise as the trials began. The major difficulty in achieving this goal was that the novice users were not members of the same discourse community as the experts. Accordingly, the manuals and the training sessions were attempts to socialize those potentially new members to the community of experts. In other words, the future users at Central Hospital had to gain membership into the community of assist pump experts. This is a learning process because discourse communities shape thinking among their members, and this influence has practical manifestations within the organizations that embody such communities:

These communities establish paradigms that discoursers adhere to or, often at their risk, depart from. . . . The paradigms reign like prelates and governments reign: they set an agenda and attempt to guarantee its meeting, often rewarding those who do and discouraging those who don't. They legislate conduct and behavior, establishing the eminently kosher as well as the unseemly and untoward. The legislation itself takes the form of institutional norms. . . . A computer company such as IBM will have one set of norms, and however similar it may be to IBM, Digital (or Hewlett Packard or Apple) will have another. Each organization is a different culture and each has different rules. And though each will use the English language and write the English language, the writing (and the attitudes about and behaviors during the writing) may very well be different. (Freed and Broadhead 1987, p. 156–57)

In other words, what constitutes good writing in any one community may not be good writing in another. The elements of quality are not necessarily agreed upon from one community to the next. For example, in their analysis of clarity in business writing, Suchan and Dulek (1990) argue that traditional conceptions of what constitutes clarity are inadequate because those conceptions posit *only* absolute standards that supposedly span organizations or disciplines. Instead, they argue that clarity is largely context dependent and therefore governed by the characteristics of the members of specific discourse communities. To illustrate this point, they describe an engineering design group within a defense-oriented aircraft manufacturer. A major facet of the design group's work is to build systems that contain redundant (backup) systems within a product to take over the functioning of the product should the first-line system fail. This commitment to redundancy has its influence throughout the group's work—from the way the organization is managed to the way some of its members dress. And, most important for our interests, redundancy influences the company's internal documents:

To outsiders, the communications contain needless repetition of words, restatement of ideas, and a belaboring of points that are already made clear. But to the design engineers, redundancy is synonymous with clarity [a backup system of ideas] and effectiveness; to write in any other manner is ineffective, not "failsafe." New hires or engineers transferring into the design department cannot become full-fledged members of the community until they quickly start to think and write in a redundant fashion. In fact, the code of redundancy is so strong that any other way of thinking is seen as aberrant and dangerous—to the professional esteem of the group and to the pilots who fly planes for which the group designs systems. (p. 94)

It is this latter point—barriers to membership in the community—that is crucial. If one is to learn how to work in a new environment, one must gain entrance not only into the new physical world but also into its discourse community. In their study of one writer's learning the demands of a new discourse community, Berkenkotter, Huckin, and Ackerman (1988) point out that individuals have memberships in many discourse communities simultaneously. The fact that individuals communicate within and across a multitude of communities and subcommunities indicates that it is difficult to isolate any one person acting in ways that are dominated totally by that individual's membership in a particular community.

Therefore, it is important to ask this question of the heart assist case study: did the people, organizations, and cultures across this transfer constitute differing discourse communities? I could argue that the participants from RMS to Biomed to Central were all working within the community of cardiac medicine and within the community of biomedical technologies geared to support cardiac surgery. Conversely, I could argue that each group represents a different type of community: a university whose mission is basic research, a corporation whose mission is product development and sales, and a hospital whose mission is community health services. These are not the only similarities and differences among the participants. The participants shared memberships in discourse communities, and they were also members in differing communities. My focus is on the community of assist pump expertise. How did the users I studied, Mark Ivers and Arie Fagan of Central, begin to become members of that group?

One of the first difficulties in gaining membership has to do with the assist pump community itself. As discourse communities go, it is a fledgling group. Reza and Morris recognized that one of the difficulties in training potential operators is that there does not exist a widespread "community of people," as Morris put it, who understand the subtleties of the technology. Not many practicing surgeons, nurses, and medical technicians have had any experiences with this technology. As a result, there are virtually no ready-made resident experts to help integrate this new technology to a new site. What is far more typical in a hospital is the scenario in which a new product is actually just a version of an already in-use product, say, a new type of balloon pump. As a result, there would be a number of expert balloon pumpers already in-house, and the training arranged by the manufacturer for the new device could be facilitated by the customer's own experts. In contrast, the assist pump technology was different enough to other pumping technologies that the resident experts were not already in place at Central. (For a discussion of the importance of resident experts in the adoption of a new technology in an organization, see Mirel 1988.)

In this case, it was the job of the manufacturer to develop and expand that community through its clinical trials. Rob and others had to make clear to the future users that the assist pump technology, while similar to other pumping technologies, is fundamentally different from them. This task, in fact, was of some concern to Reza, who worried that the future users might confuse some of the fundamental assumptions of the assist pump technology with the fundamental assumptions of the balloon pumping technology.

Disparity of Technologies   In order to become part of the drive unit team, the trainees at Central had to have had experience with other heart-assist technologies, both balloon pumping and the blood oxygenation procedure. But certain fundamental principles that underlie those technologies and influence decisions during their use are different from some fundamental principles in assist pumping. Thus, users cannot rely on their experiences with other similar technologies, especially when they must make quick decisions based on their interpretations. How do those other abilities match up to the demands of operating the assist pump drive unit? The answer is that operating the drive unit is far more complicated.

In order to understand the potential for confusion, it is useful to recall, once again, our story. You were going through bypass surgery, and your heart could not be revived sufficiently after the new veins were grafted to your heart. The surgeons called for a balloon pump to help your heart pump. When the balloon pump is required, the surgeon inserts it into the patient's aorta. The balloon can then expand and contract in a way to help the natural heart pump blood. It does this by inflating and deflating precisely in conjunction with the heartbeat. When the heart is ejecting blood (systole), the balloon deflates. This makes for lower pressure, and it is therefore easier for the heart to pump that blood out of the heart. After the heart has ejected the blood, it moves into the other part of the stroke (diastole), and the heart expands and fills. That is when the balloon must inflate to force blood out of the aorta away from the heart and into the system. That produces a pressure pulse that the heart could not do itself. The job of the balloon pump operator is to make sure that the balloon pump inflates and deflates at the correct moments in conjunction with the patient's heartbeats.

The operator does this by looking at an oscilloscope that shows a waveform of the patient's heart. This waveform provides a visual representation of systole and diastole. In this visual, certain key points in the systole and diastole are marked by blips in the wave. In addition to this wave and its blips, the oscilloscope shows the augmentation wave which represents the inflation and deflation of the balloon pump. The job of the balloon pump operator is to match the balloon's inflation and deflation points to certain points in the heart's waveform, so the primary job for the operator is to turn one of two control dials and watch as the balloon pump's inflation or deflation moves closer to the appropriate point in the heart's wave. That is the extent of the adjustments that the balloon pump operator must make—far simpler than those of the assist pump drive operator. In addition, the pumps are based on a fundamentally different operating principle. The goal of balloon pumping is to time the pump precisely in terms of the patient's heartbeat. The goal of the assist pumping is to fill and empty completely in order to achieve a desired blood flow regardless of the relationship of the assist pump strokes to the patient's heartbeats. Reza was concerned that neophyte users would make adjustment decisions based on a need to synchronize the pump with the patient's heart. You may remember that the pump has a heart-synchronous mode, but that is an option to be used in certain situations. The key here is that synchronicity is not a goal but one of a number of means to a different, more crucial goal.

The concern that Central Hospital users may not differentiate between the subtleties of these juxtaposed technologies is enhanced when we consider the differing amounts of time that different users could devote to developing expertise. The RMS engineers' level of expertise *as users* was facilitated by their continual work with the technology. They were focused on the assist pump in much of what they did every day on the job. In contrast, the time available to the Central Hospital users was less conducive to developing expertise. The users were involved in a variety of different tasks, many of which had little direct relationship to this technology. Yet these users eventually began to develop expertise. We can gain some insight into this development by examining how the differences in users across the transfer were overcome.

Disparity of Users   The differing characteristics of adult readers who must read to do their jobs have been explored in a number of recent studies (e.g., Sticht 1985; Rosenbaum and Walters 1986; Spilka 1990; Mikulecky 1990). Traditional conceptions of the act of reading characterize it as a process of decoding—figuring out the meaning of each word and then stringing meanings together to discover the meaning. In contrast, current theories of reading describe processes that are interpretive and interactive. Reading is not passive reception of meaning; it is active construction of meaning. Haas and Flower (1988) note "a growing consensus in our field that reading should be thought of as a constructive rather than as a receptive process: that 'meaning' does not exist in a text but in readers and the representations they build. . . . That is, when readers construct meaning, they do so in the context of a discourse situation, which includes the writer of the original text, other readers, the rhetorical context for reading, and the history of the discourse" (p. 167). Thus, the nature of a reader's construction depends on the extent of the reader's membership in the discourse community of the writer and others involved in the discourse situation.

Given this new definition of reading, traditional concerns about the audiences of functional documents must change too. Technical communicators have traditionally been concerned with who readers are. How old are they? What is their education? What level of prior knowledge do they bring to the reading task? But if we accept a constructivist conception of reading, we need to understand better *what readers do*—how they construct meaning during the act of reading. This change in the way a writer characterizes readers should not be exclusionary but expansive: "Certainly reader identification is crucial to the writing process. But I want to argue for a shift of focus from reader identity to reader action—what readers do that writers need to know about. In particular, I believe that we need to know more about readers' *responsive* acts as they try to make meaning from a text" (Roberts 1989, p. 136). In order to investigate these responsive acts, Roberts collected read-aloud protocols of individuals reading functional documents. His results enabled him to classify readers' responses by various levels of understanding and confusion. He argues that writers should try to anticipate the types of confusion that readers may encounter and take steps to eliminate that confusion beforehand. The advice appears sound, but fully anticipating reader confusion is usually impossible. The whole concept of the constructive, interpretive, creative nature of reading indicates that writers cannot predetermine readers' responses to a text. What is more important is for writers and trainers to try to help readers become rhetorical readers (Haas and Flower 1988).

Rhetorical reading is something beyond what we traditionally characterize as skillful reading. Haas and Flower describe this disjunction in terms of college teachers and students: "Many of our students are 'good' readers in the traditional sense: they have large vocabularies, read quickly, are able to do well at comprehension tasks involving recall of content. They can identify topic sentences, introductions and conclusions, generalizations and supporting details. Yet, these same students often frustrate us, as they paraphrase rather than analyze, summarize rather than criticize texts" (p. 170). Rhetorical reading, argues Haas and Flower, is a form of critical reading. It requires going beyond simple recall or comprehension to develop detailed constructions that place the text within the complex discourse situation of the reader—that is, within the world of texts that the reader knows. Therefore, a rhetorical reader's constructions are intertextual not merely intratextual (see Porter 1986 for an overview of the theory that supports the concept of intertextuality). And while those constructions may involve misapprehension or confusion, they are nonetheless critical, engaged, complex interpretations. The rhetorical reader is able to infer claims that the author may be making, both explicit and implicit, because the reader can place the text within a context. The reader who is not a member of a discourse community may have difficulty placing a text within a useful or illuminating context. The full member of the discourse community cannot help but read rhetorically because for that reader all texts within that community are interdependent. "We understand a text," says Porter, "only insofar as we understand its precursors."

Is rhetorical reading something that one *develops* as one becomes a more *skilled* reader? Haas and Flower suggest that rhetorical reading is a skill that should be able to be taught. Porter, in contrast, characterizes the change from the inexperienced member of a discourse community to the experienced, critical member as a change from presocialized to socialized to postsocialized individuals (Kaufer and Geisler 1989; Lutz 1989; Anson and Forsberg 1990; Winsor 1990a, 1990b, 1990c). Although Porter discusses these stages in terms of writers, it is clear that they describe the progression of readers also. In this progression, presocialized readers are not a part of the discourse community within which they are reading. "They do not know what can be presupposed, are not conscious of the distinctive intertextuality of the community, may be only superficially acquainted with explicit conventions" (p. 42). Socialized readers are full-fledged members of the discourse community within which they read, and postsocialized readers are those "who have achieved such a degree of confidence, authority, power, or achievement in the discourse community so as to become part of the regulating body. They are able to vary conventions and question assumptions—i.e., effect change in communities—without fear of exclusion" (p. 42). Thus, it is experience within appropriate discourse communities that determines the ability to read rhetorically. The development of expertise is not in a specific reading skill; it is in the knowledge of the community or communities with which the text is interdependent.

I examined the responses of the novices, Mark and Arie, as they read the instructional materials. Even in their presocialized state, they were able to employ some rhetorical reading strategies. Possibly their abilities to read rhetorically in a presocialized state paved the way for them to achieve socialization in the discourse community. My major problem, however, with attributing a high value to their rhetorical reading abilities is that the presocialized claims and assumptions that they made while reading were as likely to be inaccurate or irrelevant as they were to be perceptive and useful. The most important difference between the experienced users at RMS and the novice users at Central was the role that each played in terms of the technologies and instructions. RMS engineers are used to thinking and acting creatively with the technology. At Central, the respiratory therapists are trained to follow procedures. As Rob told the RMS engineers when they were discussing how to improve the Biomed manuals, the clinical trials users are intelligent people who will tend to fixate on what the manuals say. Those manuals, then, would play an important role in the novices' socialization.

Postsocialized Reading   Recall Reza's and Morris's comments about the problems with the Biomed manuals, comments made as they read two different versions of the Biomed manual as well as an early version of Mark Ivers's in-house manual. Their readings were highly rhetorical. In Haas and Flower's terms, "Rhetorical reading strategies include not only a representation of discourse as discourse but as unique discourse with a real author, a specific purpose, and actual effects" (p. 178). For example, when Reza read an instruction in the Biomed manual that he thought would be misleading, he said, "A technician who is being trained specifically for this project would read this more literally [than I or Rob Florio would]—trying to follow the directions more precisely." Here he is constructing both the point of view of the author and a point of view of future readers. He knows an expert interpretation of the passage and knows that it should not be taken, as he put it, "literally." He suspects that the users he constructs in this reading will "read this more literally." The disjunction between how he reads the passage and how he projects the future users/trainees will read the passage is the source of his critical reading. At one point in Morris's reading of the Biomed manuals, he noted that a passage describing the function of a power supply battery did not emphasize a point strongly enough. He justified his critical reading by saying, "I've seen perfusionists ignore batteries." Like Reza, Morris constructs a reading and the effects of that reading based on his knowledge and experience. Overall, it is no surprise that they were postsocialized readers. They were leaders in the discourse community of assist pumpers. The challenge for Rob Florio was socializing the Central Hospital personnel into that community.

Overcoming the Barrier

My first discourse-based interview with Mark Ivers took place shortly after he began Biomed's training so that he could train the Central Hospital respiratory therapists. Some months after he wrote his version, Mark performed a read-aloud protocol during his first reading of the revised Biomed manual. I later observed Mark working with Arie Fagan during a individualized training session. And, finally, I was able to interview him regarding an actual-use experience that he had. Through these methods I was able to get a glimpse of his growth to a socialized reader.

Presocialized   Early in his own training, Mark's reading revealed that he had little knowledge or experience that would enable him to question what Biomed told him. But he was an experienced reader of technical instructions and showed signs of an ability to read rhetorically. Of the following three examples of his responses when reading the manuals, the first two illustrate his presocialized state, and the third illustrates his ability to read rhetorically while still in this presocialized phase:

Example 1: Mark read a statement that instructed the user to start pumping at a certain rate. He then read a comment from one of the RMS engineers who noted that the Biomed manual had stated a different starting rate elsewhere in the manual. The engineer suggested that Biomed should choose one rate (different from one the Biomed manual had stated) and use one consistently when discussing starting the pump. Mark's response was, "Well, as you know, I haven't actually used the pump on a patient, so basically I'm just going on the recommendations of the manufacturer." He went on to wonder about what a safe starting beat rate would be. He was not readily recognizing that the issue of consistency may have been a useful strategy in this part of the instructional manual. This example illustrates a nonrhetorical reading in a presocialized state.

Example 2: Mark read a statement about the backup power system that would provide battery power for the drive unit (for use when the patient was moved from one room to another). He then read a comment by one of the RMS engineers that alluded to a potential problem with the batteries. The problem involved a situation in which the batteries' power could be drained but not show an accurate reading of that power loss. The engineer's comment was meant to elaborate on the way the batteries could lose power so that a user could make sure that the reading of a charged battery (which would read 14 to 15 volts) was indeed accurate. Mark did not understand the comments: "I guess I really don't understand what they are driving at with that comment there. I guess it's because I don't understand much about how these batteries operate. When I look at what the [Biomed] version says, 'Verify that the Battery Voltage gauge shows 14 to 15 volts," to me that would just represent a check off, saying that I'm in a safe range." To Mark, the reading of the battery gauge was simply something to look at and recognize if it was sufficiently charged (14–15 volts). If there was some underlying issue that made the battery gauge reading contingent on other readings, he did not yet understand it. In this instance, Mark's reading of the device and the manual was limited and superficial. He lacked the experience to know the contingencies, the subtleties of either text.

Example 3: He read a statement that instructed the reader, "See that the pressure is set to get the desired arterial pressure." The pump should be adjusted in such a way that the operator could see a change in the patient's physiological status (the patient's arterial pressure). He then read a comment from one of the RMS engineers suggesting that sentence be dropped and replaced with, "Adjust the pressure and systolic duration until the pump fully empties on each stroke." This alteration said nothing about the status of the patient and focused only on the performance of the pump. Later, Mark would learn that the original statement was fundamentally flawed and would be altered significantly by Rob Florio. But at this stage in his learning, Mark preferred the inclusion of the original sentence because it provided "a goal, something that you are shooting for." At the same time, he noted that the suggested revision changed the goal and recognized that the writer suggesting the change was attempting to change his focus to a more immediate goal: "What they are trying to do when they drop that is to probably have the practitioner, the operator, focus on the issue of complete emptying and complete filling. And they want them to look at that before they look down the road to arterial pressure. But I still appreciate, nonetheless, having that goal in mind of getting the desired arterial pressure." He liked the original because it put the goal in terms of the physical state of the patient. The original statement "gives you an idea of what you are doing with that control, you know, why are you making that adjustment. And the effects that it will have on the physiological parameters of the patient." Mark recognized the strategy of the reviewer (to attempt to change his goal) but preferred a version that enabled him to construct the process in terms of the effects on the patient. (Mark went on to include the original in his in-house documentation; later he altered it when the RMS engineers objected to it, and Rob Florio rewrote the Biomed manuals to eliminate the original statement.) Although he could read a passage rhetorically—perceiving the rhetorical strategies that were being played out by the writer and the reviewer—he still did not understand the device enough to make an authoritative judgment on a subtle issue. At that point in his development, Mark may have been able to read rhetorically but not in a critically useful way with the practical effects that Rob and Biomed would hope for. Mark was not yet socialized.

Socialized   Some months later after going through quite a number of training sessions as both a trainee and as a trainer, Mark was sent the revised version of the Biomed manual—the version that resulted from Rob's meeting with the RMS engineers. As he read parts of that manual for the first time, we can begin to see signs of a more sophisticated, socialized reader. First, he validated the rhetorical strategies that Rob and the engineers agreed on when he recognized that the practice of elaborating a principle can be useful for him and his trainees. He read an elaboration that explained why the drive unit operators could make a mistake by applying too much vacuum to the pump when they want to pull blood out of the patient. The statement read, "Vacuum will help fill the pump, but only to a point. Excessive vacuum can draw the wall of the vessel or chamber down onto the cannula tip, actually *reducing* the inflow." He responded that he had been teaching the trainees that they should not apply too much vacuum but he had not been teaching them *why*: "The statement about how vacuum helps fill the pump only to a point . . . is something that I understood, but I can see where that would need more emphasis in the way I would present this training. I mean we haven't really spent a whole lot of time talking about what excessive vacuum could potentially do in terms of reducing inflow. We've always spoken of a limit you know of vacuum but never really *why* you have a limit in the amount of vacuum that you want to utilize." He also recognized that elaborations on underlying principles would be useful for certain members of the team who may lack some knowledge that he and a few others had. The elaboration read, "Pressure and duration are interdependent; higher pressure can be used to empty the pump in less time, longer duration will allow complete emptying with less pressure." He believed this elaboration would be something that he would incorporate in his training sessions: "And that statement in terms of understanding how pressure and duration settings work. . . . As a respiratory therapist the interdependence of pressure and duration is something that's very understandable. But spelling it out in the text here makes a lot of sense for folks who don't have that kind of background. Again, that statement is good to have spelled out, and it would be certainly something that I would want to communicate to them [the trainees]."

While there were some elaborations that he was happy to see and would inform his teaching, he expressed some doubts about other information in the revised version. He was gaining some confidence in his ability, and he could make evaluative judgments based on his growing confidence. For example, the text read, "An extended sac-is-full signal is not necessarily a problem; it may be desirable sometimes." This statement presented new information that he was not ready to accept: "That is brand new information to me, and I really wonder what they mean by that. I always had understood that an extended sac-is-full signal would indicate stasis of blood and potential for clot formation, so I'd like that clarified in my communication with Rob."

He seemed to be most confident when his understanding of the assist pump intersected with his intimate knowledge of Central Hospital procedures. For example, one passage in the revised manual explained how to adjust the device if one was going to leave it in the control of others who were not on the drive unit team. Mark rejected this idea completely: "So what this is saying is that you want to give yourself a little bit of a hedge if you plan on just leaving the unit in a critical care area without somebody monitoring it moment by moment. I don't think we'd be in this situation. . . . I think in a critical care unit where conditions can change from moment to moment, that this isn't a sufficient hedge. I really do believe that you have to have personnel there to make the adjustment on pressure and duration on a moment-by-moment basis. At least that's going to be our practice until we develop a little more confidence with this instrument." In contrast to when he first started on the project and would typically defer to Biomed's expertise on all issues, he was gradually becoming a critical reader. Probably the most sophisticated rhetorical reading ability that he had developed as he became socialized was an increasing ability to place new and possibly radical information within a context. He was beginning to be able to work out conflicting ideas and extrapolate beyond what he read; he was developing an intertextual sense when reading. For example, when he read the passage, "Higher pressures may be required if the patient is hypertensive or if the pump outlet is restricted," he at first responded dubiously:

[He read:] "Higher pressures may be required if the patient is hypertensive." Shouldn't that be hypotensive? Well, actually, no that makes sense if the patient is hypertensive that you would need higher pressures because the resistance of the pumping would be greater. . . . OK, well this gives me a slightly different understanding—a little clearer understanding of a patient condition and how we'd have to respond to it in terms of pressure setting. . . . You know, I guess if I had sat down and thought about this a little while, that would have been clear. But at first guess, I would have said that this is really *the opposite* of what you want. But when I think about why you would need higher pressures from the pump—higher pressures to overcome the resistance in the patient's arterial system—certainly you would need higher pressures in order to insure good outflow. [Pause] So that's a great statement. I really kind of like that statement.

He was exploring a concept that his intuition said was the *opposite* of what he should do as an operator, and he was countering his intuition, or better, educating his intuition, in the light of general advice on the goals and the means to those goals. In short, he was doing just what Reza, Morris, and Rob had hoped that the readers would do when they read the revised manual. The RMS engineers wanted Rob to provide general theoretical statements of goals and the means to those goals so that the users would be forced to think about how to use the means to reach the goals when the parameters of a situation are one way or another. Mark was showing signs of developing this creativity. He was able to wrestle with conflicting or confusing information and place that information within a context to try to work out the problems that he was encountering.

Roberts (1989) argues that writers should try to anticipate points in the information that may lead to confusion and uncertainty in readers. This advice is paradoxically both simplistic and impossible. Of course, writers want to eliminate confusion, but they can never guarantee the responses of readers. The writer's highest goal should be to stimulate the reader's active engagement in a text, and sometimes conflict and confusion may be part of that active engagement.

But if you are lying on that operating table with your chest open, you probably do not want to be treated by a user confused about the crucial issues during his or her training. The ultimate question is, How did Mark and his trainees perform during the actual use of the device? Shortly before Central Hospital was about to use it for the first time, the FDA temporarily halted all clinical trials of artificial hearts because of concerns about certain problems with the pumps. As a result, all of the uses of these pumps (not only ones developed by RMS and made by Biomed but also ones developed and manufactured by others) had been delayed indefinitely. Although the problems with the pumps were deemed serious, the manufacturers were confident that the problems would be resolved. Even so, at the time of this writing, the delay has lasted more than a year and continues.

Mark, however, was given the opportunity to observe the use of the device with an actual patient shortly before the FDA temporarily halted clinical uses. Rob Florio took Mark to another hospital that was running clinical trials using a similar drive unit and pump. At the hospital, Rob and Mark were shown manipulations of the settings on the pump that was in use on a patient. Later, Mark admitted that he was quite surprised and gratified by his experience. He was gratified because his experience convinced him that, for the most part, he knew what he was doing with the pump and that the combined Biomed/Central training was on target in preparing the Central team. He was surprised to see that the patient he observed was less sensitive to poor adjustment decisions than he had believed would be possible:

From this particular patient, and it's only one patient over a two-hour period of time, but still from this one patient we saw manipulations and we saw what I would have considered mistakes in the manipulation of that pump—and mistakes that were presented as grave mistakes—without any real, you know, deleterious effects on the patient. So that is telling me that I'm on a bit of tightrope [as a drive unit operator] but I'm perhaps, you know, not a thousand feet off the ground. I do have some leeway here. I do have some options, and every little move I make on a patient is not going to cause a nasty side effect.

The most significant thing that happened during this visit occurred when a young resident came in and made some changes to the settings and then left the room. Mark was somewhat taken aback by what he referred to as "bizarre" changes and suggested to Rob that the settings should be changed to what he thought were less extreme, safer settings. Rob agreed, and the settings were subsequently changed by a technician after Rob and Mark discussed it with the appropriate hospital staff. Mark was capable of doing an authoritative reading of the situation. He was indeed becoming fully socialized into the community.

By helping to develop Central's resident expert, Biomed was developing a potentially effective educational force. During training sessions with Arie Fagan, for example, Mark repeatedly quizzed her on the subtleties of adjusting the pump. He observed her as she set up the device and prepared it for a simulated use. Throughout the session, he played out a scenario in terms of the specifics of the Central Cardiac staff in order to prompt her responses—for example, "OK, Doctor Becker hands you the power cable and . . . ?" While she was taking what she thought was the appropriate action, he would ask her to explain what she was doing. In particular, as she manipulated the controls in a mock loop, he repeatedly prompted her to explain her goals at a given moment, what controls she had at her disposal to reach those goals, and how her actions could be safely done.

During the time that Mark was conducting these training sessions he had visited the other hospital to observe and take part in the use of the device. When I asked him if he planned to tell of his experiences to his trainees if he would change his training regimen as a result of the visit, he said that he emphasized that he planned to stay the course: "I am going to pass on, at our next review session, the fact that I was there and I dealt with the patient and I observed that the patients are a little more compliant than our impression was in the initial part of the training. But I'm still going to insist that they understand and adhere to [the Biomed/Central procedures]. . . . What I observed there may not be true with every patient that comes down the line. But it did give me confidence in terms of the way we are preparing our staff. . . . I'm going to pass it on, but I'm not going to say, 'hey, relax.'" His experience, his continual socialization, gave him increased authority to make decisions. Mark's growing authority indicates that the RMS/Biomed transfer was succeeding.

In attempting to bring new technologies to new sets of users, this case suggests that it is important for manufacturers to:

• Take an active role in the development of resident experts in the users' organizations.

• Monitor and review the users' in-house documentation in order to gauge the strengths and weaknesses of the users' developing expertise.

• Develop a flexible liason between the R&D experts and the users, enabling experts to respond to user in-house training procedures and enabling selected novices to observe experts and participate in actual sessions.

• Recognize that expertise goes beyond mere comprehension of manufacturer-prescribed standards and procedures and encompasses the ability to offer critical interpretations of the manufacturers' prescriptions.

The last suggestion indicates that the job of customer training and support personnel is not complete when the customer trainees show that they can ape the experts. The goal of customer support and training should be to produce trained customers (or at least one person who will serve as the resident expert) who are fully socialized to the new technology. The users must know the goals of the technology, be able to manipulate the means to achieve those goals, and have the ability to use those means in novel situations. This last stage is the goal that customer support personnel should try to achieve before ending their support for the customer.

Conclusion: The Constructive Nature of Technical Writing and Technology Transfers

Writing in industry—whether done by technical writers or others, like engineers, who write to do their jobs—is traditionally seen to function as a conduit, a medium through which facts flow. Writing from this point of view is thought to be a compartmentalized process, which is trotted out when there is a need to transmit information through that conduit. The ideal conduit is one through which facts flow unimpeded by rhetoric; that is, the ideal writer avoids rhetoric and writes clearly. Indeed, clarity is the highest quality to which such writers can aspire. For example, if you discussed this issue with a randomly chosen population of technical writers,

I would not be surprised that the vast majority of them would say something to the effect of, "I am paid to communicate someone else's knowl-edge to others. I am not paid to affect that knowledge."

This is the traditional point of view that practitioners have espoused. Their goal is to continually refine old practices and find new ways, often new communication technologies, to improve upon clarity. Many writers believe that they must serve this role because many work within a division of labor production system, one that tells them that writing is a tool to transfer knowledge from knowledge makers to knowledge users. Writing as transfer is not writing as knowledge making. It is the former, transfer-ring information, that technical writers in technology transfers are supposed to do. One who believes in this conduit metaphor would predict that Rob Florio's role would have been to communicate the knowledge of the designers and expert users so that the novices could learn that information. But what Rob and the other writers did was much more complex than this.

Modern theories of the constructive nature of writing and reading are fundamentally opposed to the traditional views described by the conduit metaphor. Those who espouse a constructivist view argue that the writer is not a mere conduit. All writing is constructive and the technical writer reconstructs technology through language. Dorothy Winsor (1990a) de-fines this constructivist view and points out how it is at odds with views of knowledge-making commonly accepted by engineers: "We talk, there-fore, of language, and particularly written language, as a tool for con-structing ideas. . . and of knowledge itself, including scientific knowledge, as rhetorically shaped. . . . [Those in engineering define it] as a field con-cerned with the production of useful objects. In keeping with this con-cern, engineers tend not only to see their own knowledge as coming directly from physical reality without textual mediation, but also to de-value the texts engineers themselves produce, seeing them as simple write-ups of information found elsewhere" (p. 58). In this characterization, the engineering point of view places the most importance on the physical phe-nomena that engineers and scientist work with. The constructivist point of view deemphasizes the physical phenomena by saying that all percep-tions of those phenomena are mediated by language and are therefore language constructs, not the thing itself. This view places most impor-tance on the *representation* of physical phenomena.

Fundamentally, all knowledge is mediated through language. But it is sometimes important to act as if certain knowledge about physical realities exists separate from language. Otherwise, we can easily wind up with a paralyzing critique of the nature of communication. If we take the constructivist point of view to its limits, we believe that all knowledge is idiosyncratic and arbitrary, all communication is imperfect and incomplete, all absolutes are uncertain, and, therefore, it is either an absurdity or a fiction to believe in words like, fact, correct, proven. It is either an absurdity or a fiction to believe that we can have direct knowledge of the nature and function of any physical phenomena. And we can become paralyzed by the seeming impossibility of accurate communication. We become certain about our uncertainty. As Winsor states, "For those of us who choose to work with machines, belief in their direct presence is very important because direct presence can allow direct mastery of and power over reality. That the mastery comes through language raises the distressing thought that it may be 'only' mastery of language" (1990a, p. 68). But when faced with the task of trying to save a life with a machine, we must act as if we do have mastery and power over reality. We have no other choice. Although our understandings of cardiovascular systems, the nature of heart disease, and the ways to treat heart disease may be language constructions and although all facts about assist pumping are only explicitly or tacitly agreed upon constructions that members of a community of heart assist experts have come to agree upon, we have no choice but to act upon those constructions in order to affect those physical phenomena.

Does this mean that we should abandon these politically charged beliefs that all knowledge is constructed through language and act as though language is merely a window or a conduit? No. It means that we must recognize that certain pragmatic language use is an imperfect but necessary attempt to agree upon an interpretation of technology. The work that Rob Florio, Mark Ivers, and others did in this case was, in effect, a commitment to an interpretation of the technology.

The process of developing the documentation requires that those involved in the transfer from the lab to the market commit themselves to certain interpretations of what the technology is and can do and for what purposes. This does not mean that the documentation establishes a single conception of the technology; varying interpretations of the written texts are common *and problematic*. What it does mean is that certain aspects of the functions and purposes of the technology are highly contingent on user interpretations, and the process of creating the instructional texts is an attempt to limit that contingency.

At the same time, a well-written manual and a well-planned and executed training regimen will attempt to free the users to accept contingencies and become creative in contingent circumstances. As Rob Florio recognized, novices work their ways through something akin to a contingency learning curve: novices tend to want to reduce contingencies until they begin to develop some abilities. As they develop those abilities, they begin to expand the possibilities and the contingencies. They fixate less on procedures and rely more on fundamental knowledge, which allows them to make informed decisions that go beyond the procedural (see Carter 1990 for a discussion of the relationship of "general" to "local" knowledge in the development of expertise). Limiting the manual to the procedural is a mistake, but banning the procedural is a mistake also. It is better to bring novices through procedures and move them into the theoretical arena.

Technologies such as the assist pump may be continually interpreted and reinterpreted by participants in transfer from the lab to the market. Writers who are adapting that technology to users construct a representation of the technology and its uses. But that does not seem to matter when you are lying on the operating table and a technician is looking at a readout and deciding how to turn a dial. What does matter is that the technician makes the correct adjustment. In a world of deconstructable facts, we must recognize that learning how to make that "correct" adjustment is not merely a matter of finding out what is correct from experts and stating it clearly. Technology is not transferred; it is reconstructed.

4

From Design to Use: The Roles of Communication Specialists on Product Design Teams

You've just unwrapped that shiny new programmable CD player and sleek video camcorder, fresh from beneath the pine boughs. There's only one problem: you've sorted out all the cables, pushed all the buttons, read through the instruction manuals twice, and you still can't figure out how the gadgets work. Do not question your IQ: households across the nation are in the same quandary. And design experts increasingly believe that the fault lies not with the humble consumer, but in the products themselves. Says David Kelly, a product designer in Palo Alto, Calif.: "The gap between the people designing technology and those who buy it just keeps getting bigger and bigger."
M. Rogers, 1991

If the problem of technologies that are at once amazing and frustrating applied only to the uses of day-to-day consumer products, we could characterize it as a mere nuisance. But the issue has grave ramifications for all facets of life, from the mundane to the essential to the dangerous:

The syndrome of unworkable technology is far broader: from televisions to jet fighters and nuclear power plants. In the brave new world of electronics, gadgets are growing "smarter," packed with sophisticated computer chips. This transformation has created products ranging from the ingenious—such as answering machines that can automatically forward telephone calls—to the useless, like powerful pocket computers with keys so tiny they do not fit human fingers. But in the process of getting smarter, products have grown inexorably more complex, and more difficult to operate. (Rogers 1991, p. 46)

Why is the marketplace flooded with technologies that are liberating and enslaving, indispensable and dangerous? Is there a great gulf between the creative, innovative technological experts who design products and the masses who will, and increasingly must, use those products?

Innovation, Design, and Users

Donald A. Norman in his highly popular book, *The Design of Every Day Things* (1988), argues that designers are too removed from the people who must use their designs. The problem is not that designers do not want to adapt their designs to users' needs; it is that they do not know their users well enough: "Even the best best-trained and best-motivated designers can go wrong when they listen to their instincts instead of testing their ideas on actual users. Designers know too much about their products to be objective judges: the features they have come to love and prefer may not be understood or preferred by the future customers" (p. ix). Key symptoms of such failures of design are warning labels and large instruction manuals. They are "attempts to patch up problems that should have been avoided by proper design in the first place" (p. ix). Instead of merely patching up problems with documentation, Norman calls for a commitment to usable design, which he labels "the next competitive frontier" for modern industry, and offers some principles to guide this commitment.

Norman's prescriptions may be too simplistic. In a review of his book, Carole Yee (1990) praises Norman's attempt to look at a variety of product designs from users' points of view but sees his theoretical solution as highly limited:

> The idea of this book seems to be that applying a few, simple principles will produce better designs than we have now. But given the range and variety of the human mind, this seems a highly questionable proposition. . . . The problem is that users vary enormously. The first-time user is very different from the frequent user, and the range of possible users and the interpretations they might make for virtually any product are unlimited. If there is any single principle that emerges from the contemporary picture of the modular mind, it is that no simple, easy-to-follow principles could apply to all minds. The modular mind, with its ability to invent interpretations for whatever might be going on, with its interactive, intersectional system, is simply not very predictable. (p. 170)

Furthermore, although Norman's prescription claims to incorporate the user's needs in the design, it actually does not. Norman constructs a system-centered but user-friendly design by insisting that the primary focus of design is the system. Instead, a truly user-centered system identifies the users' needs before the systems are designed (Johnson 1990).

What must technical experts do in order to design for users? How can they design for users if they are far removed from the potential users?

What does it mean to learn more about users? The simplistic answer to these questions is that the experts must gain information about users. For example, the demographics of users may be transferred to designers. A more complex answer is that the experts need to learn how users act. This knowledge can generally come from three sources: user-initiated feedback to designers through such corporation-created channels as user-mailed comment cards, users' 800 telephone calls, or corporation support staff service reports; laboratory studies of human factors that focus on usability; and descriptive studies based upon field research in users' actual work environments.

All of these sources of information may be quite helpful for designers. Nevertheless, all three types of user-related information, separately and together, fail to provide the designer with what may be the most powerful resource available: interpersonal relationships with users. The import of such a relationship has been described by Michael Schrage (1990) who argues that value is not created in an organization merely by giving workers access to more and more information. A usability problem is not solved by throwing information at it. That would be a "data-driven" attempt at solving a problem. Instead, we need to develop approaches to problem solving that are "relationship-driven."

A data-driven solution to new product design problems can be represented by the approach recommended by Chay (1989), who poses this question for R&D personnel: "If sensitivity to the marketplace is key to successful new product development, how can we help strengthen the flow of information from the customer to the company?" (p. 36). His answer is to tap more sources of information through new consumer research techniques—for example, surveys of broad environmental factors, such as cultural and social trends, demographics, and attitudinal measures, as well as surveys of consumer responses to customer-identified problems with a given company's products. In contrast, a relationship-driven approach is implicitly recommended through the findings of research by Hise et al. (1990), who investigated factors that have led to successful new products. In particular, the investigators studied the collaborative efforts between marketing and R&D personnel during new product development and concluded that members of these two groups must work together day to day to produce effective new products: "The key to improving new product success levels . . . seems to lie with additional marketing/R&D involvement in the day-to-day, nitty-gritty aspects of actually shaping the product physically, rather than with the up-front aspects of collecting and using input from the market" (p. 154). That is, marketers, who presumably know customers, should not merely provide information to designers; they must work with designers to produce new products (Gupta 1990).

If one accepts the position that organizations create value through relationships, then, in order to design for usability, one must collaborate with—develop relationships with—users. "Truly successful creativity and innovation—the type that transforms a discipline or a marketplace—is as much a social act as an individual affair" (Schrage 1990, p. 34).

For new product design teams, merely getting more information about users is a limited improvement. Relying solely on such information acquisition means placing one's faith in the myth of information transfer. What is more important is for designers to develop relationships with users so that they can work together in some shared space. For example, based on interviews at 180 companies, Szakonyi (1988) advises R&D personnel to increase their awareness of customers and their understanding of customer needs by sending R&D personnel to meet with customers at customers' sites, by inviting customers to visit the companies, and by recruiting customers to join the R&D organization. Although all three of these practices may be useful, it may be difficult to replicate them continually. These types of customer-designer interactions are ideals. An alternative is for those whose job it is to adapt technologies to users and who usually serve as user representatives (technical writers) to provide information to designers and work on par with them, developing working relationships with them so that a user-oriented product can result from the relationship. The result of that relationship is an improved product—the value that an organization produces.

Collaboration, Communication, and Politics

The value produced by an organization, argues Schrage (1990), is usually the result of collaboration among workers. But collaboration is not just people talking with each other and trading information:

For example, many companies believe that interdisciplinary groups—that mix sales and marketing with R&D and finance, perhaps—represent an effort to encourage collaboration between different parts of the organization. On the surface, that seems to make sense. Scratch a little deeper and it becomes apparent that the traditional models of communication will often render this an exercise in futility. The priorities of finance are likely to be radically different from the priorities of marketing, which are certain to be different from the priorities of R&D. These factions are little more than acquaintances in the spectrum of relationships. (p. 31)

The source of this problem, says Schrage, is that traditional communication does not work, leaving professionals in many organizations frustrated. "Despite their best efforts to communicate with their colleagues—and their colleagues' best efforts to communicate with them—the misunderstandings, ambiguities, confusions, and uncertainties triumph" (p. 31).

What is necessary to overcome these barriers is truly collaborative communication. Collaboration is not just collected individual actions or collective awareness of individual actions. Rather, collaboration is working in a shared space (Ede and Lunsford 1990, Lay and Karis 1991). That is, collaboration is shared work, not shared information: "Collaboration is the process of shared creation: two or more individuals with complementary skills interacting to create a shared understanding that none had previously possessed or could have come to on their own. Collaboration creates a shared meaning about a process, a product, or an event. In this sense, there is nothing routine about it. Something is there that was not there before. Collaboration can occur by mail, over the phone lines, and in person. But the true medium of collaboration is other people. Real innovation comes from this social matrix" (Schrage 1990, p. 40).

The key to collaboration is a social bond among participants. Those who collaborate with each other must "possess a modicum of mutual trust, the belief that they are each adding value, and a genuine desire to solve the problem at hand or create something new" (Schrage 1990, p. 43). The importance of trust among team members is echoed by Larson and LaFasto (1989), who argue that trust enables team members to communicate with each other well and eventually produce quality outcomes of the collaborative enterprise. In particular, trust enables team members to keep their focus on the task at hand; otherwise, personal political agendas may debilitate the team: "The absence of trust diverts the mental concentration and energy of a team away from its performance objective and onto other issues. The team becomes politicized. Communication becomes guarded and distorted. Alliances and personal agendas begin to take precedence over the team goal. The resulting loss of focus on the common goal is a critical factor. It wounds the team and often renders it ineffective" (p. 88). The absence of trust, they say, engenders a politicized environment; I argue that trust among team members, being a social-interpersonal dynamic that influences collaboration, is itself a political stance and, by extension, all teamwork is bound by social politics. A key question arises: What role does the social working relationship of design team members play in the design process?

This question is explored in part in a study by Kernaghan and Cooke (1990), who examined the roles of rational and interpersonal processes in R&D teamwork. By rational processes, the researchers mean "the degree to which [team members] approach a problem in a logical, systematic way, (e.g., do they set goals and objectives?)" (p. 109). An example of rational analysis is a study by Vliegen and Van Mal (1990) in which the authors build upon the work of Mintzberg and his colleagues to construct a model of rational decision making. This process is based on a strategy, tactics, and execution structure that provides an outline of a decision-making process for participants in a design meeting. By contrast, interpersonal processes, according to Kernaghan and Cooke, "reflect how well members interact with one another as individuals (i.e., do they listen to each other?)" (p. 109). The results of Kernaghan and Cooke's study illustrate the influences of both processes on teamwork. Yet regardless of whether it is the most powerful element or, one of the central components of collaboration is the social nature of the working relationship among collaborators. This is a key element, whether the task is to create new knowledge or to solve problems.

These two types of tasks—innovation and problem solving—involve two types of collaboration, according to Schrage (1990). On the one hand, there is "conceptual collaboration," which occurs when participants collaborate with the goal of creating "concepts, ideas, themes, metaphors, [and] analogies" (p. 61). This occurs, for example, when market researchers and product engineers speculate about innovations that can address an emerging market. On the basis of the conceptual collaboration, "technical collaboration," the process of adapting the concepts to specific applied tasks, follows: "These are the collaborations where one requires an expert. A design engineer needs to know the stress tolerance of a material and seeks a mechanical engineer for the answer. A software programmer consults a mathematician on how best to write a certain segment of an algorithm. An advertising copywriter goes over the polls with the agency expert on market research. In these instances, the collaboration creates a shared understanding about the solution to a very narrowly defined problem" (Schrage 1990, p. 62).

New product design teams must often engage in both conceptual and technical collaboration, and these types of activities lead me to ask two questions: Should technical writers be involved in either conceptual or technical collaboration with technical designers during new product development? Do writers have anything to add to that process, and does that process add anything to what we traditionally see as the work of technical writers in industry?

Writers on Design Teams? Expert Opinions

It is not a new idea that writers should be on design teams. Haselkorn (1988) speaks of it as if it is a foregone conclusion that writers are becoming part of the design process. He notes widespread dissatisfaction with documentation created in isolation at the end of the product development process. He is not alone in this assessment. Baker (1988), noting that typically writers are brought into the product development process near the end, argues that they should enter at the "investigation phase" and work through the "design phase, prototype phase, production phase" (p. 321). Chisholm (1988) surveyed technical writers and developed three models of document and product development in industry: the end-loaded document cycle in which documentation is done after the product is complete; the in-the-middle document cycle in which writers are called in to the product development process sometime after the product has been designed and has begun its development; the collaborative document cycle in which an integrated team works together from the market analysis phase through design and development. Haselkorn, Baker, and Chisholm all argue that the end-loaded process is outmoded and inefficient and most important, eliminates any possibility of incorporating the insights of documentation specialists into product development. In contrast, Haselkorn describes the changes in the industry: "Writers will be involved earlier in the process: This is not an earthshaking statement. It is already happening, in fact even our undergraduate interns working at Microsoft tell me they are working on documentation for a product that does not exist yet. In the future, the entry point of 'writers' into the product development process will continue to push earlier and earlier, all the way back to research and product conception. As experts in the users' perspectives and needs, 'writers' will play the role of 'user advocate' throughout the processes of product research, design, development, and support" (p. 8). Haselkorn puts the term writers in quotation marks because he sees that label as an inadequate descriptor of their evolving roles. It is inadequate because they are becoming adept using a variety of media to communicate technical documentation. He also sees them becoming more expert technically without damaging their communicative abilities or their unique knowledge of user perspectives.

It may seem obvious that writers should contribute to new product design and development, but not everyone in industry agrees. A 1989 survey of owners, managers, and systems analysts from 107 companies that develop computer software showed that nearly 50 percent of those companies involved technical writers at the end of the product development process (Bresko 1991). It may be that even if managers, technical developers, and writers agree that a change is necessary, these changes are not happening quickly and easily. It is very difficult to change the course of an organization. Organizational systems seem to have a momentum that is often resistant to change. And although writers' roles in industry may be in the process of expanding, it is an evolution fraught with difficulties. Some of those difficulties stem from a perceived gulf between differing cultures within industry.

Two Cultures

Shirk (1989) argues that there are two distinct corporate cultures working side by side in the computer software industry; the software engineers, programmers, and systems analysts who design and write code and the technical writers who write user documentation. Citing sources that describe deep-seated differences in perception and personality traits that typify the two cultures, Shirk notes that such cultural conflicts can occur in any organization in which technologists and nontechnologists work together. Fowler and Roeger (1986) offer an example of a typical corporate culture split. Programmers, they note, are perceived to have the most prestigious jobs and writers the least prestigious: "Programmers also seem to believe that writers are interested only in 'literary' values, that they have no notion of logic or structure, and that, given a chance, they will over-write" (p. 22).

Even with differences like these, Shirk points to two changes in the industry that are bridging the gulf between the two cultures. First is the development of on-line documentation that integrates the work of the writer and the technologist. Second is evidence gleaned from the software industry trade literature indicating that writers are becoming involved in the earliest stages of the product development process in order to stimulate the long-range vision of the product designers. These trends, argues Shirk, indicate that managers must encourage and facilitate interdisciplinary approaches to project management.

Project Management

Broad methods of project management have been applied to the work of technical writers by Killingsworth and Jones (1989), who analyze two overarching management modes: the division of labor and the integrated team modes. In a division of labor mode, managers assign employees with specialized skills to distinct tasks in a closely analyzed production process. Tasks such as the production of technical documents are undertaken in a step-by-step, linear sequence. This process is managed externally by professional managers.

The implications of this approach for documentation specialists have been explored in a study by Debs (1986), who investigated technical writing processes in a large organization. Debs examined how the organization influenced the practices of writers, noting that the segmented structure blocked writers from being involved in creating new knowledge in the organization: "In many ways, the organization's division of labor structure and development sequence assumes the writer's obligation to a pre-existing reality. Consequently, the procedures reflect the company's view of composing—the writer's job is to invent form, not content" (p. 215). In addition, when divided workers must rely on each other for certain knowledge and resources, the act of collaborating is not necessarily productive for both parties. A common division of labor problem is that writers must often learn about the product from developers; but "programmers have to be allowed to program without constant interruptions from writers or customer service representatives. However, input from writers and customers has demonstrably improved programs, so there has to be a tradeoff" (Fowler and Roeger 1986, p. 22).

In contrast to the division of labor mode is the evolving integrated teams mode, which is based on project teams made up of individuals from a variety of relevant corporate specialties. These team members collaborate to complete a task in a process that may proceed informally, recursively, and uniquely from project to project. The team either manages itself democratically or is managed by a team representative who serves as a liaison with management.

While noting the ascendance of the integrated team approach, Killingsworth and Jones discuss a survey that indicates that the division of labor mode is still dominant in most large organizations but that the efficiency and job satisfaction of technical writers is higher for those who work on integrated teams. These authors do not claim that their survey verifies that this mode improves quality of product and documentation. Additionally, they note that from a management perspective, division of labor is a more convenient system: "Managers of communication in various companies will no doubt be better able than we are to see the disadvantages of the integrated process model. From their perspective, in a field where a high rate of turnover is the norm, one drawback will be obvious. As classic economic theory suggests, division of labor is effective because it allows for easy replacement of 'interchangeable parts'" (p. 220). That is, it is easier to replace a part if its function is distinct and clearly definable. In an integrated team, the functions of all of the members may blur, even if each member begins the project with distinct skills and goals. Indeed, the nonintegrated division of labor mode may be the optimal structure for large organizations:

Organizations in which it may be best to have information development in a separate organization include those that have a large number of information developers (large enough to warrant the overhead associated with any organizational hierarchy) and those that have a dynamically and rapidly changing workload. In these situations information development work can be parceled out and moved around within the existing information development organization rather than moving the information developers around to the different hardware and software development groups with which they work. (Grice 1988, p. 139)

A division of labor mode that operates through a centralized writing group offers other advantages, according to Grice. The centralized system offers synergism for writers: they can support each other and improve the writing/publishing processes; they can follow a career path that would lead through stages within the writing group; the group as a whole can reaffirm its status as a profession and career choice.

The major disadvantage of such a system in a large corporation lies in the possibility that it isolates writers from developers and can engender an "us-them" mentality, especially "when resources must be competed for, which is a common occurrence" (Grice 1988, p. 139). An us-versus-them environment does not engender collaboration, and a number of experts emphasize the collaborative imperative of writers and designers. Writers and designers can and must work together. The question is, still, in what mode? Those who favor the integrated team mode argue that writers have much to offer those teams.

Writers' Contributions to the Design Group

A number of experts point out that writers already understand a general process that guides both product design and development and documentation development. Hosier (1989) describes a generic process of analysis, design, development, testing, and release, which governs both the creation of products and their documentation. Similarly, Houghton-Alico (1991) models a generic system that shows documentation and software going through parallel development. Wimberly (1983) also describes a product development process within which the documentation is developed concurrent with the software product. Both development processes begin at the same time, and the writer interacts with technical experts and others involved in the process from the time the product is conceived to completion. Such a parallel development system actually helps to mark technical development milestones in a system described by McDaniel and associates (1991).

When the work of writers and designers begins concurrently, writers can contribute to the designers' work in addition to carrying out their traditional tasks. They can help the technical designers by affirming the customers' needs through audience analysis and by providing the "conceptual overview" of the product (Wimberly 1983). Writers have unique abilities that can contribute to the product development process in two ways (although they are rarely allowed to do so): they can write systems specifications that define and describe the proposed system so that developers can create it, test it, and implement it and they can provide program documentation describing the logic and coding of the system: "Clear, well-planned [program] documentation provides the means for developers of a system to communicate with each other and leaves a useful record for those who will modify the system in the future" (Dunkle and Pesante 1988, p. WE-52). (A third contribution to the process, writing operational documentation, is their traditional role.) Writers can help in the first two stages because they are sensitive to users' needs and can make connections between the design and the users.

Integrating Writers and Designers

A number of experts suggest ways to integrate writers into product development groups. Mirel (1990) urges writers to take proactive steps to gain both formal and informal entries into such enterprises. Levine (1988) believes that writers who get involved in the product development process can increase their stature and visibility within an organization. The more that writers contribute, the more they will be seen as contributors and the more that their contribution will be expected or sought out. From this base, writers can expand their influences in the product development process. In order to instigate such changes in corporate cultures, Levine offers several suggestions:

1. Situate writers physically with developers (develop a strategic knowledge of building resources and realignments and subtly attempt to interject writers into realignment plans).

2. Place writing groups within the same organizational divisions as the product development groups; do not place them within product support and marketing groups.

3. Have writers write product specifications: "Specification writing poses an extraordinary opportunity for documentation people to get involved and give something back to their information sources *during product development*" (p. 161). But, notes Levine, specs are not always meaningful documents in all organizations; sometimes they are not done and sometimes they are done only for show. The writer can substantiate the process by doing it well and making the spec useful to all.

4. Institute a writer-to-developer ratio of about 1 to 2 (ideal) or 1 to 5 or 10 (adequate).

Three key factors enable writers to contribute to software development teams (Smallwood 1986):

1. Technical knowledge: Writers must develop technical proficiency. Unfortunately technical proficiency in one area does not carry over well to other areas in the data processing industry. Nevertheless, writers should commit themselves to learning as much as they can about the technical aspects of the product under development, an effort that will enable them to gain the respect of the technical experts.

2. Flexibility in the light of design changes: Writers must be ready to cope with changes that will affect their own documentation development schedules. They should not take the attitude of "when it's ready, call me." Instead, they should understand that design changes are not errors but part of a normal design process.

3. Rapport with designers: Writers must show that they appreciate what designers do well, and designers will return the sentiment.

Advantages and Disadvantages

Should writers join design teams at the start of product development? Grice (1988) offers differing arguments, pro and con. The advantages of an integrated team approach are that it encourages synergism among a multifaceted product development group; writers can develop technical expertise because they work with technical experts; and the differing goals of the varied members of the integrated team may merge as they collaborate. On the other hand, separating writers from writing groups and placing them with design groups may inhibit technical writing as a distinct profession, limit the career potential of writers, disperse any political and organizational weight that they might have in a corporation, and make of the writers second-class technical developers. Worse, they may become just like technical developers and lose the unique perspective that they have as communicators.

Change, Conduits, and Constructivists

Most of the issues Grice and others have raised come into play in the following two case studies. Each study presents an organization that is breaking down the distinctions between technical writing and product development by integrating information specialists into design processes. The first case describes a single product development project in a large company and illustrates how the company switched from division of labor to integrated teams very quickly. The second case examines an overall approach to changing the organizational structure of the product development process and discusses how a corporation is undergoing a more gradual change to integrated teams. My overall purpose here relates to the discussions in the previous chapters of writing-as-conduit versus writing-as-constructive. The following studies in particular and the chapter as a whole illustrate why technical writing as a profession has been relegated to the status of conduit for so many years—so long that even many of the profession's defenders argue that its highest goal is to transmit information clearly between sender and receiver. This myth of the conduit is the product of the separation of technical writers from technical experts is the major reason that writers typically have a relatively low status within organizations. The case studies illustrate why and how writers are attempting to change that myth. But keep in mind that the primary goal of this change is not to improve the status of technical writers, it is to improve product development.

Case Study

ABC Company: The Sudden Change

What do you do when your company attempts to respond to the demands of the market as quickly and comprehensively as possible, and something goes wrong? One response is to double the speed to correct what went wrong and still meet the customers' needs and deadlines. The following case reveals some of the challenges that face technical communicators when they are involved in the design (and redesign) of new products. It is the story of a company that broke down the barriers between distinct functional groups (software development, marketing, customer support, technical documentation) in the successful attempt to resolve problems and improve product quality. The challenge that faced this company typifies the kinds of problems that are endemic to high-tech industries: when the products are complex, the attendant difficulties with those products are complex. Situations such as these demand multifaceted, integrated teams to solve such problems.

The Company

In 1988, ABC Company was producing a large-scale software product. As part of that development project, the company installed the prototype for a customer as a prerelease test. The product was slated for release to the market in October 1988, but in July some significant problems were revealed when the new software was being tested at the customer site. With the product scheduled to be released in two months, a crisis response team was organized to solve the problems and keep the prerelease customer's operation afloat.

What makes this story interesting and ultimately useful is a combination of factors. First, the crisis response team was truly interdisciplinary. It included programmers, marketers, technical writers, managers, field engineers, customer support personnel, and actual customers/users. Second, the extent of the problem was not known when the team was formed. Indeed, the size and complexity of the problem and its solution were developing throughout the team's response to the crisis. Much of the work of the team was research oriented: trying to learn the extent of the problems and testing potential solutions. Third, because of the time demands, the project provides a telescoped picture of an integrated team approach to product design and development.

The case description was constructed from interviews with the two principal technical writers on the project, Walter Truman and Corrie Boyle (pseudonyms), seasoned technical writers who had been with the company between five and ten years. Both had been hired as writers, but they had significant technical knowledge of the company's software—significant for technical writers, that is. The project that this case describes plunged them deeper into the technology than they had ever gone before. Therein lay the challenge.

The Challenge

Learning the Extent of the Difficulty

The problem was large, and it involved ABC Company's largest customers. Furthermore, this product was designed to precede a future product that was already in development and could not be completed and released without having the first product in place and working well. The flawed product involved a massive amount of software that was supporting a system tying numerous user sites and levels of use. The hardware functions and software code were complex. It was this complexity of code that made problems difficult to analyze and fix. The team had a name for this difficulty. "We called it brittle code," said Walter, "because you made one change to it, and it fell apart, caused fifty problems for every change you made." Ultimately, ten thousand lines of code were involved in the redesign.

When the problems surfaced, the company immediately moved in to the prerelease customer and helped them to scaffold their system in order to keep it running effectively until the problems could be resolved. This quick-response action characterized the company's larger effort to fix its problems and produce what was ultimately a product of high quality. It took an extraordinary effort by all involved to achieve that quality, and the stakes were high, as Walter noted: "We were just about to make the product generally available, in field testing, the final phase of the product development. We were only two months from actually saying 'here world, here's this wonderful, new product.' If we had shipped [the flawed product], imagine the implications for our largest customers' installing this product and having it fail. It would have been devastating."

For the first three weeks, project participants were merely trying to gauge the extent of the problem. But they decided quickly—after two days—that the product had to be reworked, and the accompanying documentation that was being written would have to be significantly altered. The task was formidable, as Walter described it, and it had a major effect on customers' ability to use the product effectively: "When you're talking about thousands of lines of problem code, that's bad enough, but when you're talking about thousands of lines of code that involve customer interfaces . . . ten lines of problem code could have a tremendous effect on product externals [customer interfaces]." In addition, more than twenty technical publications would be affected by the prospective changes. The time to do this massive task was short; they had to redesign the product in two or three months.

The company was able to support its prerelease customer immediately and then redesign and produce a high-quality, fault-free version of the product by Christmas 1988, a little more than two months after the product's original release date. While completing this task in such a limited time was a major challenge, the company's prerelease program succeeded at what it was designed to do. One of the major purposes of the program is to catch problems in time to fix them before releasing a product to the market. In that sense it serves as a safety net. The difficulty in this case was that the problems began occurring late in the testing process, and the time remaining was too short to allow for redesign and release by the original target date. In addition, the prerelease customer had integrated the new product extensively into its daily operations. The product's failure threatened some of the customer's own products and services.

Developing a Team as the Problems Emerged

In August the company organized a task force. Although a number of individuals from a variety of sources eventually contributed to the effort at differing times, the team was primarily composed of three main programmers, two system designers, two function testers, one system tester, several field engineers at the customer's site, and two technical writers (Corrie and Walter). An upper-level manager—a manager above the departmental level—took direct control.

Corrie and Walter were chosen for the project because both were knowledgeable about the product. Corrie knew more about the inner workings of the product, and Walter knew more about the user interfaces. As the project progressed, both learned more about this product than any other on which they had ever worked. The day-to-day process of redesigning the product, writing the design specifications, and subsequently developing the user documentation brought about their technical expertise.

Working under an Intensive Development Schedule

The product was originally set to be released by October 1988. Once the team was formed, a goal of a November 1988 release was discussed, but when the team began to explore the problem, the members agreed that November was too soon. Management was supportive but also wanted the team to set an aggressive target goal: "When we resized the work effort, we went back to management and said that we could not deliver in November of 88. We could deliver in December of 88 or January of 89. Management came back to us and said that's not doable. They said that such a schedule would delay an entire new product line. That's when the intensity increased. That's when upper lines of management became heavily involved and started managing the problem directly." But regardless of what schedule was chosen, the team could never be sure whether the plan would ever relate to reality. Scheduling, said Walter, was like trying to hit a moving target. And he believed that the fact that the team finished the product by Christmas was "phenomenal."

The Process

Working Day to Day

The team's work began with the customer and the company's field personnel informing the newly developed team about the primary problems appearing in the field tests of the product. Walter described a palpable sense of urgency:

> Early on the problem unfolded hour by hour. We were meeting in war rooms trying to understand the scope of the problem. We had our people at the customer site, holding conference calls with us back here at the lab, quite dramatic actually. We had our programmers, our best field support personnel out at the customer's site. Once a day they would call the lab, and about six to nine of us, at least one or two representatives from every major function, would sit and listen as they would describe each new problem; we were learning about the extent of the failure, one problem after another.

After the major difficulties with the product were identified by the customer and the field engineers, the team met daily to work out the sources of the problems and begin to redesign the product to overcome these difficulties. Throughout this process, the team met from four to ten hours a day, with Walter and Corrie writing the user documentation at night. Typically the team met in the morning and continued all day in a small conference room equipped with a white board. They sat around one large table with the lead system architect presenting one out of the hundred or so subproblems that they faced. The architect and others diagramed on the board the possible logic paths the team could take in order to fix that problem. They might spend a half-hour working through one logic path and decide they had hit a roadblock and it was really an unworkable solution, and they would erase it and start over. This was the process for every problem.

When these sessions ended, the team broke up, with each member going off to work on his or her part of the project. Then, typically in the late afternoon, a group with representatives from every function met in a conference room. They were not always the same people who had been in the morning design group. Walter was one of the people in both groups. The rest of the group consisted of planners, managers, and a variety of technical people. Representatives of the design group explained what they were doing and why they were doing it. For roughly an hour, the group reviewed the current state of all the problems, the solutions, and the requirements to enact those solutions.

Then the marketing and field support representatives stood up to present the next new set of problems that had cropped up overnight. These problems came to the company from reports quickly written at the customer's site. For each problem that arose at the site, one of the company's representatives filled out a report and transmitted it electronically to the company. The reports were meant to outline a particular problem and to show where in the code that problem occurred. In practice, the reports were sometimes a bit cryptic and sometimes sketchy, containing mostly a number of customer comments, (e.g., "The system is doing this and that, and it's not working right"). These comments gave the team clues to help them find the sources of the problems. Sometimes these were severe problems. The pressure was unrelenting.

With this meeting over, Corrie and Walter typically got something to eat and went to their respective offices, writing into the evening. As they wrote, they were dealing with information that they had learned and discussed that day with the technical experts on the team. They were gathering input from the programmers and their revised code. They read the programmers' comments in the code and during the group meetings discussed the code in detail. "We would talk on a module level," said Walter. "For example, a programmer would say, 'Oh, I had this module, and this part of the code wasn't working right, so I had to move it to this module.' And we gathered input that way, which is quite unusual. It's not the way most writers write user manuals." Nevertheless, writing from this vantage point proved to be quite effective.

In November the team had representatives from the early release customer and several other customers review the in-progress design at the company's lab site. Corrie and Walter had done drafts of parts of the user documentation at that time, so the customers could review the design specification and some of the user documentation as well. Customers were able to provide information about the problems with the original version of the product and take part in the design of both the software and the documentation.

The Technical Writers' Role in the Team

Walter and Corrie contributed significantly to this process in several ways. They developed the technical publication information plan and integrated it into the overall product development plan. This, of course, was not unique to this project; writing the information plan for any new product would normally have to be done by technical writing personnel. What was unique about this particular process was that they helped programmers write both programming documentation and certain types of programming reports that were sent to customers. Furthermore, Walter and Corrie participated in writing the product design specification. Finally, they wrote some of the user documentation and consulted with other technical writers—writers who had not participated in the team project— for help in writing the remaining user documentation for the product. In this capacity, they served as what they called scout writers—writers who went off into unknown technical territory and brought back technical knowledge that the other writers could tap into.

Developing an Information Plan When Corrie and Walter joined the team, one of their first tasks was to define the information objectives for the new version of the product. That is, they had to identify the extent of new information that was developing with the new design, which existing technical publications would be affected by this redesign, and what the writing and production schedule must be to make the Christmas target date. These items were impossible to pin down until the problems began to be sorted out and the new design began to take shape. Because Walter and Corrie did not know the extent of the problems and solutions as they unfolded, the information plan was a dynamic, evolving document that they developed over the course of the first month of the project.

They did make some key early decisions that paid off later. One was to scrap certain publications that had been underway and start them anew. So much was going to change that it did not seem as if revising those works would be efficient.

One of the most difficult aspects of information planning involved all of the interdependencies between the technical writers and the other functional groups participating in the development of the software and the publications. Corrie and Walter continually had to watch how their publication development schedule was integrated with product testing and with publication printing and production. They met daily with representatives of all the functions in the product development process. "We all had plans," noted Walter, "and we met every afternoon to see if our plans were still accurate. There was a lot of give and take between the groups." They developed what Walter called a "living plan" that could be altered daily:

I would update it based on what we learned that day, what new problems cropped up, how much more documentation was going to be required to solve the problems that we identified only four or eight hours previously. I'd meet with my manager to try to identify new interdependencies [with other groups]: like, if we were going to attempt a December date, we weren't going to be able to use our traditional printing houses, for example. We were going to have to find local printers that could turn our publications around in six days and drop ship the library to customers within three more to make the general availability date.

Because the situation was so fluid, the normally tricky task of coordinating a variety of functions was made much more difficult. Furthermore, there were other products in varying stages of development that were interdependent with this one, so team members had to inform their counterparts on those other projects what was happening with this one. "We had to inform other product groups of our situation and keep them abreast of what our dates were. They could not release their products until we released," said Walter. "So we had that hanging over our heads, as well." Thus, in addition to negotiating the new design, the writers had to do much more than just develop clear and accurate information. They had to negotiate a number of other considerations in order to get the publications printed and sent to customers' site with the code by the scheduled delivery date.

Helping to Write Programming Documentation and Reports   Although the information plan was an indispensable part of the writers' work, the most important job of the team was to redesign the product. The writers contributed to that process in several key ways. One of those contributions centered on helping the programmers write the programming documentation that accompanies the new code—documentation known as prelims—and the programming reports—commonly called repair reports—to the customers on that new code.

Prelims, short for "preliminary documentation," are notes that precede each module of code describing what that piece of code does. It describes its conventions and how it works with other programs and other pieces of code. This type of documentation is not intended for customer use, although the customers are not restricted from reading it. Primarily this documentation is written so that if a module needs to be revised later, the programmer can reconstruct the nature of the module. The prelims are also heavily relied on by those who test the software and by the technical writers; both can learn about the product, in part, through the prelims. Therefore, prelims need to be highly precise, and some of them must be quite detailed in their explanations of the module's function. Normally this type of documentation is written by the programmers who are writing the code. Because Walter and Corrie were so involved in the design process so early, they were able to offer to write some of these prelims for the programmers.

Well-written prelims were particularly useful when the team members were trying to discover the nature of the problems with the original code. "When we had good documentation prelims," noted Walter, "we were easily able to follow the design of the module." Therefore, when the team identified a couple of new modules that would be particularly critical to the success of the product, Corrie and Walter offered to help to write the prelims. This occurred sometimes well after the design had been agreed upon and the coding had begun. Even after all of the design meetings took place, design decisions had to be made during the coding because the programmers sometimes face new problems that could not be solved with the design. The programmer would have to redesign during the coding process, and Corrie and Walter would work very closely with the programmer to find out what changes were being made and update the prelims accordingly. Although they were not required to do such work, Corrie and Walter believed that it was beneficial to both the programmers—because some of the burden of writing was taken from them, not to mention that the prelims were being written by skilled writers—and the writers—because they developed a detailed understanding of how the code worked.

The other type of programmer documentation that the Corrie and Walter wrote were the programmers' repair reports to the prerelease customer. These reports contained explanations of the altered software that the team sent to the customer throughout the redesign. This work helped to keep the customer from having computer downtime during the two months that the product was being revamped. The information that the writers included with the software was essentially derived from the information that the writers were developing for the user documentation. By volunteering to write these reports, the technical writers were, in a sense, having the customers test out some of their information before the publications were completed.

Writing the Design Specifications   Although the technical writers' participation in the writing of the prelims and repair reports was useful, both activities were tangential to the primary activity of the team: developing a new design specification. As members of the team, Walter and Corrie helped to write passages of this document—work that had a profound impact on the quality of the subsequent user documentation.

Under normal conditions, design specs were written by the technical experts who were developing a new product. In this case, writing the design spec was a joint effort of the technical designers and the technical writers. Walter and Corrie wrote most of what they refer to as externals— the aspects of the product that users will see and interact with. For example, they wrote the parts of the design specifications that described how the user interface and the user message system worked. The designers wrote the parts that described the logic design and internals—descriptions of the ways that the product was going to function internally. These parts of the software would never be used directly by customers. The central challenge to Corrie and Walter was that they lacked the sophisticated technical knowledge that some of their teammates had. As a result, they did not contribute immediately. But the more they listened and learned, the more they began to see how the problems and proposed solutions would affect the use of the product. They were quick to examine the proposed designs from the user's point of view. As Walter noted, it did not take them too long to begin to be heard during team discussions:

We didn't contribute immediately, not in the early stages, not in the first day or couple of days but very quickly thereafter. In time, we became acclimated to the problems and to the program logic. We would begin to pick up on certain keywords, especially when it involved externals. And we would immediately jump in and say "but that means you're going to require operators to use this command and to do this and that. That's not a good idea." That would not be an adequate solution from a usability point of view. [We argued that] we shouldn't have to document our way out of problems; we should solve them in the product design. So we would at least identify the usability issues and, if nothing else, cause them to rethink the logic paths.

The writers attempted to represent the ease-of-use concerns of their customers. Indeed, their primary concern was for the redesigned product to be highly usable so that the function of the manuals would not be to make usable a difficult-to-use product. This type of issue enabled the writers to begin to contribute to the redesign of the product.

As the days went by, the writers continued to volunteer to write parts of the design spec. As Corrie described it, during each of the daily meetings, certain members took on certain writing tasks. The writer-reviewer roles were shared by all. "Someone would sign up to write a piece," she said, "to take notes and write narrative on what we had discussed for the day." After taking notes, "you'd go up to your own office and write it into the spec. Then programmers would review it, and the system architects would review it and give comments. And we would review things that they had written."

Overall, according to Corrie, she and Walter contributed significantly to the design: "We were able to help programmers write better message text, improve the interfaces, establish consistencies across commands, and develop easily understood names for modules within the product." All of these came from looking at the product from a user's point of view. "Sometimes programmers just think about what the product has to do," noted Corrie, "but they don't think about what the customer would actually have to do to implement that function."

As the team hammered out parts of the design, the coding and testing began on those parts. "Unfortunately," noted Walter, "there were some designs that would affect other parts of the design since everything was interrelated. Sometimes coding that had already begun had to be reworked. That was the only way we could possibly meet the deadline." Regardless, the designing, coding, testing, and technical writing were moving ahead concurrently.

Writing User Documentation and Serving as Scout Writers   Typically technical writers begin writing user documentation with the design spec as a guide; it is a source for information but not a source for actual text that is incorporated in the user documentation. But in this case, Walter and Corrie lifted passages from the spec and built upon them in the user publications. They were able to do this because they had written those parts of the spec to begin with and were able to produce text that could do double duty. This was a major time saver. They saved more time because they did not have to track down technical information from the programmers; as members of the design team, they had learned nearly all they would ever need to know to write the users' manuals. Because Corrie and Walter were technically astute, the technical reviews that programmers routinely do of all manuals before production went very quickly. The technical writers knew what they were writing about far better than they ever had before, and although they had spent time doing, in effect, nontechnical writer work (writing prelims, repair reports, and parts of the design spec), they were able to produce highly accurate user documentation quickly.

The distinction between the spec and the technical documentation was becoming blurred. Indeed, writing user manuals was not the writers' primary concern. Rather, it was to develop usable technical information. "We weren't looking at it as writing an individual publication and updating that individual publication," said Walter. "All we cared about was that we had this huge body of information that we had to write. Where it was eventually used was a secondary consideration. We were responsible for, in effect, producing the spec."

As they developed the technical publications, Walter and Corrie served as each other's peer reviewer before any of their documentation was reviewed by programmers for technical accuracy. They also served as peer reviewers for other technical writers who were not directly involved in the design team but who were writing technical publications that were affected by the changes in this product. There were several writers whose work would be affected by these events. It was for them that Walter and Corrie served as scout writers.

This project affected a number of other publications under development. In order to help other writers, Walter and Corrie tried to keep them informed about the project as it unfolded. Eventually they sent those writers chunks of the information that Walter and Corrie were writing so that the others could adapt that information to their own publications. "Whenever we finished documenting a task," said Walter, "we would give it to the other writers on the team as well. So not only was it going into the spec, but it was also going to whoever was writing a particular publication." In addition, Walter and Corrie served as technical resources, a role usually played by technical experts. That is, they established a new communication pattern for verifying technical information: "We would prepare the information up to a certain level and then hand it off and educate others. We tried to keep all internal technical publication education coming from Corrie and me and not bother the programmers. We didn't want the other writers to trouble the programmers with technical questions because Corrie and I were already very well versed in the technical issues. We could answer probably 99 percent of those questions. So there was a hierarchy of communication in which Corrie and I served as the central technical contacts for the rest of the writing community."

By becoming members of the design team, the writers became technical expert surrogates, a role that helped to hasten the writing process. By having other writers as expert sources of technical information, the inquiring writer could more easily track down needed details and explanations. These new experts were more accessible than programmers and spoke the same language as the other writers. Not only had Walter and Corrie become technical experts but they were also expert at adapting that knowledge to the needs and demands of the writing community far better than could programmers, who worked within a differing discourse community.

The Outcome

Before the product could be deemed ready for general release to the market, it had to go through several weeks of error-free tests in the field, the prerelease customer's site. For these field tests, the writers had to provide a complete draft of the documentation. The writers had to plan for packaging and distributing those publications. The key problem, according to Walter, was that they lacked the time to have the publications printed by their usual suppliers. But they were able to make other printing arrangements and shipped drafts of the documentation for the field tests and completed documentation for the general release to the market. There were a few tangential parts of the software and documentation that were not completed by the Christmas deadline, but they were soon finished and available. By January, what had been once seen as a crisis was now resolved. To the outside world, there was a minor lapse in the original schedule, but the product went on to become successful and is still the primary product of its type in the market today.

Within a year after the project, the company surveyed customers to assess how they rated the quality of some products. This particular product showed the greatest gain in customer satisfaction of all new or updated products. Clearly the work of the integrated development team was not merely a quick and dirty fix to a big problem. It was a serious response within an abnormally short time frame, a time frame that engendered a new way of developing a product. That process was new not only for the development of the software but for the development of the publications also. It integrated both, breaking down distinctions between software design and information design.

Implications

Corrie and Walter came out of this experience with fresh views of the role that technical writers must play in the development of new products. Walter was particularly concerned with the education of writers, Corrie with the need for writers to be seen as potential contributors to product design by gaining equal status with technical developers and becoming involved early in the product development cycle. Finally, both valued the collaborative nature of experience.

The Education of Writers
This project made it clear to Walter that a practical technical education is important for writers, but it is not easily achieved. It is not that writers do not need to learn theoretical technical knowledge, but that type of knowledge alone will not help them contribute to the problem-solving rigors of product design. After learning some theory, writers need to develop detailed practical knowledge of the use of the technology. The difficulty is that few companies and even fewer universities can offer enough of what would be very specific classes. The only recourse is for writers to learn the pragmatics on the job; the problem is that writers in any large high-tech company rarely stay with a single product long enough to develop a masterful, practical, expertise, a situation that results from a variety of dynamics and may be beneficial to certain aspects of a writer's

ability, productivity, and job satisfaction. But, argues Walter, if a writer wants to join a design team—and writers should do just that—he or she must expect to work with the technology for years in order to develop the needed expertise.

First, you need product-specific education. After writers are hired, they are taught basic programming concepts and languages over the course of two months or three months and then they learn about the internals of the system. The problem is that most writers do not take the opportunity to learn how to use a product in a practical sense. . . .

Writers must develop technical knowledge. I mean practical knowledge, not theoretical knowledge, not the kind of knowledge you get when you go to programming school where you learn operating system theory. This has to be working knowledge of the product, day-to-day experience. That's critical.

In most cases, that kind of education is simply not the norm. It's rarely available, so the only alternative is to work on the product library for a period of time to gain that. You cannot have people moving from product to product, as is common today. Too often a writer is brought in who has one or two publications for a year or two and then goes to another product. All that training period is lost plus they've never had a chance to work on other publications so they could get the benefit of seeing what happens in other publications. You need to have people that stay five and six years. That's the critical thing, that's something that can be done to effect a change. . . .

A large operating system takes several years to learn. You need to have experienced writers who have been on a product for at least, in this case, several years. They must have the technical depth and understanding across the entire product design to be able to make the interconnection between one function and another and be able to piece it together for the customer in a usable fashion. Products of this size are comprised of many subfunctions; in this case, there are twenty-seven large subfunctions to this product. Most writers only get to write about one to five functions throughout the whole course of their participation in writing for that product. . . .

People need to write as many different publications in a product library as possible to obtain a broad perspective of the whole library.

For a writer who wishes to participate in integrated product design teams, the heart of that writer's education begins after formal schooling ends. Such writers must also become expert in another area as well—an area that separates them from the technical experts with whom they will collaborate during the design process. This unique area of expertise centers on users' needs and abilities.

The fact that a customer was involved with the redesign of the product in this case was an important ingredient in balancing the product's technical viability with its usability. Walter argued that it is one element that should be repeated in other product development cycles. But whether customers can directly influence the design of products, the technical writers can serve as the customer's advocate during the design process. The design team writer must be educated in both the theory and practice of the technology and must know who the customers are, how they think, and what they have the ability to do with the technology:

It's also critical that writers learn not only to become very technical but they be able to switch between being very technical and being able to simplify, externalize, and not contaminate the external documentation with their knowledge of product internals. To look at it [the design] from a customer's perspective, to document it from a customer's perspective and be able to say, "Gee, it [the design] is wonderful, the code's beautiful, but that's not what it needs now." Developing that ability, to be able to not contaminate your writing with your technical knowledge is an extremely difficult skill to develop.

Writers must continually interact with users—actual customers and laboratory test users—throughout their technical education. The writer thus becomes the boundary spanner between the naivete of the customer and the expertise of the technical developer.

Walter's experience shows that in companies that produce large-scale, complex, high-technology products, technical writers can play key roles in the design of new products—if those writers develop an expertise that balances theory and practice. That pragmatic expertise usually comes only from lengthy and varied experience with a particular type of technology and/or product, as well as first-hand knowledge of customers' uses of that technology. With that education, a writer can bring unique and valuable perspectives to the product development process if the writer is allowed to participate early in that process.

The Quest for Equal Status with the Technical Developers
In many corporations, design usually happens a year to three years ahead of the implementation of that design. If writers do not participate in the design, they enter the project a year or two after the technical experts have left the product, a situation that poses a double problem. First, the writers have difficulty reconstructing necessary technical details that may have been glossed over in a design specification by technical developers who did not realize that writers and users may not fully understand a certain aspect of the technology. A writer who is trying to track down a technical detail two years after it was dealt with, may have difficulty even finding the developer who worked on the project initially. And if that per-

son can be found, who knows whether she or he will remember the detail quickly and completely? Second, writers may have some useful input into the design but at such a late stage that the chances that the input could be heard, discussed, and possibly implemented is greatly lessened.

One of the difficulties associated with writers' entering the process during the design stage is their relative lack of status within the design team. Corrie was concerned with that. Yet she noted that because she and Walter worked hard at learning the technology, they gained respect, and their contribution was recognized: "From my perspective I thought that they really appreciated what we had to contribute. I felt it was the first time that Technical Development had looked at us as an equal partner in the development process. It was the first time that they looked at us as anything other than a secretary who just simply took what they had done and rewritten it to suit our needs. We were finally thinking people." Corrie also admitted that the unthinking-secretary stereotype was understandable given the fact that in the past writers had rarely contributed substantively to the design process.

By joining the team, Walter and Corrie paid a price. Echoing Walter's discussion of the extensive education that the design team writer needs, Corrie described the amount of work that early involvement required of the writers:

We had to work hard to be earlier involved. We had to do a lot more background work to understand the problems and to understand the function before we even walked in on the design sessions because we had to be equal to the developers. To know as much technical knowledge. We had to step up to that in order to keep up with the technical sessions that they had.

We had to learn something about every aspect of the product while certain developers had their own piece and didn't really have to understand everybody else's piece. But in order to understand, to get an overview of the package, we had to understand all the pieces. So our knowledge had to be more extensive, and because we had a small amount of time to understand it, we had to really concentrate our efforts. . . .

I don't think that I worked less than twelve hours a day, and there were some days that I worked sixteen or eighteen hours a day during that time cycle. Sometimes I was here until five o'clock in the morning, writing, looking at codes. And that wasn't really expected of me, not by management or by the technical developers. That was something that I wanted to contribute to the project.

It took that amount of effort to gain the respect of the developers and become a substantive contributor to the team.

The Need for Free and Flexible Collaboration

Neither Corrie nor Walter wants to work in a crisis response mode on a regular basis, but they nevertheless valued the experience. One of the aspects that seemed to be most interesting and rewarding was the level of collaboration. If this integrated team design process was to be replicated within a normal product development process, the key, according to Walter, would be the myriad of interactions among team members: "I don't think it would have been impossible to do it in a normal cycle, but we still would need excellent working relationships with all the different groups. Those relationships were critical. As a writer on such a team, you need to speak frequently to your testers, developers, architects, and other writers. You must have meaningful discussions with them, and you need to review each other's work. There needs to be that tight working relationship."

Although everyone on an integrated team may have a distinct responsibility, the disciplinary walls between those team members must be brought down. It may be easier for such collaboration to flourish during a crisis when the disparate participants realize that they must pull together for the short term. A key challenge for any large, high-tech company is to foster free and flexible communication among representatives of differing parts of the organization during normal product development cycles, when those representatives are not motivated by the unique demands of a crisis.

Melding Division of Labor and Integrated Teams

I entitled this case "The Sudden Change" because a new product development process was suddenly created ad hoc, but that title is really not an accurate descriptor. A better, albeit less dramatic, title may have been, "The Partial Change."

Schrage (1990) argues that a representative team structure is not collaborative; simply establishing a team of individuals representing differing constituencies does not mean that they will actually collaborate. In this case, we see a representative structure: each functional group had a representative on the team who reported back to others who were not directly involved in the teamwork but were doing work on the project; for example, programmers on the team reported back to programmers not on the team who were working on code for the product. This representative structure is a variation on the division of labor mode. Employees with specialized skills are systematically assigned distinct tasks, each of which fulfills a different part of the project. Most of those employees are centrally housed with others of the same specialization, and they are all managed in a hierarchical fashion by professional managers.

At the same time, however, the work of the team began to break down those divisions between team members. Tasks normally completed by members of one specialty function became shared by others outside that function. Individual members of the team developed interpersonal working relationships and worked together in a shared space on the basis of mutual trust. In Schrage's terms, the team members truly collaborated.

From the writer's perspective, the role of scout writer embodied this melding of the two modes. It was a representative role that served to supply information to other writers and a collaborative role that brought the writers into the worlds of other functional specialties. It may be that this type of change in structure and process is the way that large organizations must evolve: variations on the past in response to crises and external pressures—sudden jumps into partial changes. In contrast, the following case describes a different type of organizational evolution for technical writers; a company in which the writers are involved in moving from division of labor to integrated teams gradually.

Case Study

XYZ Corporation: The Grass-Roots Change

How can a system be changed when the system excludes those who can make the change? How can a corporation reorganize when there is an institutional bias against the reorganization? How can a group be allowed to contribute their useful expertise to a process that needs that expertise, when, by definition, that group is not counted as a contributor? How can a technical publications group, some of whose members can play key roles in product development teams, be enabled to contribute to those teams when the corporation does not include them in the product development division of the company? These questions describe the dilemma faced by the technical publications group in XYZ Corporation.

The Corporation, Writers, Designers, and the Design Process

XYZ Corporation

XYZ Corporation designs and develops products for the telecommunications industry. Its technical writers work on a variety of products, from telecommunications hardware and software to computer-aided design systems for the corporation's own design engineers. The corporation contains a technical publications group that is attempting to become part of the product development although the technical communicators are not housed within the product development division of the corporation. The publications group is housed, instead, within the product support division. The technical communicators must develop a process that will enable them to move across organizational barriers and into the product development process. This transition is evolving through a grass-roots campaign that is bringing about significant organizational change from the bottom up.

This case study describes the evolving documentation system and analyzes the implications of this evolution for the product development processes and the career development of technical writers. These discussions and analyses are the result of a number of interviews with a variety of writers and several designers within the corporation. All of them work in many different parts of the corporation, and no two writers' experiences are exactly the same.

This case is a qualitative compilation of interviews. Although I include a variety of views and opinions, not every interviewee expressed all of the opinions noted here. However, all of the writers and designers expressed relatively similar opinions about the need for technical writers to be involved early in the product development process. There are some differences of opinion about how and when writers should undertake that involvement and what the benefits are to the writers and the corporation.

The Changing Role of Technical Writers in the Product Development Process

In the past, XYZ Corporation operated under a traditional division of labor system that separated the development of technical publications from product development. There was little ongoing contact during the product development process, and, accordingly, the development of the publications lagged behind the development of the rest of the product. The work of technical publications in the eyes of the development group was seen to be that of a word processing shop. But as the system is changing, that image is also changing.

The evolving system is beginning to bring technical writers into the product development process earlier and earlier. Typically, the writers enter the process when the product specification is nearly complete. The product spec is the document that describes a future product and its uses. In a few cases, the writers may be involved in writing that spec. Either way, the process of designing and developing the product is still largely separated from that of developing the documentation. Although some writers work with the developers when the product is being designed and developed, most work with other publication personnel to do their primary job: developing the documentation. Whether the two developmental processes become significantly intertwined, both proceed toward their parallel goals: producing products and the publications that support those products.

The writers who do become involved early in the process take part in the creation of one of two types of product specifications: the design spec, which represents the new concept, the innovation that may become a new product, and the feature spec which represents the detailed functions that give body to that innovation. The feature design phase begins when people begin thinking about how to achieve the design. Usually writers enter the process after the design spec has been completed and the feature spec has been started. Writers often contribute to the reviews of drafts of the feature spec.

Although writers may not write the feature spec, they can influence it in several ways: they can formally criticize features, commenting on their usefulness or design; they can formally request features when they see that the product may not serve the customer as well as they hoped that it could; or they can informally meet with design managers (those with whom the writer has developed a trusting working relationship) and offer a range of suggestions regarding the proposed features of a new product. The influence that the writers have on the feature spec can be informal, through the working relationship with the design manager, or formal, through the feature review meeting. Because the corporation values consensus decision making, it wants everyone to sign off on the spec. Typically, a group meets in a conference room to review the entire package of features. Said one writing supervisor, "We tend not to leave the room until everyone is reasonably comfortable with the decisions." The writer has as much voice as anyone else in that meeting. "They [the design managers] will often ask you questions, and after you develop your working relationship they'll actually phone you and ask 'what do you think about this feature?'"

Nevertheless, many of the design teams do not easily yield control over the design and features of the new product. "The feature design groups," said one writer, "tend to like to control quite closely the writing of the feature design specifications. When they're happy with what they've got within their own department, they present that formally in the review meeting." So although writers may be allowed to become involved before the product's features are agreed upon, the process of reaching that agreement may still be controlled primarily by the developers. Even that is changing because of one key move: a mid-level managerial decision to place, or co-locate, writers in the same rooms with development teams.

The Importance of Co-location

Regardless of when the writers enter the process. the co-location of writers with developers has begun what I am calling the grass-roots evolution of writers in the design process. Rather than house all writers in a separate, centralized location, some managers are placing writers in the same offices as the developers with whom they must work. Although the writers are removed from the centralized writing group, high-tech publication tools enable quick updates and portability so that writers keep other writers and production people informed and updated.

A writer who is co-located with a development team—even if a writer is assigned to a project after the product is fully designed—is close to the key expert sources of information about that product and can more easily interact with those experts, both formally and informally. Co-location has enhanced both the development of the documentation and the development of the technical innovation, the new product. It has helped the documentation process in two ways. First, it has helped writers find, learn, and write about the information that will comprise a product's documentation. Whether by interacting with developers on a daily, informal basis or by having the evolving product available for use, writers have more opportunities to discover and learn what they need to know to do their jobs. Second, it has helped writers stay abreast of the constant flow of technical changes in a product during its design and development. Because changes are frequent, writers cannot rely on early specifications as the sole sources of information for their documentation. By being located with developers, the writers are better informed about those changes early and thus avoid inaccuracies and late changes to publications that may be well into production.

Co-location has also improved the ways that writers can contribute to the technical development in two ways. First, because the writers are particularly attuned to the needs of the end users, they can contribute usability insights to the emerging product. This role, which I call the usability writer, is commonly attributed to documentation specialists. The nature of the job requires that writers continually envision ways to adapt the technology to users better. Writers who see how the application of the technology can be altered to become more usable can influence the design of the product, particularly the user interface. Writers in this capacity serve, in effect, as interface watchdogs. Second, if writers become integrated into design teams, they can serve as liaisons among the technical experts on those teams. This role, which I call the design writer, helps designers keep in touch with one another and with the myriad of issues and changes generated in the design process. As one writer at XYZ put it, writers on the design teams serve as the information manager of the team.

Although these two roles sound like good ideas, several questions remain: Can writers serve in both capacities? What is needed to implement these roles? What impediments do the writers face? What are their limitations as contributors to the design process?

The analysis indicates that while the effectiveness of writers serving in either capacity is significantly affected by the writer's communication and technical abilities, their success or failure as contributors to design teams is also centered on social and political issues. The attitudes of designers vary from design group to design group: some accept writers; some do not feel that they need them. In the face of opposition, writers can help to spread the word that they are useful by proving themselves with technical designers. That is, designers may not see the worth of technical writers by definition, but they can learn their worth in action.

The Writers' Roles on the Development Team

Usability Writer: Interface Watchdog

The writers at XYZ Corporation have an advantage that writers in many other corporations do not have: easy access to their customers. In fact, customer representatives are involved in an advisory capacity in the product development process. Therefore the writers develop relationships with actual users, which helps the writers see potential products from those users' points of view. Writers can examine users' working environments and learn first-hand what they do on the job, what problems they have, and how much they know about the XYZ Corporation's technologies. This close contact with customers combined with a knowledge of effective user interfaces can help writers contribute to the design of user interfaces for new products (Sankar and Hawkins 1991).

The products are complex, and the users are relative novices who typically have a minimal educational level. Although some writers produce documentation for engineers, most gear their work for technicians with a tenth-grade education. Typically users do bring carry-over knowledge to the use of new products. To put it another way, new products typically build on or alter previous products. As one manager noted, "There is never a quantum leap in our new products—neither a technology quantum leap nor a quantum leap into a totally different application."

Even so, many of the products and their interfaces are challenging. For example, "A maintenance interface can be quite complex," says one manager, "complete with alarms and error messages. We've had some badly designed systems in the past where alarms have been hexadecimally coded, and the operator has to refer to a three-hundred page manual to decode it, and meanwhile the system is dead in the water. Not a good situation."

In order to head off such situations in the design stage, writers can serve as the customers' usability advocates. Because most writers do not have enough technical knowledge to understand data structures and data hierarchies, writers tend to fixate on user interfaces. "We bring an outsider's view as well as a certain level of literacy," says one writer. One designer noted that it is the questions that writers ask—even the simple explanatory ones, like "How do you do X?"—that help the designers to refocus on the overall product. This inability to see the overall product is a common problem for designers because they are usually focused on their little part of it and consequently are often unaware of user needs. The major difficulty that a writer may face is convincing the designers that the writer's ideas are valid. This challenge depends on the attitude of the design team. Some embrace the writer's opinions about the user interface; some will not invite writers to the review meetings, and writers have to make an issue of it.

In one instance, a writer asked for a user interface to be added to a particular software product. The designers said that one was not needed because another module (another product) would have the interface that covered this product's function. But the writer sensed a real need for an interface for that particular module and continued to argue for it; eventually it was added. For a variety of reasons, the production of the other module was delayed for a year and a half, and the inclusion of the interface on the original product saved the entire product from uselessness and delay. In another instance, a writer in hardware development noticed that the designers did not need long electrical cables to power the developing product in their labs. The writer knew that users—not working in conveniently designed labs—might very well need lengthy cables. Something as simple as this can head off major redesigns.

Writers are thinking of the practical uses of the device and can raise questions about use that designers might miss. The writer knows to look at these aspects because he or she needs to know how the user thinks. "The user isn't interested in the implementation features," argues one writer. "He doesn't even know that they exist. What the user is interested in is the process of his work. [In the past] we used to describe how the system works; now we describe how they [users] should do their work with the system. The old type of documentation was nothing more than an advertisement for the ingenuity of the design." Current documentation practices attempt to be eminently practical.

By being involved in the design phase, writers address these types of issues at the conceptual stage instead of having to deal with redesign problems when the product has been manufactured and is being installed. While the latter has happened, "we don't have any less respect for the designers," notes a writer, "because we know that they have to focus very narrowly on the function they are creating. A function, say for software, may involve hundreds of thousands of lines of code, and [a designer] can't possibly think about all of the implications." The writers must.

Design Writer: Information Manager
A far less developed and less typical role for writers is that of the information manager on a design team. The genesis of this role has been the increasing complexity of some of the technologies that XYZ is using to develop new products. Because future users must learn more and more about the increasingly complex technologies, writers are finding that they must become much more technically knowledgeable. Like the designers, they must become specialists in a particular technology or application, although the writers' expertise may not reach that of the designers. In effect, writers' expertise must go beyond the user interface. One writer who works in a computer-aided design (CAD) development division noted, if this new role is to evolve, writers must enter the design process early: "We've been calling for this for years because one of the things we're learning is that we can no longer be jacks of all trades. The learning curves are too long. They were short when all we were talking about was user interface issues. But now since we're working in the CAD environment, when we're describing to engineers how to design integrated circuits with our tools, we're not talking just interfaces any more; we're talking pretty complex design issues."

As a result, managers at XYZ are beginning to place writers into design groups to develop the information needed to produce a product's documentation and to serve as an informal information manager among a group of designers who are all focused on their own piece of the design puzzle. The goal of the design writer is "to provide the information glue for that team so that they know what they are all talking about and they know where they all are and so that we have a coherent epistemology and a coherent set of goals," says one writer. "The upshot of that for the documentation process is that our documents will have a higher level of accuracy and understanding of the [product] environment."

Co-locating potential contributors to a team is generally considered a useful practice, but it is becoming more difficult to enact in large organizations. Co-location is not always achieved even among designers. The resulting problems of lack of proximity for team members are large. In these situations, the information manager role that technical writers play becomes even more critical. The writer can keep everyone within a group informed and updated on everyone else's progress. "If the writer is co-located," says the designer, "the writer could continually produce an updated documentation of the current stage of the project. It would centralize the process, and it would bring disparate individuals together."

The design process is thus facilitated by the writer, and the writer's information development process is facilitated by taking part in the design process. It sounds ideal. Writers, who should already be usability experts, become technology experts, join design teams, and live happily ever after. Is this happening at XYZ? In some cases, yes. But it is not without its difficulties.

Advantages and Disadvantages of Both Roles

Although it was the overwhelming opinion of all who were interviewed that the early involvement of writers in the design process was an overall benefit to XYZ Corporation, some writers and designers raised some difficult issues regarding this involvement. A number of benefits and caveats need consideration.

Benefit 1: Improved Product

Everyone interviewed agreed that writers in the design process can help improve the product—both the hardware or software and the accompanying documentation—although one manager pointed out that those involved have not attempted to assess this claim systematically. Most agreed that writers who enter the product development process in the design stage can help to improve:

Accuracy: Writers learn more about the technology and are better equipped to produce accurate documentation. They are better able to perceive technology and documentation errors and fix them early in the documentation process.

Consistency: Writers who have greater technical knowledge are better able to assess consistency across two different types of texts: the user documentation and the product specifications. For the former, writers on the design team may be able to head off inconsistencies that could crop up across a product library. For the latter, writers can review for consistency the specs written by a number of people and therefore potentially inconsistent in concepts, terminology, and style. Writers can be one of the first reviewers who can flag such problems.

Usability: Writers involved in the design phase can request features that improve the user interfaces. When design groups are producing software that contains on-line documentation or hypertext, the separation of the software product and the documentation is potentially indistinguishable. Usability is central to the technical development of the product and writers must be involved in the design.

In a time when corporations are trying hard to measure quality, writers are finding it difficult to quantify what makes for high-quality documents. Improving the relationship of writers and the technical experts is one, largely nonquantifiable, way to improve the chances that writers will produce high-quality documentation. "One can measure readability and retrievability," stated one technical writing supervisor, "but a high level of knowledge of technology is the best insurance of technical documentation quality, whether it is the spec or the user documentation— and that is a strong argument for early involvement."

A Caveat   One writer cautioned that writers' contributions at the design phase can be important but are fundamentally limited because writers are not designers: "Writers themselves are not good at writing design specs because they don't dream products. They research products, they pour over products, they handle products, and they teach other people how to handle products, but they don't create products very well." When developers are actually creating the product based on the design spec, writers can help developers, but at the conceptualizing stage, writers do not know enough to create new knowledge. When writers hit a problem, they consult designers/developers. When developers hit a problem, they try to create a solution. Writers are not attuned to creating new ways of doing things. Another way of looking at this issue is to recall Schrage's (1990) two types of collaboration: conceptual and technical. According to the writer cited above, writers are not good at conceptual collaboration, which involves speculative thinking about new ideas—creating new knowledge. On the other hand, writers are particularly good at technical collaboration, which involves adapting new ideas for practical uses.

Benefit 2: Improved Process
By including writers on design teams, the process of developing products can be made more efficient and less time-consuming. The length of time allotted for product development cycles is decreasing at XYZ; the corporation is producing products at a faster rate. Accordingly, the time needed to develop the technical documentation for a product can be shortened because the writer on the design team is learning about the product earlier and, potentially, better. If the team has a writer who acts as an information manager, the design spec can be written more quickly and the design process itself can move forward more efficiently. Three processes are improved: the writers' learning processes, the designers' writing processes, and the design process.

Writers' Learning Process   When writers are a part of the design phase, they are, by definition, in the loop. They are better positioned to learn the design objectives and the technical market requirements and can stay abreast of changes during and after the design phase of product development.

When co-located with the design team, the writer has numerous opportunities to learn about the product, the technology, and the design process. Says a writer, "A lot of learning comes by just being around— listening, talking informally, hearing something over a divider." Writers develop relationships with the designers, and when the inevitable changes in the design occur, writers are positioned to be a part of the discussions. Most important, the writers may be able to understand the nature of the changes immediately. Because they are on the team, they get to know the key technical people on a project and are able to continue informal contact in order to stay informed. Writers can stay in touch after the design phase is over, when key changes still may be made in the product.

One key benefit is that the designers get someone who becomes knowledgeable and remains with a project, so that the designers do not have to deal with new and unknowledgeable people later in the process when the user documents are developed. Overall, writers can research and learn more efficiently: "You are part of a team, your suggestions are heard, you can obtain information from reticent sources more easily. As a team member you are able to deal with people who may be slow in developing the information that you need, and you can more easily keep on those people."

Designers' Writing Process   Writers on the team can help designers produce a better spec because designers are not necessarily good and efficient writers. "What happens is that the designers often don't have the skills to do it very well," notes one writer, "and they often spend more time with it than it really deserves. They also find it painful, and it may not be the best use of their time." Even so, the designers spend a significant part of their jobs writing. An internal audit revealed that typically technical designers spend roughly 60 percent of their time documenting their work. The writer can help to take away some of this burden.

As the corporation moves to a more and more structured environment, staff have to account more carefully for what they do and when they do it. A writer on a design team helps to make their work more efficient. One writer believes "it would probably be far better for a designer to develop plans in an initial way, then provide it to a writer, who could then make them far more coherent and know whether those plans have any coherent relationship to what all the other designers are writing in their documents." Another writer noted that "designers can turn to the writer for guidance in terms of 'what should I be putting in this document?' Even though the format is formalized, it is a format of categories: functional description, technical description, etc. But what actual information should go in there and in what detail, the writer can advise the designer." If much of the designer's work involves writing and if writers' main concern is the usability of the product and the documentation, it seems natural that both writers and designers influence each others' work.

The Design Process   Each designer on a team must focus so narrowly on his or her specific tasks that few of them ever stop to consider the product as a whole. Writers' questions often force them to expand their focus and consider larger issues of usability and consistency. The earlier these questions can be asked, the earlier they are addressed. One developer noted, "An experienced writer helps us by asking questions that change our focus from the details to the entire product, the big picture. These are issues that we will have to look at, but the writer gets us looking at them earlier than we might naturally do and that helps the process. For example, writers' user-interface questions would help right from the very conceptual stages of the design process."

During the design stage, writers ask a number of questions:

- What is the user supposed to do?
- What happens automatically here?
- What is the user interface?
- What are we going to prepackage and close off from the user so the user doesn't have to worry about it?
- What are the aspects that need to be elaborated?
- Exactly which button is the user going to press?
- Exactly what command is the user going to issue?
- Is this the kind of user who is going to be doing this, or is it a different kind of user?
- When we did this on [a previous, similar product], there was an issue about the X. How are we going to solve that on this product?

Writers' concerns for users and user documentation serve as a heuristic for designers. In the earliest specifications, the product is described in relative generalities; Many details are glossed over and are left for the feature specification stage. When a technical writer enters the process, the writer brings questions that get at the details and brings issues to the surface. Notes one designer, "When you are forced, as a designer, to think about this, you realize that you better change the design as it is evolving to handle these issues." While both writers and designers were quick to note that the technical writers can clean up the spec for style, they all agreed that the best use of the writer comes from them asking—ahead of time—all the questions that need to be answered in order to produce the documentation.

Caveats   Writers and designers see three problems when writers enter the design process. The first is timing. Writers often need to see the user interfaces for products, and designers may not be able to get to that until late in the design process. A writer who is on the team from its inception may spend a good while just waiting for designers to progress to a point at which the writer can fruitfully interact with them and the product design.

The second problem is that not every new product design phase is right for writers to work on it early. If the design is to proceed through an iterative prototyping (a trial-and-error process of producing and scrapping a series of provisional prototypes on the way to solving certain design problems), the writer may end up documenting nothing more than a history of the group's failures. Thus, the writer may produce much user information that is scrapped. This may be a situation in which the writer should not be involved early.

Finally, in an environment of limited resources (need for office space, for other hardware and lab resources), a writer may drain some of the budget away from a group when they could use resources other than the writer. With products becoming more and more technically challenging, the designers can use all of the technical expertise that they can get. When a writer is on the team, another space is taken up by a nontechnical person.

Benefit 3: Improved Status and Satisfaction for Writers

By showing what they can contribute to design teams, writers can gain respect and influence with technical experts. Historically, writers at XYZ had been considered word processors with little technical knowledge; that is the role they played. "The designers are not looking at us so much as enemies," says one writer. "Their attitude is more a lack of respect for what we can do for them. What they discover is that we can indeed do things for them. We can relieve them of oppressive burdens. We can assist them in their design—make their lives easier and make their profits better, make their clients happier, and get them higher raises. This all helps to make us part of their team and in the end it becomes obvious qualitatively that there is an enormous improvement for all."

A writing supervisor describes the evolving ideal relationship between designers and writers: "By being able to draw on us for expertise in what we know well, they come to view us as experts. This is a world of experts we live in. The renaissance man is gone. We have ours, they have theirs, and we work together to complement each other. I find that most designers come very quickly to appreciate that. And it becomes a mutually supportive relationship. They are a font of technical information, and we are expert at putting it all together. They enjoy being able to bring that cohesion to the whole process, and it shows up all the way to the end when they see the satisfaction of the client and the feedback they get." If the designers have historically dealt with passive, nontechnically astute writers, that impression has to be overcome. The old impression still holds for many, and early involvement is a way to undermine that historical image.

Caveats   While the writers clearly believed that early involvement was a boon to them and design teams, they also pointed out that it may be a liability professionally for three reasons. The first concerns isolation. Leaving the comfortable confines of a writing group in order to work—that is, to be co-located—with a design group may impose a feeling of loneliness upon a writer. The writer is the outsider coming into a group of technical designers. When working with other writers on a daily basis, a writer gains a professional identity and has a political and professional base from which to work with other nonwriters. But a writer may feel that that base of support is gone when working on the design team.

A key issue here is the ways that writers are socialized within the organization. If writers gain their professional identity only from their abilities to craft prose, they may never feel at home in a design group. If, however, they gain their professional identity from their abilities to solve problems, they may find the design team a stimulating and secure place to work. Another writer noted, "If you see your kind as being a writer, then you will have problems with this. If you see yourself as a creative information person, as integral a part of the design as any other, then you're not."

If a writer does become an integral part of the design process, another problem arises: becoming overly socialized into the technical world. All of the writers noted that it is possible for them to get sucked into a design way of thinking and a design language and lose the user perspective: "Depending on which design group the writers have been with, they get so imbued with the jargon that is relevant to that particular kind of thing. It might be a particular operating system, or a particular application, or a particular kind of hardware. What things are called and how they are referred to come out in the document. I can pick up a document and say, 'this guy [writer] has been with a bunch of Unix people for too long.'"

To balance this problem, advise several of the writers and managers, the writers must stay in contact with customers, continually learning anew the ways that customers think and the ways that they use language when using technology. In effect, writers must become like field anthropologists, working with two different types of natives (designers and customers), learning to speak in both of their languages in order to mediate between the two.

That writer who goes off to live with those design natives may become valuable to that group but may not get rewarded for it. The writer works with the designers but not for them. His or her manager is housed in a writing group, and, as one writer put it, "out of sight, out of mind." There are no career advancement opportunities in a design group for a writer. "One of the things about this career is that there is no career path to it," says one writer. "Either you are a technical writer, or you are a manager of technical writers. The problem is that you never move anywhere. You can move from technology to technology, but you never have a sense that you are moving to a higher plane." Although joining a design team is a kind of a step for an experienced technical writer, it is not officially recognized as such.

Overcoming the Institutional Bias Against Integration

Regardless of the difficulties, XYZ Corporation is witnessing a healthy evolution of its writers from wordsmiths to design writers. Although the writers are not formally a part of the product design and development process, they are involved in a grass-roots expansion of status, responsibility, and skill. It is conceivable that in a large organization, such as XYZ, the integration of writers in design teams can occur only through a bottom-up movement. It may not occur otherwise for two reasons. First, because the organization does not house writers in R&D but places them into support divisions, most of the work that the writers do is considered merely support for others. This predisposes writers to perform only support activities, and therefore they are seemingly where they deserve to be. The underlying assumption is that somehow the communication can be separated from the science and technology—a modern holdover from the age-old separation of rhetoric from science.

Second, technical writers are not educated for design writers' roles. They are educated to be support writers. Support writers know much about support writing technologies but not as much about technology. However, as technologies demand a greater usability and employ more usable interfaces writers must become far more technologically expert. This is what is happening at XYZ Corporation.

Perhaps the answer lies not with educating writers to become part of the design team but educating the designers to become better communicators. At XYZ, however, the problem of lack of expert communicators on the design team is not solved by having articulate designers for two reasons: designers themselves are split in a division of labor organization and have trouble seeing beyond their own tasks and therefore are not positioned to serve as the informational glue that a design writer can, and writing today means more than just articulation; it involves detailed knowledge of communication technologies as well as visual design. In other words, writers develop a technical writing expertise that includes much more than eloquence.

At XYZ Corporation, writers are developing these expanded abilities through their growing relationships with the technical experts. These developing interpersonal and social relationships of writers and designers constitute the grass-roots movement that is changing the way that products are developed. As one writer put it, "There is an excellent new culture developing, ad hoc."

Conclusions

The Social Factor: Rational versus Interpersonal Collaborative Strategies
Some theorists and researchers argue that design teams need to improve the ways that their members work together. One aspect of this issue is the rational process of design team inner workings: do the members attack problems through systematic strategies and tactics? Another key aspect is the interpersonal, or social-political, component of teamwork. Both case studies provide clear evidence that all participants work within enterprises based on rational problem-solving systems. What is most clear is that it is the quality of the social-political facet of their work that makes the rational system succeed or fail.

In both case studies, the technical writers' contributions to the design process were minimally enabled by the rational, problem-solving system that was already in place. It was only through the interpersonal strategies that they employed that they were able to establish themselves within the problem-solving system, and it was only through their interpersonal working relationships that they were able to begin to break down the barriers between them and the technical developers.

Resolving Two Cultures

In both case studies, the participants perceived a significant wall between technical developers and technical writers. Many argue—both experts in the literature and participants in the case studies—that this wall must be dissolved. But on a closer look, we can see that total dissolution may not only be impossible but may be undesirable as well. For example, when considering the issue of technical expertise, most commentators point out that writers need to become more technically astute in order to expand their contributions to the product development process. At the same time, many point out the advantages of having a writer who is somewhat naive technically.

Bosch and Levine (1985), for example, discuss the ways that technical writers can participate in the design process without having much technical knowledge. In their views, writers serve as information facilitators by recording information, and offering and requesting clarifications, explanations, summaries, definitions, examples, and compromises. Their ability to communicate clearly and to understand when technical information is not being communicated clearly serves technical writers well when trying to contribute to a design team. In this way, the naive writer can serve effectively as both usability writer and information manager.

In contrast, Walton, Dismukes and Browning (1989) have reported on a pilot project that places a technical expert as an information specialist on an R&D team in a research division of Exxon. This specialist is typically a research engineer or scientist who has had extensive experience at technical information retrieval. The major tasks of the information specialist are to retrieve technical and scientific information that may be relevant to a given issue in an R&D project, assess the information and issue, and recommend a strategy relating to the issue. These tasks are part of the process of bringing the research to the market. "Each input anticipates or responds to an issue that must be addressed in order to move the innovation toward commercialization" (p. 34). With this system we see, in effect, a technical expert serving as an information manager. The advantage of this system is that the technical expert may be better equipped to assess technical information than a writer who has achieved even a high measure of technical expertise. The disadvantage could be that the technical expert may not be as adept at looking at design issues from the perspectives of the marketplace (the users). In an organization in which resources are scarce, R&D enterprises will most likely not be able to afford both types of communication specialists on design teams. In such cases, the choice of one type over the other comes down to a matter of emphasis. An organization that chooses the technical expert as the communication specialist emphasizes the development of the technology; an organization that chooses a writer who can play the roles of usability writer and design writer emphasizes the adaptation of technology to users.

Boundary Spanning and the Rhetorical, Constructive Nature of Design Writing

The writer who can play both roles—usability and design—is someone who can bridge gaps between innovations and the eventual users of that innovation as well as the gaps that may develop among technical designers. It is in these functions—the latter especially—that writers serve as boundary spanner (Allen 1977, Tushman and Nadler 1980, Harrison and Debs 1988, Peterson 1989, Peterson, Zimmerman and Muraski, in press).

Although technical writers do seemingly transmit information to those who will need it, they do not serve as mere conduits of that information: "The importance of boundary-spanning individuals goes considerably beyond their ability to act as conduits for information flow. . . . Boundary spanners make sense out of information as it gets disseminated" (Harrison and Debs 1988, p. 11). The effective boundary spanning role that technical writers must play is not to move information; it is to serve as a force to mediate differing worldviews among constituents, whether those differing views are internal to design groups or are between design groups and others, such as marketers or customers. Ginn and Rubenstein (1986) found that barriers to technology transfers are not overcome just by liaisons—individuals who merely pass information back and forth without participating. More effective are agents of change who can ameliorate differences among stakeholders early in a project.

Design writers can serve this function and act as filters and interpreters—rightly or wrongly, effectively or ineffectively—of the information that they deal with. They present some information in ways that seem to validate or invalidate that information. They select and edit. They construct conceptions of problems; they construct arguments; they are creative agents. And when they do these things, they are not violating any principles of clarity. Any communicator, skilled or not, can fulfill none other than a constructive function in the role of design writer. The design writer is a rhetorician.

The quality with which writers play this role depends on the extent of their education—the skills they have and how much they know about rhetoric, technology, and users. A career path and education program will improve the capabilities, status, and potentially the contribution of design writers.

Career Paths and the Education of Technical Writers

Neither of the organizations discussed in the case studies had clear career paths for writers who wish to join design teams. If organizations wish to encourage such expansion of writers' responsibilities, they must encourage design writing careers to grow by nurturing, educating, and rewarding writers along a clear career path.

Postsecondary educational programs that claim to graduate technical communicators must also develop a curriculum that prepares students for design and usability writers' roles. Students in those programs must do work in rhetoric, visual design, communication and usability research, product design, and science and technology. Future technical communicators must work with a variety of students in other major fields of study if they are to begin to learn how to collaborate effectively as they all practice to construct and reconstruct the technological worlds that they will inherit.

5

From Student to Expert: Praxis, Product Innovation, and the Teaching of Technical Communication

I'm sick and tired of visiting plants to hear nothing but great things about quality and cycle time—and then to visit customers who tell me of problems.
John Akers, 1991

Concerning technical communication theory: I did stop and think about my job, just as you had asked, and I'm sorry to report that my conclusion is still the same. We must remember my point of view, however. For the most part, the rhetorical theories seem to explain why we communicate, how we do it, the forms of communication and the patterns of miscommunication. For my job, little of this is relevant. . . . For a computer documentor, such as myself, there is very little theory involved. I obey a certain set of rules dictated by the software I am writing about. It basically boils down to writing a set of facts, no more, no less. How [clearly] I express these facts makes all the difference but they are facts nonetheless: unchangeable. No matter how I word them, they will still be unshakable truths. . . . All I have to worry about is how to make these facts as clear as possible and how detailed to get when explaining them. Basically common sense.
Excerpt from a letter in response to some questions posed by one of the writer's former college professors, 1990.

Educators must prepare future technical communicators to become substantive contributors to new product ventures and to help break down walls between participants in technological innovations. Technical communicators must go beyond traditional roles so that they may bring their unique and potentially valuable perspectives to innovative technical enterprises. To do so means bringing practical rhetoric to the heart of the enterprise, not to its periphery.

Rhetoric: An Expertise on the Fringe

The outmoded theory of communication that technical writers are merely documentors marginalizes technical writers in industry. This attitude is a product of the system that educates most students who go on to become technical writers. It is an apolitical version of communication that has, ironically, profound political consequences for technical communicators. It places them on the periphery of the "real work" that they will merely write up and edit.

This antiquated view is not suddenly imposed upon new writers when they enter industry; they learn it when they are in school. In an analysis of a group project that he assigned to three students at Purdue University, James Porter (1990) discusses the way that a student majoring in "professional writing" interacted with two students from the school of business who were "retail" majors as they collaborated to write a document: "The two retail majors regularly 'outvoted' the professional writing major on issues related to project conception and informational content. . . . The professional writing major was primarily relegated to editing and proofreading the document. Though a less capable editor than the retail majors, they believed that because he was a professional writing major, he should handle editing and that because they were retail majors, they should handle 'content'" (p. 19). These students, according to Porter, are carrying out an ideology of academic disciplinarity. When individuals of differing disciplines work together, they enact an ideology that determines the relative status of each discipline. The rules of disciplinary status are based on perceptions of specialized skills and expertise. A system that produces specialists encourages clear distinctions among specialties. Those specialties each have a differing role and status depending on the situation; generally the expert has a higher status than the nonexpert when they are working together. In addition, some expertise is valued more than others.

Such hierarchies are engendered by economic and educational systems that encourage more and more specialization. In every discipline, the amount and type of specialized knowledge that students need to learn is increasing far faster than any curriculum can keep pace with. Much of the impetus for this trend comes from industry personnel needs. Companies want to hire new employees to fill certain slots, and the companies increasingly want employees who have specific knowledge and skills. I teach in an undergraduate, degree-granting technical communication department. Our graduates are often sought by a number of companies because of the rise of the "profession" of technical writing throughout industry. Although there are still relatively few degree-granting programs in technical communication, the number of courses, programs, concentrations, undergraduate majors, and master's and doctoral programs centering on technical communication has grown dramatically since the mid-1970s.

The specialty of technical communication has been cast as something secondary to the enterprises it serves. Indeed, *serves* is a key verb. Technical writers live to serve, not enact, creative endeavors. Another way to describe the same view is that engineers do not do their jobs via rhetoric; rhetoric merely supports the engineering they do. In the light of this commonly held (and practiced) view, I restate the central argument of this book: rhetorical practices must play substantive roles in the processes of technological innovations, technology transfers, and the developments of new products. These roles are played by individuals and groups throughout differing phases or types of these endeavors—from the decisionmakers whose vision conceives, funds, and plans transfers, to the scientists, engineers, technical writers, and trainers who create and implement innovations, to the technical designers and technical writers who adapt technologies in the development of new products. But much of what goes on in industry and academe either does not recognize or does not enhance the role that rhetoric plays in these enterprises because technical communication has historically been seen as a skill and not a practice, as *techne* not *praxis*.

Techne and Praxis

Carolyn Miller (1989) notes that technical communication has historically been taught as a skill or art, which, borrowing from Aristotle, she labels techne. Miller calls for technical communication education to be based on more than just techne; it must be built on the concept of praxis: technical communication as social action. Technical communication must become a practice geared toward the social ends, the social impact of the communicators' work. Techne implies work to produce a well-crafted document, a necessary and important ability. Praxis implies work to produce a social good.

A key question that must follow is, What is the social good? Is it the good for the corporation? the employees? the community? the government? the environment? Sullivan (1990) argues that it must be for the greater society and encourages teachers to incorporate critical thinking exercises designed to help students question technological and industrial decisionmaking. But the good for the greater society is not always a clear-cut end. (See Karis and Doheny-Farina 1991 for a discussion of the debate of the environmental concerns of two neighboring communities as they were involved in the writing of proposals to cut pollution by local industries. The question of what is the good was answered very differently in each community.)

Looking at technical communication as praxis means that we can no longer view it as merely the skill or art of information transfer. We must view technical communication as epistemic, as creating knowledge, as action for the good of a larger purpose: "Understanding practical rhetoric as a matter of *conduct* rather than of production, as a matter of arguing in a prudent way toward the good of the community rather than of constructing texts, should provide some new perspectives for teachers of technical writing and developers of courses and programs in technical communication. . . . If praxis creates knowledge, academics should indeed know about non-academic practices" (Miller p. 23). If their students are to go on to play substantive roles in the creation of knowledge, then those who teach technical communication must understand praxis in business and in industry.

It is not only the education of technical communicators that can be enhanced by the concept of praxis. Other disciplines, too, will benefit by being cast in this new light. Roland Schmitt, the president of Rensselaer Polytechnic Institute and a noted expert in technology transfer, recounts a conversation he had with a graduate of Rensselaer who was 87 years old and had been "a co-founder of Texas Instruments, mayor of Dallas, Texas for seven years, [and] a philanthropist whose visionary ideas are spread from coast to coast. . . . He said, 'You must continue the rigorous professional education . . . but in today's world you must also produce graduates who know what ought to be done as well as how to do it.' I believe that charge summarizes as succinctly as possible the case for the humanities and social sciences in a technological education" (Schmitt 1989, p. 20).

The converse is equally valid: the Grand Old Man's point succinctly calls for science and technology in a humanities or social sciences education. In the light of the constructive nature of rhetorical practice in industry, it makes sense that we encourage two practices in technical communication education. First, students who are developing some expertise in technical communication must also be developing some level of knowledge in a technical and/or scientific discipline—for example, students who are majoring in technical communication must minor in a scientific or technological discipline (Bresko 1991). And students whose primary developing expertise is in technical communication must be given opportunities throughout their programs of study to collaborate on course projects with students whose primary developing expertise is in sciences or technology—for example, technical communication majors should collaborate with science and engineering majors regularly (Tebeaux 1985, Ross and Karis 1991).

Second, students in technical communication courses must become aware of the constructive nature of rhetoric and must *practice* the constructive roles that technical communicators can play in the development of new knowledge and new applications in industry. That is, they should practice the substantive roles that they can play *as rhetoricians* in situations like technology transfers and new product development projects.

I am suggesting a fairly straightforward attempt to break down disciplinary walls, but let us make no mistake—the forces that compartmentalize individuals into areas of distinct specialties are powerful. Universities and corporations are rigidly structured, and even if interdisciplinary programs are on the rise in universities and rigid division of labor systems on the wane in industry, the systems are still highly structured. Nevertheless, technical communication programs in universities and technical communicators in industry can cross boundaries in substantive ways. Teachers of technical communication must expand curricula, ensure that students can work substantively in technical and scientific realms and influence those realms, and can contribute in attempts to answer both questions: "How to?" and "What should?"

But few, if any, students will graduate from college with the abilities to contribute immediately to the efforts to answer those questions. The on-the-job education and interdisciplinary experiences of writers must be extensive if they expect to contribute to new product development projects. No technical communication student will ever learn enough about specific technologies to be able to begin a career as an accomplished design writer. Yet in a curriculum based on praxis, students will begin to learn how to collaborate in innovative environments.

Writing as techne is the production of texts; writing as praxis is the process of taking part in the discourse of a community. Courses on writing as techne teach how to write particular types of documents. Courses on writing as praxis try to socialize students to a community so that they may engage in the ongoing conversations of that community and eventually contribute to the evolution or change of a community. Learning to write as praxis means learning the boundaries, customs, and languages of a community, learning what counts as knowledge, learning what counts as appropriate forms, appropriate styles, and valid lines of reasoning, and deliberating on the means and goals of a community. Techne involves producing a clear document. Praxis involves living and contributing to an enterprise.

Praxis has been illustrated throughout this book. Chapters 2 and 3 illustrate new communities forming; chapter 2 describes the rise of a new company in an relatively new industry, and chapter 3 describes a small but growing group of experts in a new type of biomedical technology. Chapter 4 discusses the difficulties that face members of one community, a company's technical writing group, who are attempting to become socialized and gain membership into a different group, technical development and design. The socialization of those technical writers holds the promise of potentially changing the way the development groups work.

It is probably impossible for students to have similarly intensive socializing experiences like those of the individuals and teams that I describe in this book, but it is possible for them to experience some forms of socialization to the practices of business and industry. The remainder of this chapter explores some issues and techniques involved in teaching technical communication as praxis. I discuss issues that concern the transitions that students must go through as they move from school to work and conclude with a discussion of some of the benefits and caveats associated with university-industry collaboration in the education of technical communicators. Following this chapter is an appendix devoted to classroom applications. The appendix provides an extended fictional case that attempts to simulate a few of the challenges that individuals might face when collaborating with others in industry to produce a vision of a new product.

Transition from College to Career

Most research into technical and professional communication practices is conducted in industry, in laboratory studies (Carroll, Smith-Kerker et al. 1988), or in schools (Beard, Rymer, and Williams 1989; Rubens and Rubens 1988). Most conclusions about the disparities of the demands of the workplace and technical communication education come from implicit comparisons of what we know about both environments. Very few have examined individuals crossing the boundaries from school to work in order to understand the demands of both. The few studies that have attempted to understand the rigors of making this transition have been based on the experiences of interns who are nearing the end of their college careers and working for a semester or two as a writer in business or industry.

Internships are a fairly common way to enhance a technical communication curriculum in ways that may be difficult to do otherwise:

Although traditional programs in technical writing have successfully incorporated new methods of analysis, recently developed theories of writing, and advanced procedures for document design, the structure of these programs may limit their ability to introduce the situational "ins and outs" of professional practice. We know that the classroom context cannot adequately approximate the rich environment of the workplace. The organization or company is a very specific kind of context where social interactions can alternately contribute to or impinge on the individual's writing process. Assignments stop, start, and switch midstream; committees may be used to establish the sequence of a document; and a writer's choices can often depend on debate about absent audiences. To provide more fully for students' professional development, an increasing number of programs in technical writing at both the graduate and undergraduate levels now offer or require at least a semester-long internship. (Harrison and Debs 1985, p. 275)

One of the key aspects of an intern's experience is to analyze the organizational roles that the interns must play in order to do their jobs well. Coming to this understanding means undertaking self-conscious analyses of writers' roles in organizations, the ways that writers are socialized, the influences that sponsors and orientors have on writers, and the composing processes of writers. The experience may help some interns become better at their craft, but the more important aspect of the experience is the enculturating one (Bosley 1988).

The process of enculturation has been explored in several studies of interns who were crossing boundaries from academe to the job (Lutz 1986, 1989; Doheny-Farina 1989; Winsor 1990b, 1990c; Anson and Forsberg 1990). Lutz and Winsor surveyed students in industrial internships and argue that the movements from academic to nonacademic settings require socialization that affects writing processes. As Lutz (1986) says, "The newly hired writer, like any foreigner in a new land, must be socialized. She or he must learn the way the organization does things, the way it wishes to speak, and the way it wishes its writers to speak for it" (p. 188).

Writers began to become socialized through formal and informal orientation processes, according to the respondents to both Lutz's and Winsor's surveys. Winsor reports that more than a third of the interns said they learned to write on the job by interacting with supervisors, and nearly a quarter reported that they learned to write by interacting with co-workers (1990b). The majority of respondents said that they learned by imitating models. Winsor argues on this basis that the communication practices of skilled writers served as a guide for novices and are a key element in the process of socialization. Similarly, the interns whom Lutz surveyed read policy manuals, attended staff meetings on policy issues, wrote documents on the basis of models, and received feedback from members already indoctrinated in the conventions of the communities.

In another study of intern technical writers, Anson and Forsberg found that interns go through three stages: expectation, disorientation, and transition and resolution. In the first stage, preinternship writers have developed idealized conceptions of the job, especially if they have performed well as writers in college writing classes. The interns may be quite motivated and somewhat apprehensive. In the second stage, interns may become disoriented as they attempt to discover their role in the organization. They can become frustrated and feel as if they are failing at the job: "Some interns undergo a period of alienated independence, a sense of having to do things all on their own, of being expected to know already how to execute tasks and being apprehensive about consulting others, and of not knowing how or when it is appropriate to ask for information" (p. 208). In the final stage of development, the interns begin to adapt to their environment and establish roles for themselves. They begin to take on initiative and act more substantively within the organization.

The development of novices was also central to Lutz's findings. She notes that as they developed, they became aware of the organizational demands on them as writers. They learned the corporate voice and, more important, they learned that they must subordinate their persona to that of the organization. Lutz notes that in order to become "a company person," some interns had to write in ways they felt to be ineffective. Eventually, however, as they became accepted members of the organization, they began to negotiate for their points of view: "Early in the intern's tenure, such situations [conflicts between what the intern thought to be best and what the intern thought the group would think to be best] were typically resolved by the intern acquiescing to the organization's guidance. Later in the intern's apprenticeship, however, each was more likely to negotiate the text he or she thought best. Thus, such data suggest, organizations may adjust to the employee even as the employee adjusts to them" (1986, p. 189). Here again we see the reciprocal relationship of rhetorical action and the organizational environment: "Writers stand at the juncture among disciplines and among various interests and perspectives outside and inside their organization. They may enter the organization, come to understand its values, and with or without encouragement from those in charge, come to differ with either the organization's values or how communication about these values should occur, perhaps in response to audience or employer needs. Insofar as writers are effective in convincing those within the organization to change, they become effective agents of that change and advocates for the organization's audiences" (Lutz 1989, p. 120).

Throughout this book we have seen writers become advocates for change. In chapter 2 we saw the reciprocal relationship between writing processes and the processes of organizing a new venture. In chapter 3 we saw the hospital trainer become socialized to a point where he could offer critical interpretations of the process of heart assist pumping as he was developing the pump operator's manuals. In chapter 4 we saw the writers trying to become socialized in the world of technical design so that they could alter traditional design practices with input from their unique perspectives.

The benefit of the internship experience may be that writers learn the power of rhetorical action in context. They may become aware of how organizational cultures shape the way they write and how they may evolve to the point where they can shape that culture in some way.

This emphasis on learning organizational cultures is not universally accepted. The issue has been debated in an exchange between Lipson (1986, 1987) and Parsons (1987). In the initial thrust of this debate, Lipson presented two case studies of writing in a nonacademic organization. Both cases highlighted what she labeled the "cultural context" for writing in those settings, and both contexts were imbued with what she labeled "cultural" obstacles for writers. Teaching students to read those cultures, says Lipson, is an essential part of a technical or professional communication course: "Whether we teach courses to students who will become future technical writers, or service courses to future professionals in other fields, we should make sure they become aware of the cultural effects pertaining to their writing. I would hope students could become adept at reading cultures and not just at reading texts. Such sensitivity to culture should form part of their decisions as to how to write appropriately in and for these cultures. Beyond that, I would want them to become aware of the effects of the particular practices of a culture and of the ideology underlying these practices" (pp. 321–322). Lipson goes on to argue that reading cultures is not simply another way of analyzing audience: "I have seen new technical communicators move from one group to another within a company, failing to recognize that the local culture has changed, as have the norms pertaining to communication. The issue here goes far beyond what is traditionally termed audience analysis. The conditions affecting success of a technical document can change drastically in different contexts even if the audience of the document does not vary" (p. 322).

Those who can read cultures, according to Lipson, have a skill that gives them an advantage over writers who are unaware of such dimensions. As an example, Lipson cites the experiences of a student intern "whose writing was not very strong" but who was considered for a permanent position with the company at which she interned "precisely for her ability to deal across cultures." Because this ability is so

important, Lipson urges teachers to "help future communicators understand and master the communication contexts they must maneuver
within" (p. 323).

In response to Lipson's argument for teachers to increase students'
awareness of differences among discourse communities, Parsons (1987)
claims that it is unrealistic to assume that students can become adept at
reading cultures in any significant way. The ability to become aware of
cultural forces at work within organizations is a sophisticated skill, the
fruits of which are by no means clear—even to expert ethnographers.
Observations of organizational cultures provide snippets of information
that "are fraught with virtually insurmountable difficulties of accurate
interpretation. To think untrained and inexperienced interns could produce a useful ethnography of corporate culture which would be viable
presumes a competency beyond what any single [or several] communication courses might provide" (p. 266).

Since we cannot hope to teach students to observe and analyze the
organizational cultures they will enter, let us stick to what we can do
best and assume that students will develop sensitivities to the nuances of
culture as they grow older. According to Parsons, "Our teaching aims
should be set at teaching them textual expertise—with the hope that, in
time, and through more experience, they will be able to have sufficient
credibility and expertise in their own discipline to exercise 'cultural'
influence over their co-workers" (p. 266). Because students need so
much help in developing text-based skills and because educators' time
with these students is so short, argues Parsons, the focus should be on
teaching these skills so that students go into other environments
equipped with the ability to communicate clearly.

Lipson, given an opportunity to respond to Parson's critique, notes
that the issue at hand does not question the assumption that there are
differing cultural forces that affect writing in differing environments.
Instead, the primary issue involves teachers' ability to prepare students
to deal with these changing environments. But, argues Lipson, if not
teachers, who? If not now, when? Since effective communication
involves making choices in the light of local cultural factors, then it is
educators' duty to make students aware that they will face such factors.
Her interns keep journals in which they must "attend to cultural factors" on the job.

[They] have been doing so for some time now, and still have had very successful internships. All but two have received reviews of excellent or very good in performance as technical writing interns by all of the companies involved. Those two had problems not because they gave attention to cultural factors in their journals, but precisely because they gave too little attention to values and attitudes and practices of the groups they were dealing with. They tended to want to just sit and write, to use their textual expertise, and not take cultural factors seriously. Their efforts, as a result, created difficult situations in which their supervisors had to intervene. (p. 270)

Lipson concludes that skills without context are at best a limited set of skills. I, and many others, concur. Clearly if those of who teach technical communication follow Parson's prescription, the result will be writers who see themselves as neutral channels of communication and as otherwise ineffectual. These are not the writers who will play key roles in the improvement of American technology. Students need to understand the practices of rhetorical action in the workplace. We need to continue to break down walls between the university and industry.

University-Industry Cooperation

The case studies in this book represent one aspect of an increasing cooperation between academics and professionals in fields relating to technical communication. We have seen a tremendous growth in the amount of cooperation among academic researchers, teachers, and technical communicators in industry. Little (1985) describes a number of ways that university-industry collaboration can influence writing programs—for example, simulating industrial working environments in the classroom, internships for technical writing teachers (as well as students), and industrial advisory committees involved with curriculum and program development. Stewart and Gibson (1990) list approximately seventy avenues for university-industry exchanges involving both research, consulting, and pedagogy. Couture (1985) describes an extensive collaboration between local industries and the writing program at Wayne State University. Gates (1989) describes a course designed and taught by a group of university writing professors and business professionals. Kelly and Barnum (1987) describe how their work as technical writers prepared them to teach technical writing in college. And Southard (1990) describes a series of business and technical communication course assignments geared to teaching students about verbal and nonverbal corporate protocols so that they better understand "the intricacies of these discourses" (p. 79). The appendix that follows this chapter presents some examples of the pedagogy that can evolve from industry influences on technical communication curriculum. The classroom applications in the appendix concern ways to integrate issues in technology transfers and new product developments into the technical communication classroom.

These budding relationships are not without their pitfalls. There are some fundamental differences in purposes and methods between academe and industry. Indeed, while recognizing the worth of industry influences on technical writing research and pedagogy, Miller (1989) warns not to assume that because a practice exists in industry it should be studied and copied:

> But the academy does not have to be just a receptacle for practices and knowledge created elsewhere. The academy itself is also a set of practices, including those of observation, conceptualization, and instruction—practices that create their own kind of knowledge. Such knowledge allows the academy to provide a standpoint for inquiry into and criticism of non-academic practices. We ought not, in other words, simply design our courses and curricula to replicate existing practices, taking them for granted and seeking to make them more efficient on their own terms, making our students "more valuable to industry"; we ought instead to question those practices and encourage our students to do so too. (p. 23)

In direct response to this warning, Lutz (1989) argues that students must be prepared for the worlds they will enter so that they can look at them critically and change them, if possible, from the inside: "However, teachers can more adequately prepare writers for their professional roles by sensitizing them, as prospective corporate employees, to the theoretical notion of corporate culture and to the issues surrounding socialization. Such sensitization would provide a theoretical framework for students to analyze and work within the constraints of particular cultures and ultimately to contribute fully to documenting, enhancing, or, if need be, changing the organization's writing policies and practices" (p. 132).

Even if educators would like to see students eventually challenge the practices of industry, they still need to know more and more about the complexities of industrial environments. Sullivan (1990) describes a technical communication course in which he enables students to practice writing in simulated worlds of work for part of the course and then asks them to debate in a public forum controversial technological and business practices. His goal is for students to develop abilities to do the writing of the workplace and to develop a critical stance toward workplace practices and ethics. Echoing Lutz, I argue that it is only by knowing the practices of the world of work that teachers take on either of Sullivan's two approaches. And only by preparing students for those environments will they be able to become viable, possibly powerful, actors within those realms.

The potential for collaboration is large and should be approached with hope and caution. Universities are not merely training grounds for future employees. Yet at the same time universities must be places where students explore the inextricable relationships among rhetoric, innovation, and technology.

Appendix
Classroom Applications

One way to help technical communication students learn more about the relationship of rhetoric to technology is providing them practice with what will seem to some to be a very industry-specific task: participating in projects that simulate the development of new products. Such a task may serve as an excellent way to help students practice the rhetoric of the workplace.

It is noteworthy that even in schools of business relatively few programs offer extensive study of new product development processes. Apple and Vanier (1988) report that while the number of programs is growing, only 20 percent of 574 schools surveyed offered a course or courses in this area. It would not be far wrong to suggest that few technical communication programs include any work in new product ventures. Nonetheless, the conceptual and practical demands of such activities have spawned several pragmatic but substantive approaches to teaching technical communication.

Raven (1990) presents a technical communication course based on "new venture management techniques" that allow "students with diverse goals to interact with each other towards a common goal. Students can learn what constitutes acceptable interpersonal and written communication—they can learn effective techniques for small group interaction, they can practice formal speaking by giving presentations of their new product or service, and they can practice good writing by constructing a business plan" (p. 127). In this course, students work in groups to develop a new product or service to market. The potential for the success of this venture "must be established through four primary means: research and development specifications, marketing survey, advertising and sales projections, appropriate sales estimates" (p. 128). All of this work must be summarized in a business plan.

Birchak (1988) describes a technical communication course based on seven stages of new product development: (1) generate ideas, (2) initiate program, (3) prepare feasibility study, (4) develop prototype, (5) test in field, (6) develop pilot series, and (7) release product. The students develop a fictional product during the course, and for each stage they engage in the communication activities necessary to complete that stage. "Entrepreneurs in high tech companies need technical writers familiar with the communication for all 7 stages of new product development. Although some students in the advanced course I have described may not enter the high tech field, they will acquire expertise in coordinating corporate communication. As technical writers, they will possess the potential to become valuable members of any planning team by guiding management in scheduling and gathering information to ensure timely development and release of reports" (p. 41).

A third approach to the role of new product ventures in a technical communication course is the subject of the rest of this appendix. The following sections are devoted to a single teaching case that I wrote in 1985, reprinted from *Collaborative Writing and Group Projects for Technical Writing Classes* (Louth and Scott 1989) with permission of the Association of Teachers of Technical Writing (ATTW). The case is composed of an introduction that explains how the case can be used in a writing course and the three booklets that make up the case itself.

A Case for a Business or Technical Communication Course

Two key assumptions underlie the case: (1) within organizations, there are many points of view that are all competing to be heard and followed; (2) collaboration among representatives from differing divisions within a corporation is necessary to design new products. The following case in effect pits representatives of different divisions within a corporation against each other in order to write a preliminary design document for a new product. In some ways, this case is a cartoon version of life. It is big and broad and at times a bit contrived, but it is also quite complicated and has proved to be a challenge for students. Primarily this case can be used to introduce students to some of the messy realities of intrafirm projects and politics. And in order to simulate differences among internal divisions, the case somewhat simplistically separates the new product development process into three quite distinct areas: production, finance, and marketing. Even so, the case can serve as a reasonably complex exploration of the relationship of rhetoric to product design. Overall, this case is constructed to achieve collaborative goals like those listed by Ede and Lundsford (1990):

Most substantial collaborative writing assignments . . . share the following characteristics:

1. They allow time for group cohesion (but not necessarily consensus) to occur and for leadership to emerge.
2. They call for or invite collaboration; students need to work together in order to complete the assignment effectively . . .
3. They allow for the evolution of group norms and the negotiation of authority and responsibility . . .
4. They allow for and encourage creative conflict and protect minority views . . .
5. They allow for peer and self-evaluation during and after the assignment.
6. They call on students to monitor and evaluate individual and group performance and to reflect on the processes that made for effective—or—ineffective collaboration. (pp. 123–124)

I believe that this case and others (Louth and Scott 1989, Tebeaux 1991) can be used to achieve these goals.

SECRET PROJECT AT SOFTEC

Notes for Instructors

Introduction
This case attempts to foster differing points of view among each member of a three-person documentation team. That is, this case attempts to stimulate substantial conflict among team members—conflict over the goals, facts, and methods discussed in the case. Thus, all three members must negotiate with each other in order to complete the team's assignments. The purpose of this case is to foster an environment that necessitates interpersonal negotiation during the group writing process. In addition, there is no absolute right or wrong decision in this case. Reasonable arguments can be made on either side of the key issues. As such, this case is

an attempt to simulate the kinds of issues and obstacles that collaborative writers in industry must face and overcome in order to succeed.

Each team member works for a different division of Softec, a micro-computer software company. One member works for the marketing division; another works for finance; the third works for production. These three representatives are brought together to collaborate on the design of the final phase of a secret product development project.

Each team member learns the point of view of his or her division by reading the appropriate case booklet. Each booklet contains an *introduction* and the *transcript* of a meeting that the member "attends" by reading the transcript. The introduction explains the history of the company and each member's previous experience with the company. The "meeting" that follows is attended by the vice president of the member's particular division and the VP's administrative assistant. These two executives speak to the reader and to each other throughout the meeting. The transcript contains only what these two executives say—with no narration or commentary.

The topics that the vice presidents and administrative assistants discuss do not follow an organized line of reasoning. Instead, sometimes a speaker goes off on a tangent; topics are discussed, dropped, and picked up later; irrelevant or unnecessary information is interspersed throughout. Only some of the information needed to complete the report is included in each case book: Finance has some information that Marketing does not have and vice-versa; Production offers information that neither of the other two has. In addition, each VP holds a differing point of view of the project and as a result offers some differing opinions and dates. Thus, each member must first learn the point of view and data offered by his or her constituency—the VP and assistant. Then each representative must collaborate while armed with differing opinions and data.

Because the case presents several rhetorical problems that can be resolved in many very different ways, I have not developed a teacher's key for the case. However, if you wish to read an analysis of (a) the major differences among Softec's divisions, (b) the key questions that the collaborators must answer, and (c) the theory that underlies the case, see Doheny-Farina (1988).

Assignments

1. A team-written report to the president of Softec: The team must provide a detailed analysis of the new product, its features, functions, and costs. This report will also provide a rationale for the team's decision.

2. Memos written by each member to his or her vice president, explaining the results of the collaboration: each member must report to his or her boss on what decisions the group made and why. This assignment ensures that each member is held accountable to his or her immediate boss. Some members will report that the team enacted all of the VP's wishes; others will have to report that the team modified or rejected the VP's wishes.

3. Other assignments: Teachers may ask for progress reports, or teachers may adapt the case by adding or withholding information, which will require teams to write to request that information. In fact, teachers may wish to set themselves up as consultants to the groups—a consultant who must be approached and hired in a businesslike manner. This consulting role will be useful for students who may complain that they know very little about the supposed areas of expertise: the insurance industry and/or computer software design. Even though the case has been written so that the students do not need any specialized information, teachers may still be able to provide students with some useful advice about the industries within which they are working. As complicated as this case already is, it still allows an innovative teacher plenty of opportunities to adapt or extend its requirements.

Procedures

I suggest that you work this case into your class over a two-week period. Of course, this time period may vary for many reasons: you may wish to concentrate on nothing but the case and take less class time, or you may wish to integrate the case with other course work and extend it. Regardless, I suggest that you allow students the better part of a week to collaborate. In general, I advise you to do the following:

1. Before telling your students who their teammates are, group the students in threes and give each member of the group a different case booklet. If your class is not divisible by three, then you can choose one of three alternatives:

• Allow for a group of four in which two students will work for one of the three divisions.

• Allow for a group of two; one student will represent finance, one will represent production, and they will both read the marketing division booklet. (I have never done this and I am afraid this option will water-down the major thrust of the case).

• Use this case simultaneously with other group assignments so that you will only have groups of threes working on this case.

2. Assign each student to read and analyze the booklet before the next class session. I suggest that you tell students that they will not be able to keep the booklets and therefore they should take detailed notes. If you want to be strict about this, you may decide only to let them see the booklets in class or in your presence. You would do this to keep collaborators from later sharing the differing booklets with each other. Again, you can create a situation in which you hold information that individuals or groups may need and must request in writing from you.

3. After students know their roles, identify the students' teammates, and let them meet to begin collaborating.

Following that, I suggest a hands-off approach to collaboration, which allows the groups to work out the case problems with little interference from you. Of course, you may wish to serve as a source of advice or further data. Class discussions of the problems involved may be useful while reports are being written, but I advise you to hold off on such discussions until after drafts have been completed. Class discussions (among differing groups) before drafts are written may foster very similar reports with very similar conclusions. If each group's members do not discuss the case with other groups' members, I would anticipate that different groups will produce very different drafts that arrive at opposing conclusions. After such drafts are written, class discussions between groups may be vigorous and enlightening.

Grading

My standards for grading these assignments are no different than they would be for any other case assignments. I am sure that you can adapt the case to fit within any grading scheme that you prefer. One way to increase each student's commitment to his or her division (and increase the potential for conflict) is to award some sort of bonus to the individuals who best satisfy the demands of their immediate division boss. Such an incentive may make the case a bit too cutthroat for many students' and teachers' tastes. In contrast, you may wish to reward the group that best defuses Softec's internal conflicts.

While the latter may make for a more pleasant experience for everyone, I'm not sure that—for better or worse—such practices are necessarily rewarded in the win-or-lose mentality of American big business. Regardless, whether you wish your students to engage in or defuse internal competition, this case will certainly help you raise this issue in your class. And it will help them to see how their skills as writers will play a central role in their ability to handle conflict on the job.

CASE BOOKLET FOR THE MARKETING REPRESENTATIVE

Introduction

You are sitting by yourself in a small but plushly furnished conference room waiting for a meeting to begin. The conference room is located in the large modern building that serves as the national headquarters of Softec, Inc., in Westbrook, New Jersey. In four short years, Softec has established itself as one of the largest independent producers of software for IBM and Apple microcomputers. Of course, the relative size of the company is deceptive. Even the largest independent software companies are struggling to survive in today's computer products markets. Softec is no exception.

Although you have worked for the company for two years, you are a bit nervous. This is your first official function in your new position of assistant developer in the marketing/sales division. For the last two years you have been stationed nearly a thousand miles away in Softec's Chicago sales office. During that time you sold mass-market software (video games, business graphics packages) to software distributors throughout the Midwest. Two weeks ago your good work paid off, and you were promoted back east. Now, after a one week vacation, you're facing a new challenge.

You are not exactly sure what today's meeting is about, but you think that it has to do with some new, super-secret product that the company is developing. One thing you do know is that producing and selling microcomputer software is a highly competitive, even cutthroat business. In the early 1980s, when microcomputers were first hitting the mass market, it seemed as though anyone could make a fortune in the computer business. Not anymore. You have seen first-hand how tough the business is. Each company is continually trying to get an edge on its competitors just to survive. There is little room for error. You have heard that Softec nearly went bankrupt last year when one of its new products, a business graphics software package, failed to sell well when it first hit the market. The software was designed to give business persons the means to produce complex graphic presentations of financial data. For example, by feeding yearly sales figures into the computer, a user could create a full color line, bar, or pie chart that showed yearly sales trends in a very professional manner, rivaling what a professional graphic artist could produce. Yet the product failed to sell.

You and your sales manager both agreed that the main problem with the product was that it had cost too much to develop and as a result it was overpriced. You also had an opinion as to why it was overpriced: it was too fancy. The product was designed to do too many functions, far more functions than the customer wanted. For example, a user could have created pie charts that contained 50 different colors. While a pie chart that contains 50 colors may be pretty, it would be impossible to read. Most people only need 3 to 5 colors when making a pie chart. If the company had developed a simpler product, you thought, we could have sold it for a lower price and it may have succeeded. You wondered how the people back in New Jersey could make such a fundamental mistake in designing a product. You do know, however, that the design of new products has often been the source of many inter-company battles.

In fact, you routinely heard stories about epic struggles between the marketing/sales division and other divisions—struggles over the size, shape, and contents of new products. Recently, you were even asked to provide some information to bolster a marketing/sales argument. Late one Monday afternoon about one month ago, the vice president of marketing/sales, David Edel, called and asked you to tell him what kind of computer games you thought customers wanted. You were a bit stunned by the call and a bit intimidated. You felt that he was putting you on the spot. Even though you had not said this to anyone, you thought that Softec should get out of the computer game business. It was a fad that had run its course; there was little or no money left in that business. Several panicky thoughts ran through your mind at once: "If I say what I really think, I may contradict my boss here in Chicago. Even if I do speak my mind, it may not be what Edel wants to hear. What then?" You had to think quickly, but finally you told him your true thoughts, "Frankly, Mr. Edel, I don't think any computer game is going to be profitable anymore."

Throughout the conversation Edel didn't react strongly one way or another, and you began to have second thoughts about being so honest.

Two weeks later, however, you realized that honesty paid off. Your boss in Chicago returned from a week of meetings at HQ in New Jersey and told you that Softec was terminating all production of computer games. He said that the decision did not come easily. He told you that he sat in on some passionate, sometimes vicious, arguments between representatives of various divisions within Softec. Apparently the production division, the programmers and engineers, wanted to continue producing games because they were on the verge of developing some exciting breakthroughs in visual techniques that would make the games appear to be 3-dimensional on the computer screen. Production was anxious to apply the fruits of their research to a new generation of super-sophisticated computer games. On the other side, the representatives of the financial division and the marketing/sales division both argued that computer games were doomed to fail no matter how many "bells and whistles" could be added to a game. Production lost the argument. The next day you got another call from Mr. Edel. This time he called to offer you your promotion to HQ.

You don't know too much about HQ, but you do know that it is where the big battles are fought—battles waged in the plush conference rooms. And you are sitting in one right now.

Suddenly, the door opens and a man in a meticulously tailored, dark gray business suit walks in. You recognize his voice as you stand, and he introduces himself to you. He is David Edel. Behind him is his assistant, Sonia Miller. Mr. Edel, who appears to be in his early 50s, offers a vigorous handshake and a genuine smile. You think to yourself that he must have been a great salesman in his day. Ms. Miller, who is in her late 30s, is dressed in a dark business suit and carries a leather briefcase. After the introductions, the three of you sit down, and Ms. Miller opens her briefcase and brings out some papers.

Transcript of the Marketing Meeting

Edel: As you well know, we've been getting out of mass market software products. It's just no damn good anymore. We've said, look, let's terminate the computer games and let's put that business graphics package out of its misery. That damn thing was a failure. So instead of the mass market direction that most companies in the industry have followed, we have decided to move into software for limited markets—software for vertical markets. Now, I'm going to let you in on some big information. For the last year we have secretly put a small group of people on an important research project. Their goal was simple: find the best vertical market for us to go into. Six months ago they reported their findings, and we have decided to go with what they recommended to us. We are six months away from coming out with a product that will enable small to mid-sized independent insurance agencies to completely computerize their operations. Those agencies need to computerize, but until now there hasn't been any good software out there for them.

Well, we are going to fill that gap, and we're going to fill it soon. We are just one step away from unveiling *Insurease Software*. This last step is where you come in. Our original research team that recommended such a product has been disbanded. One person has moved up to an executive position, and the other three, well, I don't know. What the hell happened to them, Sonia?

Miller: Uh, let's see, two are still with the project. They are managing programmers, and I think the third is on maternity leave.

Edel: Yes, well, wherever they are, their job is done. Right now we need to assemble a new team to decide on the design of the last part of the entire project. And as I said, that is where you come in. After this meeting you will take the information that we give you, and you will need to meet with two others who will work with you on this. I don't know who they are, but I do know that one is from the financial division and the other is from production.

And I don't mind telling you, I'm pretty damn mad about that. I think that we in marketing should create the general design. We don't need to share the decision-making power with those other divisions. Let them support us—give us help, but let us do the design, damn it! We know what the customer wants! What the customer needs! But that's not the way it works around here. Our president is very, very concerned about this project. It is of the utmost importance to him and to the company. And he says that the design of the product must bring together the best thinking from marketing, finance, and production. So that is where we are. You will work with reps from each division.

Now, what will you be designing? Well, let me let Sonia tell you about *Insurease*. Sonia, will you explain the system?

Miller: Certainly, Dave. First, let me explain a little bit about how these insurance agencies work. The insurance agent is, in effect, the middleman between the client—the person or family who buys insurance—and the company—the big insurance companies, like State Farm, Allstate, or Travelers.

Edel: Let me just interrupt here for a second, Sonia. In general, insurance agencies are run by men who know nothing about computers and who have succeeded and prospered for years without them. But, now, you see, they are becoming afraid that they will have to computerize for several reasons. First, in many businesses computerized operations have become a fact of life in the last five years. These small insurance agents don't want to be left behind. They want to remain competitive. Second, they want to streamline their operations and cut long-term costs because their potential market is not growing anymore. They must squeeze more from the same amount of customers. This will be a key aspect of the thing you are going to do for us, but more of that later. A third reason they want to computerize is because the big insurance companies have computerized and the agencies want to be able to tap into the big companies' systems and use their resources. So the time is ripe to go out there with a software package that meets the needs of these small and mid-sized independent insurance agencies.

Miller: What our system does is enable the agent to computerize information on both clients and companies. We're going to go to a prospective agent and say, "Look, our system will handle nearly all your paperwork *and* it will enable you to link up with the computers of the big insurance companies and send and receive key information."

We are going to sell the package in a cooperative deal with one of several hardware dealers. We have both IBM and Apple versions of the package. We will allow the agent the option of getting the best hardware deal. The hardware price will vary according to the agent's location. But that's nothing that you need to worry about. Let me get to your job.

First of all, *Insurease* is based on a modular structure. Since we haven't produced any modular-based software yet, let me explain what that means. The system is composed of six parts, or modules, each of which provides a different function. For example, the central module is a data base which will hold all of the information about the clients that the agent has—information like name, address, phone, policies held, types of coverage, amounts of coverage, and any other data that the agent typically gathers about a client. The data base module is designed so that the agencies' clerical personnel can enter all of the vital information about each client and then print out lists of that information whenever necessary. Now that module, like all the modules, can communicate and share information with the other modules.

Edel: For example, the accounting module organizes some of that info from the data base. Right?

Miller: Yes, accounting organizes all credits and debits for each client and enables the agent to produce detailed financial statements. It also tallies and prints monthly bills—the premium payments—for all clients. In general, it handles any activity related to credits and debits. To date, all of the modules but one have been designed, and some of those modules are now being coded. You are going to help to design the one that's left. We have tentatively called it the "words" module.

Edel: By the way, your team will decide on a name for the module, once you do the first stage of the design.

Miller: Right, that's what we need right now: design stage one. You and your colleagues from production and finance must get together and produce a report on just what this module should do. That is stage one. We're not looking for a design of the computer code. We are a long way away from that yet. What we need is a very basic picture of what the module should look like. And we want to get you started in the right direction.

Edel: Yes, Sonia and I and others in marketing want to make sure that this module is done the way *we* want it to be done. This module will be the agents' key marketing tool. With it the agent will be able to target customers and really pinpoint his sales efforts. That is a marketing function, and I'll be damned if your team members from production and finance are going to dictate to us just what a marketing module should do!

Miller: Well, Dave, I think we're getting a little ahead of ourselves here. First of all, this module should do three things in general: First, it should give the agent some basic word processing capabilities. We don't need a full-blown word processor. The agent will only need to write one- and two-page letters and memos. All of the policy and premium forms are produced by other modules, and we don't feel that the agent will need to write longer things, like reports. So you need to design a simple word processor. That means you have to decide upon *all* of the functions that your word processor will do. Everything. In addition, you must design the word processing screens. The president will expect to be able to look at your report and get a clear picture of what the word processor will look like and do. OK, that's the first thing that this module must do.

The second function is fairly simple: the module must include a mailing label generator. That is, we want the agent to be able to print out addresses on mailing labels. Actually, it may be nice to include this within the word processor system. That will be up to you. Any printer that will come with this system will have the capability to print addresses on that paper that has the labels with the sticky backs. So, that's function number two.

Edel: Now I want to make it clear just what we expect of you. We expect your team to produce a report that lists and explains all of the functions that we've referred to, or will refer to. You can write a brief memo that introduces all of this info. Then, I suspect that your report will be broken into three or four sections, each one describing in detail each part of this module. Also, one of the sections will explain the projected costs of this module—we'll explain that in a few minutes.

Make the report as concise as you can, but be sure to justify your choices when necessary. Ultimately, this report should be persuasive. You'll have to convince people that your design will be useful. If you design certain aspects of the module for specific reasons, then you must make those reasons clear. If your choices are just arbitrary, and could be done another way, then give us an alternative way so we can judge what might be best.

Miller: All right, now the third function is the biggie.

Edel: This is the one that will set us apart from our competitors. This damn thing is top secret. As far as we can tell, no one out there is doing insurance agency software with this feature. The president is very, very interested in this last function in your module.

Miller: That's right. The third function is a customer profile system. What does that mean? Well, let's say that an agent wants to try to sell a new type of policy, such as a new type of life insurance policy. Let's say that that type of life insurance would be best for married men, ages 25 to 35, who have two or more children, and have a yearly income between $20,000 and $30,000. You know, a policy for the first-time life insurance buyer. Now, these agencies have hundreds, even thousands of clients— some of whom fit that description. We want this module to be able to sort through those clients and pick out the ones that fit that description. We want to enable the agent to say, "OK, I want to get a list of potential customers who fit this description: divorced women, ages 30 to 35, one or more children, live in X county"—or whatever. So that the agent can target his audience for those sales letters that he or she will send with your word processor. Which means that the mailing label/word processor system should be integrated with this profiling system.

Edel: One of the big questions that you will have to answer is this: which criteria will be useful? We want the agent to be able to target pretty specific audiences, but we don't want it to be so damn complicated that the agent will be intimidated. Actually, the agents themselves will probably not be using this system everyday. It will be the agents' clerical personnel. But, it is the agent that we have to sell. Either way, few if any of those people, agents and their secretaries, will have had experience with this type of thing. We want to make it appear to be a simple, easy-to-use system. But we want it to be useful as well. There's a fine line you have to walk here.

Miller: That's right. The big question is how many criteria do you give the agent to fool with and how many combinations do you let him have. That means, do you let him sort a list by two, three, four, five or more criteria? You know, age, sex, marital status, number of children, income, zip code, county, policies held, amounts of coverage, credit history (you know, do they pay their bills on time?). What other criteria are there, Dave?

Edel: Uh, job type, cars—make, model, year. I guess that's about it. As you can see this could get quite complicated. Don't make it so complicated that you intimidate the agent, but make it so that an agent will look at it and say, "Yeah, that will be useful for me."

Miller: I want to emphasize that the president will want to see what this profiling system will look like. So your team should design the screens for this. Give us a picture of how such a system should look. As it stands now we're not sure how many screens it will entail. That will be up to you and your colleagues to decide.

Edel: OK, now there is one more aspect to this whole thing: costs—costs for us and costs for the agent. Our market research has determined that this entire package—all six modules and whatever else goes with it—should be priced at $5,000. We think that that is a price that will sell. Our projections show us getting about 10 percent of the market. There are approximately 10,000 small to mid-sized agencies out there that we hope to try to sell to. So, we hope to sell 1,000 of these systems. Of course, if this product is successful, this will only be the beginning. The whole thing will grow. But, for it to be successful, we need to produce the product for a cost that allows us to sell it for only $5,000. That is crucial. You and your team members must figure out the costs, *in general*. Once you write your report and make your recommendations, then we will get a team of finance people on the project and they will come up with the specific numbers. You will only deal with the general costs. But I think that you will have to make some fundamental decisions based on those costs. That kind of information will come from the other team members. All we know now is that our market research says, don't price the product at more than $5,000. When you meet with the reps from production and finance, you will get more information on this issue.

Well, I think it is clear. You and your team members must produce a report to the president. If you haven't been told already, you will be given a deadline for that report. You should also have been given the names of the other team members. I suggest that you meet with them soon and get to work. We are counting on you.

Miller: Oh wait, there is one more thing. We will want you to write a brief memo to us here in Marketing summarizing the key decisions your team made and explaining why you made them. Write this memo privately—do not write it with your teammates. It will be a confidential memo between you and us. We will want to know how well you represented our marketing agenda in your group. We want to get our way in this project and we will expect a brief memo that tells us how successful you were in getting our way for us.

Edel: Absolutely! Good luck.

CASE BOOKLET FOR THE FINANCE REPRESENTITIVE

Introduction

You are sitting by yourself in a small but plushly furnished conference room waiting for a meeting to begin. The conference room is located in the large, modern building that serves as the national headquarters of Softec, Inc., in Westbrook, New Jersey. In four short years, Softec has established itself as one of the largest independent producers of software for IBM and Apple microcomputers. Of course, the relative size of the company is deceptive. Even the largest independent software companies are struggling to survive in today's computer products markets. Softec is no exception.

Although you have worked for the company for two years, you are a bit nervous. You are wondering why you were picked for this job. For the last two years you were an assistant to the director of plant operations. Three weeks ago you were told that you were going to be promoted to the position of administrative assistant in the finance division. You are a bit concerned because you have very little background in financial matters. But the promotion meant a sizable pay increase and you were happy to take it.

After talking to your old boss, you found out why you were chosen to fill this position. It had to do with your record of representing the plant operations division in some key inter-company battles. As assistant to the director of plant operations, you helped to put together proposals to the president of the company. These proposals argued for things that the plant operations people wanted. For example, you proposed that the computer operations center needed a better air conditioning system. After some debate your proposal was approved, purchased, and installed exactly as you wanted. Your proposal showed that a new system would break down far less often than the old did, and as a result, would increase computer operation time, thus increasing productivity. You estimated that the new system would pay for itself in three years. A year later that cost schedule is right on target.

You succeeded with that proposal even though others in the company opposed any large expenditures. So it made some sense to you when you found out that the vice president of finance, Sarah Bryan, picked you to join her division because she wanted someone who could be an effective advocate for the finance division in any inter-company debates.

From what you have been told during your first week on the job, the finance division has not often won these inter-company battles. Apparently the company, after heated internal debate, has gone ahead and produced software that the finance people argued against producing. Finance was against these projects because (a) the software cost too much to produce, and (b) it was overpriced. Several of the recent software products that finance opposed were failures—they did not turn a profit—and some people in finance said that they felt like telling the president, "I told you so," but didn't.

Those failed products were the results of serious internal battles among the marketing, finance, and production divisions. You are not sure, but you think that today's meeting involves such a debate about a new product. You do know that there has been a secret project in the works for some time and now you may be thrust into the heart of it.

Today's meeting was called by Sarah Bryan. You only met her once, the day you accepted your promotion two weeks ago. She impressed you as being highly intelligent and very businesslike—a true professional. You are sure that she'll expect a lot from you. The door opens and Ms. Bryan and an assistant come in. Ms. Bryan looks to be about 40 years old, with slightly graying dark hair. She is dressed in a dark gray business suit and carries a leather briefcase. She introduces her assistant as Joe Decola, senior administrative assistant. He appears to be in his early 30s and is wearing a dark blue pinstripe suit. You shake hands. Mr. Decola asks if you or Ms. Bryan want some coffee. You both decline. Joe goes out to get a cup and is back in a moment. Meanwhile, Ms. Bryan opens her briefcase and pulls out some papers. When Joe returns, Ms. Bryan begins the meeting.

Transcript of the Finance Meeting

Bryan: You may be aware that Softec has embarked on a new course. But you probably don't know what that course is. That's because the whole project has been a secret and will remain so for several more weeks. In fact, it will remain a secret until you complete the job that we are here to discuss. As you may or may not know, the company is getting out of the mass market software business. We had been producing computer games and business graphics packages for the general public. Well, some people in this company have finally seen the light. There is no mass market software business anymore. The boom in computer games and general purpose software peaked a few years ago, and I don't see it coming back in the foreseeable future. What we are doing now is going into vertical markets. That is, we are going to produce specifically designed software for a limited group. The potential market is smaller but it is better than the mass market because (1) you charge more per software package sold, and (2) once you sell a customer, you get a high percentage of repeat business. If we sell them our introductory software, many are going to come back and buy our advanced versions.

Now, for some specifics. For the last year we have secretly put a small group of people on an important research project. Their goal was simple: find the best vertical market for us to go into. Six months ago they reported their findings and we have decided to go with the recommendation. We are six months away from coming out with a product that will enable small to mid-sized independent insurance agencies to completely computerize their operations. Many agencies have wanted to computerize, but there hasn't been any good software out there for them.

Well, we are going to fill that gap, and we're going to fill it soon. We are just one step away from unveiling *Insurease Software*. This last step is where you come in. Our original research team that recommended such a product has been disbanded. One person has moved up to an executive position, and I'm not sure what happened to the others. Joe, do you know?

Decola: Uh, let's see, two are still with the project. They are managing programmers and I think the third is on maternity leave.

Bryan: Yes, well, their job is done. Right now we need to assemble a new team to design the last part of the entire project. And as I said, that is where you come in. After this meeting you will take the information that we give you and you will meet with two others who will work with you on this. I don't know who they are, but I do know that one is from the marketing division and the other is from production.

And I want to tell you that your job is going to be to represent our point of view on this part of the project. In the past, we have lost in many of these types of battles—and I do think that you will come up against opinions that differ from ours. Actually, I'm a little angry that you are going to have to be part of a team of this project. I mean, I think that when it comes to deciding the crucial financial issues for any new product, the finance division should have ultimate authority to make those decisions. Why have our people haggle things out with reps from marketing and production? Let us handle the financial matters!

Anyway, let's discuss what you will be working on. Joe, will you explain the system?

Decola: Sure, Sarah. First, let me explain a little bit about how these insurance agencies work. The insurance agent is, in effect, the middleman between the client—the person or family who buys insurance—and the company—the big insurance companies, like State Farm, Allstate, or Travelers.

Bryan: Let me just interrupt here for a second, Joe. In general, insurance agencies are run by men who know nothing about computers and who have succeeded and prospered for years without them. But, now, you see, they know that they will have to computerize for several reasons. First, in many businesses, computerized operations have become a fact of life in the last five years. These small insurance agents don't want to be left behind. They want to remain competitive. Second, they want to streamline their operations and cut long-term costs because their potential market is not growing anymore. They must squeeze more from the same number of customers. This will be the key aspect of your project. A third reason to computerize is that the big insurance companies have computerized and the agencies want to be able to tap into the systems of the big companies and use their resources. So the time is ripe to sell a software package that meets the needs of these small and mid-sized independent agencies.

Decola: What our system does is enable the agent to computerize his or her information on both clients and companies. As I'm told, our sales people are going to go into a prospective agency and say, "Look, our system will handle nearly all of your paperwork *and* it will enable you to link up with the computers of the big insurance companies and send and receive key information."

We are going to sell the package in a cooperative deal with one of several hardware dealers. We have both IBM and Apple versions of the package. We will allow the agent the option of getting the best hardware deal possible. The hardware price will vary according to the agent's location. But that's nothing that you need to worry about. Let me get to your job.

First of all, *Insurease* is based on a modular structure. Since we haven't produced any modular-based software yet, let me explain what that means. The system is composed of six parts, or modules, that each provide a different function. For example, the central module is a data base which will hold all of the information about the clients that the agent has—information like name, address, phone, policies held, types of coverage, amounts of coverage, and any other data that the agent typically gathers about a client. The data base module is designed so that the agencies' clerical personnel can enter all of the vital information about each client and then print out lists of that information whenever necessary. Now that module, like all the modules, can communicate and share information with the other modules.

Bryan: For example, the accounting module organizes some of that info from the data base.

Decola: Yes, accounting organizes all credits and debits for each client and enables the agent to produce detailed financial statements. It also tallies and prints monthly bills—the premium payments—for all clients. In general, it handles any activity related to credits and debits.

To date all of the modules but one have been designed and some of those modules are now being coded. You are going to help to design the one that's left. We have tentatively called it the "words" module.

Bryan: By the way, your team will decide on a name for the module, once you complete the first stage of the design.

Decola: Right, that's what we need now: design stage one. You and your colleagues from production and marketing must get together and produce a report on just what this module should do. That is stage one. We're not looking for a design of the computer code. We are a long way away from that yet. What we need is a very basic picture of what the module should look like. And we want to get you started in the right direction.

Bryan: Yes, Joe and I and others in finance want to make sure that this module is done the way *we* want it to be done. I think that we need not develop this entire module in-house. Our production people work too slowly and cost us too much. We can go out and buy certain parts of this module from other software companies and then adapt those parts to what we already have produced here. I feel very strongly about this, and I know that production will not want to go along with this plan.

Decola: Well, Sarah, I think we're getting a little ahead of ourselves here. First of all, let me explain what we need. This module should do three things in general: First, it should give the agent some basic word processing capabilities. We don't need a full-blown word processor. The agent will only need to write one and two page letters and memos. All of the policy and premium forms are produced by other modules, and we don't feel that the agent will need to write longer things, like reports. So you need to design a simple word processor. That means you have to decide upon *all* of the functions that your word processor will do. Everything. In addition, you must design the word processing screens. The president will expect to be able to look at your report and get a clear picture of what the word processor will look like and do. OK, that's the first thing that this module must do.

The second function is fairly simple: the module must include a mailing label generator. That is, we want the agent to be able to print out addresses on mailing labels. Actually, it may be nice to include this within the word processor system. That will be up to you. Any printer that will come with this system will have the capability to print addresses on that paper that has the labels with the sticky backs. So, that's function number two.

Bryan: Before we go into function number three, I want to tell you how you are to represent finance when you plan these first two parts of the module. First of all, Joe and I know that you are under orders to design the word processor and the mailing label generator. Fine. Do so. But, we think that Softec would be foolish to take the time to actually develop these things. Instead, what we should do is this: After your team decides just what we need in a word processor and mailing label device, Softec should shop around and buy from another software company a system that is similar to your design. Then our programmers will adapt that word processor to our system. It will be much cheaper to do it that way. If it is cheaper, then we can keep the price down on the entire package.

Decola: I think we should make it clear just what kind of report we expect of you.

Bryan: Right, we expect your team to produce a report that lists and explains all of the functions that we've referred to. You can write a brief memo that introduces all of this info. Then, I suspect that your report will be broken into three or four sections, each one describing in detail each part of this module. Also, one of the sections will explain the projected costs of this module—we'll explain that in a few minutes.

Make the report as concise as you can, but be sure to justify your choices when necessary. Ultimately, this report should be persuasive. You'll have to convince people that your design will be useful. If you design certain aspects of the module for specific reasons, then you must make those reasons clear. If your choices are just arbitrary and could be done another way, then give us an alternative way so we can judge what might be best.

Decola: Now, how can we estimate the price from the costs? Well, your team will only deal with general numbers. Once your team produces this report—and if that report is accepted by the president—then a team of finance accountants will do a detailed financial analysis and decide on the actual price.

Actually, most of the costs are already fixed. You only have to decide upon about 5 percent of the entire budget.

This is the way the whole *Insurease* project is budgeted: We expect to sell 1,000 systems at $5,000 each for a total revenue of $5 million. We hope to have a profit margin of 35 percent, which means we would like to make $1,850,000 in profit on those 1,000 sales. That means that 65 percent of our total revenues is what it will cost us to produce and sell *Insurease*. Now most of that 65 percent is already accounted for. Ten percent is budgeted for marketing the system. That is, we have budgeted $500,000 to market *Insurease*. Five percent, or $250,000, will be spent on quality control, the process of debugging the software and assuring that we are manufacturing perfect disks and packages. Ten percent, $500,000, is budgeted for the manufacturing and packages process. Those costs, totaling $1,250,000, are already budgeted, and you don't have to worry about them. The largest cost is for programming. To program the entire *Insurease* system, we have budgeted $2 million, or 40 percent of the total revenues. Of that $2 million, 95 percent is already budgeted for the other five modules. That leaves $100,000 for programming the sixth module, the one your team will be designing.

Now, our finance people have estimated some figures that show that we should not pay our own programmers to produce word processing and mailing label generating software. We can save some money if we buy someone else's software and adapt it to our system.

The first thing you must know is this: we estimate the costs of producing a piece of software in terms of man-hours. Our division has recently reported to the president that it costs us $100 per man-hour to program software. That cost includes everything: salaries, cost of computers, supplies, maintenance. Everything. Therefore, if we have $100,000 budgeted for this module, that means we have the equivalent of 1,000 available man-hours. Based on past performance by our production people, we estimate that it will take them 450 man-hours to produce their own word processing and mailing label software. That's a cost of $45,000. If we buy that software and adapt it to our system, we will use 50 man-hours and spend approximately $35,000 to purchase adequate software. That totals $40,000, a savings of $5,000. Which then leaves us with more money to complete the third and last element of the module.

Bryan: The third function is the most important part of this entire module. It is the one that will make our software unique. As far as we know, no one out there is doing insurance agency software with this feature. The president is very, very interested in this last function in your module.

Decola: That's right. The third function is a customer profile system. What does that mean? Well, let's say that an agent wants to try to sell a new type of policy, such as a new type of life insurance policy. Let's say that that type of life insurance would be best for married men, ages 25 to 35, who have two or more children, and have a yearly income between $20,000 and $30,000. You know, a policy for the first-time life insurance buyer. Now, these agencies have hundreds, even thousands of clients— some of whom fit that description. We want this module to be able to sort through those clients and pick out the ones that fit that description.

We want to enable the agent to say, "OK, I want to get a list of potential customers who fit this description: divorced women, ages 30 to 35, one or more children, live in X county"—or whatever. So that the agent can target his audience for those sales letters that he or she will send with your word processor. Which means that the mailing label/word processor system should be integrated with this profiling system.

Now, I think that your team will have to design what the screen will look like with this function. You know, what will the user see and how will the user choose the criteria. Isn't that right, Sarah?

Bryan: Yes, the others in your team should have more information on that. But one of the big questions that you will have to answer is this: how many criteria can we afford to include in this system?

Decola: Right. But let me tell you some more about it before I tell you how to estimate the costs. You have got to decide how many criteria you give the agent to fool with and how many combinations do you let him have. That means, do you let him sort a list by two, three, four, five, or more criteria? You know, age, sex, marital status, number of children, income, zip code, county, policies held, amounts of coverage, credit history (you know, do they pay their bills on time?). What other criteria are there, Sarah?

Bryan: Job type, cars—make, model, year. I guess that's about it. As you can see this could get quite complicated.

Decola: And expensive. Now how to estimate the costs. Really, it's very simple. We estimate that for every criterion, it will take 45 man-hours to produce. So, with some figuring you will see that it is going to be a close call. You must try very, very hard to make a proposal within the budget limits.

Bryan: Let's put it this way. If your report proposes that the module go over budget, then there better be some very good reasons for doing so. Got it? Well, I hope so. Good luck.

Decola: By the way, since your report is going to be sent to the president, you will probably want to draw up a chart that shows the total financial picture. Show him how your module fits within the overall scheme. He is interested in those figures but probably hasn't seen them all together yet.

And there is one more thing. We will want you to write a brief memo to us here in finance summarizing the key decisions your team made and explaining why you made them. Write this memo privately—do not write it with your teammates. It will be a confidential memo between you and us. We will want to know how well you represented our finance agenda in your group. We want to get our way in this project and we will expect a brief memo that tells us how successful you were in getting our way for us.

Bryan: Yes. Do a good job for us.

CASE BOOKLET FOR THE PRODUCTION REPRESENTATIVE

Introduction

You are sitting by yourself in a small but plushly furnished conference room waiting for a meeting to begin. The conference room is located in the large, modern building that serves as the national headquarters of Softec, Inc., in Westbrook, New Jersey. In four short years, Softec has established itself as one of the largest independent producers of software for IBM and Apple microcomputers. Of course, the relative size of the company is deceptive. Even the largest independent software companies are struggling to survive in today's computer products markets. Softec is no exception.

You are a bit nervous. Although you worked for Softec for two years, this is your first official function in your new position of administrative assistant in the production division. For the last two years you have served as an assistant personnel analyst in the personnel division. Your duties in personnel consisted mainly of analyzing the company's personnel needs, writing proposals and reports concerning those needs, and making presentations to the company's executives about the status of Softec's work force. Since you were not the only personnel analyst, you concentrated your work on the needs of the production division. That is, you continually analyzed the performances of Softec's computer programmers and their managers.

Before you began to focus on the programming work force, you knew little about computers. Your background is personnel management. But you think that you learned some basic things about computer programmers in your previous position. You learned that programmers sometimes underestimate the complexity of the programs that they must write. As a result, it sometimes takes them longer to write a program than they said it would take. Usually, the programming manager bases the production schedule for a new piece of software on the projected completion dates given to him by his programmers. When the software is not done when the manager says it will be done, the manager gets in trouble with superiors. Sometimes managers and programmers are fired when deadlines are missed. Even if no one is fired, many people in the company become quite upset when deadlines are missed.

At Softec the production personnel have developed a very bad reputation for not meeting projected deadlines. The managers and executives in the other divisions have complained, loudly at times, that the programmers are always holding the company back. You have been told by the vice presidents of both marketing and finance that the programming managers and their programmers are keeping Softec from getting its products out on the market in time to beat the competition. As a result, say these executives, Softec loses any advantages it could have had over its competitors—and ultimately Softec loses money.

You know about these complaints well. You have recommended some firings in the past. You have also recommended that some production managers and programmers not be fired when they miss deadlines. You have come to understand why those deadlines are often missed. It is not always the fault of the production personnel. Sometimes it is the fault of the marketing or finance divisions. They have interrupted production of software in the past. There have been several incidents when a manager or executive from one of those divisions has said, in effect, "Wait. We need to add this feature to or delete that feature from this product." Most production changes take time, and in the highly competitive computer software business, time is what Softec has least to spare.

Your defense of production personnel in a few of these incidents brought your name to the attention of the vice president of production, Sam Lentz, and a few weeks ago Sam Lentz called you on the phone. He told you that he had asked permission from your boss in personnel to offer you a promotion. He was looking for someone who was not a computer programmer or an engineer but could represent the production division effectively when new products were being planned. Although he didn't come right out and say it, you knew what he meant. He wanted someone who didn't carry that production personnel stigma. He wanted someone who would have some credibility with others in the company when it came to planning company projects. Your record of standing up for production personnel in some past confrontations made you a logical choice.

Still, you are nervous about handling this job. You really don't know many details of programmers' jobs. You just understand that it is difficult to predict accurately how quickly programmers can produce software—especially when that software has never been produced before. When Softec's programmers have tried to write programs that are similar to existing software, then they generally have kept very close to their original timetables. When they have tried to create software that has not been done ever before, then their projections are less reliable.

These projections are made in what you like to call "person-hours," but are known by most programming personnel as "man-hours." A man-hour at Softec is one hour of work done by one programmer. Your name for the term stems from the fact that slightly more than half of the programmers employed at Softec are women.

The programming managers estimate their projects by estimating how many man-hours it will take to complete a project. For example, if a project is supposed to be completed in 40 man-hours and a manager has four programmers working on the project, then that manager will estimate the project to be completed in 10 hours of work. You have discovered that the more man-hours estimated, the less reliable the estimation. Specifically, you have never seen a projection of more than 200 man-hours work out as projected. If a job is estimated in terms of hundreds of man-hours, then you are automatically suspicious of the projection—no matter who makes it. If that same job were broken into smaller ones, with smaller man-hour projections, say 10 jobs each lasting 20 man-hours, then you are more confident in the predicted work schedule.

With all this in mind, you are anxiously waiting for this meeting to begin. Suddenly the door opens and in walks Sam Lentz with his assistant, Mary Hayes. Sam, a solidly built man who appears to be 50 years old, is not wearing his suit jacket, and he has rolled up the sleeves of his white dress shirt. You notice that his dark blue tie has imprinted on it tiny insignias of some sort of professional computer society. Mary, who is in her early 30s, is dressed in a conservative business suit and carries a briefcase. You have met both of them before and you like them. You shake hands. Mary opens the briefcase and pulls out some papers. After exchanging a few pleasantries, the meeting begins in earnest.

Transcript of the Production Meeting

Lentz: You may or may not know that Softec is close to a major change in direction. We are getting out of the mass market software business. That means we will not be producing any more computer games and general business software. The people in marketing and finance have told us that there is no market for those things anymore. They tell us that computer games were a fad that has long since reached its peak. Unfortunately, some of my programmers have recently made some astonishing advances in computer graphics that would lead to a new generation of super-sophisticated, three-dimensional computer games. It is a shame that we can't go ahead with that technology. We are not happy about the situation, but we do what we are told.

The new situation is this: Softec is going to produce software for vertical markets. That means we are going to produce specifically designed software for a limited group. The potential market is smaller, but I am told that it has a tremendous potential for repeat business. If we can sell an introductory software package, there is a good chance that the customer will be interested in advanced versions of that software.

Let me give you some specifics on this whole thing: During the last year, Softec has secretly put a small group of people on an important research project. Their goal was simple: find the best vertical market for us to go into. Six months ago they reported their findings and we have decided to go with their recommendation. We are six months away from coming out with a product that will enable small to mid-sized independent insurance agencies to completely computerize their operations. Many agencies have wanted to computerize, but there hasn't been any good software out there for them.

Well, we are going to produce it, and we are just one step away from unveiling *Insurease Software*. Now this last step is where you come in. Our original research team that recommended such a product has been completely disbanded. Is that right, Mary?

Hayes: Yes, Sam. As of last week they've all moved into other projects.

Lentz: Yeah. So their job is done. Right now we need to assemble a new team to design the last part of the entire project. And, as I said, that is where you come in. After this meeting you will take the information that we give you and you will meet with two others who will work with you on this. I don't know who they are, but I do know that one is from the marketing division and the other is from finance.

As you know, I hired you to represent us in such situations. Production has taken the heat many times in the past, and I want to make sure that others in this company take what we want to do seriously. I probably don't have to tell you that you are going to go into the meeting and receive some opposition from your team members. I have a feeling that the finance person, whoever it is, will probably oppose us on some key issues. Actually, I'm a little angry that you are going to have to be part of a team on this project. I mean, I think that when it comes to planning a new product, the production people should have the authority to design it as we see fit. Sure, we need to get input from marketing and finance, but we're the ones who know how to produce software. We should be the ones who design it, too.

Anyway, let's discuss what you will be working on. Mary, will you explain the system?

Hayes: Sure, Sam. First, let me explain a little bit about how these insurance agencies work. The insurance agent is, in effect, the middleman between the client—the person or family who buys insurance—and the big insurance companies, like State Farm, Allstate, or Travelers.

Lentz: Let me just interrupt here for a second, Mary. In general, insurance agencies are run by people who know nothing about computers and who have succeeded and prospered for years without them. But, now, you see, they know that they will have to computerize for several reasons. One of the big reasons concerns their need to streamline their operations and cut long-term costs. I have been told by the original research team that the potential markets for these insurance agencies are not growing anymore. They must squeeze more from the same number of customers. This will be a key aspect of your project. So it seems that the time is ripe to sell a software package that meets the needs of these small and mid-sized independent insurance agencies.

Hayes: What our system does is enable the agent to computerize information on both clients and companies. As I'm told, our sales people are going to go into a prospective agency and say, "Look, our system will handle nearly all of your paperwork *and* it will enable you to link up with the computers of the big insurance companies and send and receive key information."

We are going to sell the package in a cooperative deal with one of several hardware dealers. We have both IBM and Apple versions of the package. We will allow the agent the option of getting the best hardware deal possible. The hardware price will vary according to the agent's location. But that's nothing that you need to worry about. Let me get to your job.

First of all, *Insurease* is based on a modular structure. Since we haven't produced any modular-based software yet, let me explain what that means. The system is composed of six parts, or modules, that each provide a different function. For example, the central module is a data base which will hold all of the information about the clients that the agent has—information like name, address, phone, policies held, types of coverage, amounts of coverage, and any other data that the agent typically gathers about a client. The data base module is designed so that the agencies' clerical personnel can enter all of the vital information about each client, and then print out lists of that information whenever necessary. Now that module, like all the modules, can communicate and share information with the other modules.

Lentz: For example, the Accounting module organizes some of that information from the data base, right?

Hayes: Yes, Accounting organizes all credits and debits for each client and enables the agent to produce detailed financial statements. It also tallies and prints monthly bills—the premium payments—for all clients. In general, it handles any activity related to credits and debits.

To date all of the modules but one have been designed and some of those modules are now being coded. You are going to help design the one that's left. We have tentatively called it the "words" module.

Lentz: By the way, your team will choose a name for the module, once you complete the first stage of the design.

Hayes: Right, that's what we need now: design stage one. You and your colleagues from finance and marketing must get together and produce a report on just what this module should do. That is stage one. We're not looking for a design of the computer code. We are a long way away from that yet. What we need is a very basic picture of what the module should look like. And we want to get you started in the right direction.

Lentz: Yes, Mary and I and others in production want to make sure that this module is done the way *we* want it to be done. I think that the finance people are going to argue that we shouldn't develop this entire module in-house. They think that Softec will save money if we buy certain parts of this module, and not develop it ourselves. Well they are wrong! We can produce better software than anyone else out there, because we can tailor it to our specific needs. And, despite what the finance people will tell you, we can also do it within budget. I feel very strongly about this.

Hayes: Well, Sam, I think we're getting a little ahead of ourselves here. Let me explain what we need. This module should do three things in general: First, it should give the agent some solid word processing capabilities. We have already been told by marketing that this word processing program should be designed for producing only short documents, like memos and letters. We should have no problem producing a very useful system—one that will enable the agent to write letters or memos up to four pages long. It will have all of the basics that a word processor needs, you know—insert, delete, move, center—and the rest of the essential commands.

By the way, the results of your team's design will be written in a report to the president. That report must describe all of the capabilities of this system. That means you have to decide upon *all* of the functions that your word processor will do. Everything. In addition, you must design the word processing screens. The president will expect to be able to look at your report and get a clear picture of what the word processor will look like and do.

Lentz: Yes, I should make it clear just what we expect of you. We expect your team to produce a report that lists and explains all of the functions that we've referred to, or will refer to. You can write a brief memo that introduces all of this info. Then, I suspect that your report will be broken into three or four sections, each one describing in detail each part of this module. Also, one of the sections will explain the projected costs of this module—we'll explain that in a few minutes.

Make the report as concise as you can, but be sure to justify your choices when necessary. Ultimately, this report should be persuasive. You'll have to convince people that your design will be useful. If you design certain aspects of the module for specific reasons, then you must make those reasons clear. If your choices are just arbitrary, and could be done another way, then give us an alternative way so we can judge what might be best.

So, as we said, make sure your team designs the basic screens for this system. And let me also add that we can include some very useful features to the system—features such as a spelling checker. You know, we can program in an entire spelling dictionary and include a search and replace function to check spelling. Uh, let's see, what other special functions can we add to this system?

Hayes: We can have several formats of memos and letters already in the system so that the agent writes a letter and memo and the system formats it automatically. That way the user won't have to do all of the indenting and the spacing. Of course, we can also enable the user to design his or her own formats, by providing all of the basic functions including the ones I mentioned a moment ago. Actually, we can incorporate any word processing function in the system.

OK, so that is the first function that the module must provide. The second function is fairly simple: The module must include a mailing label generator. That is, we want the agent to be able to print out addresses on mailing labels. Actually, it may be nice to include this within the word processor system. We can do that with no problem. So, that's function number two.

Lentz: Now before we go on to the final and most important function of this module, I want to explain to you why we must produce this word processing and mailing label system ourselves. You realize, of course, that if we don't do it ourselves, we will have to adapt some other company's word processor to our whole *Insurease* package. But if we create our own word processor, it will fit into our system more smoothly and efficiently. First of all, since our own system will be system-designed to our software, it will use up less memory and it will allow us to store more text and addresses in the system. Second, it will be simpler to use for the agent. Our own word processor will have only one- and two-key functions. Also, we'll be able to create some preprogrammed function keys that will do things like call up the preformatted memo or letter screens. If we adapt another company's word processing software to our *Insurease* system, we will probably not be able to use preprogrammed function keys and I'm sure we'll end up with some three-key functions. As far as I'm concerned,

I know that we can produce a product that is far superior to anything we can buy.

Hayes: Another important issue in this whole debate is the time it will take us to produce our own system. We estimate that we can do the basic word processor in approximately 350 man-hours. For special additions, like the spell checker, add 50 man-hours. As a rule of thumb, for any major additions beyond the basics, add 50 man-hours. When you talk with the finance rep, you will be able to figure out just what that will cost and how it will fit within the project's budget.

Lentz: Yeah, the budget is important. I'm sure that finance will hit you with that. I know we can produce our own system within finance's budget.

Hayes: OK, the third and final function is a biggie.

Lentz: Right, the third function is the most important part of this entire module. It is the one that will make our software unique. As far as we know, no one out there is doing insurance agency software with this feature. The president is very, very interested in this last function in your module.

Hayes: The third function is a customer profile system. What does that mean? Well, let's say that an agent wants to try to sell a new type of policy, such as a new type of life insurance policy. Let's say that that type of life insurance would be best for married men, ages 25 to 35, who have two or more children, and have a yearly income between $20,000 and $30,000. You know, a policy for the first-time life insurance buyer. Now, these agencies have hundreds, even thousands of clients—some of whom fit that description. We want this module to be able to sort through those clients and pick out the ones that fit that description. We want to enable the agent to say, "OK, I want to get a list of potential customers who fit this description: divorced women, ages 30 to 35, one or more children, live in X county"—or whatever. So that the agent can target the audience for those sales letters that will be sent with your word processor. Which means that the mailing label/word processor system should be integrated with this profiling system.

Now, I think that your team will have to design what the screen will look like with this function. You know, what will the user see and how will the user choose the criteria. Isn't that right, Sam?

Lentz: Yes, the big question that you will have to answer is this: how many criteria should be included in this system?

Hayes: You have got to decide how many criteria you give the agent to fool with and how many combinations do you let him have. That means do you let him sort a list by two, three, four, five, or more criteria? We can enable the agent to target some pretty specific audiences, but we must be careful that it doesn't get so complicated that the agent will be too intimidated to use it. Your design should make it easy to use.

Lentz: You can incorporate a number of criteria including age, sex, marital status, number of children, income, zip code, county, policies held, amounts of coverage, credit history (you know, do they pay their bills on time?), job type, and cars, including make, model, and year. As you can see, this could get quite complicated.

Hayes: Again, you will have to consider the development time for this profiling system. It is really very simple to calculate. We estimate that for every criterion, it will take 40 man-hours to produce. Check with the finance person to see how that fits within the project's budget.

Lentz: My biggest fear with this project is that finance and marketing will not take our opinions seriously in this project. Look, no matter what has happened in the past, we will live up to our claims on this project. You yourself know that our reputation isn't totally deserved. We can do this entire module ourselves. We need not go out and buy someone else's software.

Hayes: Oh yes, there is one more thing. We will want you to write a brief memo to us here in production summarizing the key decisions your team made and explaining why you made them. Write this memo privately—do not write it with your teammates. It will be a confidential memo between you and us. We will want to know how well you represented our production agenda in your group. We want to get our way in this project, and we will expect a brief memo that tells us how successful you were in getting our way for us.

Lentz: The president is watching this module very carefully. I have confidence that you will represent us well. Don't disappoint us.

References

"A business that defies recession." (1982). *Business Week*. October 25, 30–31.

Allen, T. J. (1977). *Managing the flow of technology: Technology transfer and the dissemination of technological information within the R&D organization.* Cambridge, Mass.: MIT Press.

Anson, C. M., and L. L. Forsberg (1990). "Moving beyond the academic community: Transitional stages in professional writing." *Written Communication* 7(2):200–231.

Apple, L. E., and D. J. Vanier (1988). "Product development: An assessment of educational resources." *Journal of Product Innovation Management* 5:70–75.

Baker, L. D. (1988). "The relationship of product design to document design." In *Effective documentation: What we have learned from research* (317–327). Edited by S. Doheny-Farina. Cambridge, Mass.: MIT Press.

Barabas, C. (1990). *Technical writing in a corporate culture.* Norwood, N.J.: Ablex Publishing.

Bazerman, C. (1988). *Shaping written knowledge: The genre and activity of the experimental article in science.* Madison: University of Wisconsin Press.

Bazerman, C., and J. Paradis, eds. (1991). *Textual dynamics of the professions: Historical and contemporary studies of writing in professional communities.* Madison: University of Wisconsin Press.

Beard, J. D., J. Rymer, and D. L. Williams (1989). "An assessment system for collaborative-writing groups: Theory and empirical evaluation." *Journal of Business and Technical Communication* 3(2):29–51.

Bell, G., and J. E. McNamara (1991). *High-tech ventures.* Reading, Mass.: Addison-Wesley.

Berkenkotter C., T. M. Huckin, and J. Ackerman (1988). "Conventions, conversations, and the writer: Case study of a student in a rhetoric Ph.D. program." *Research in the Teaching of English* 22(1):9–44.

Birchak, B. C. (1988). "Coordinating communication for new product development." *Technical Writing Teacher* 15, (Winter):37–48.

Blumenstyk, G. (1990). "Pitfalls of research parks lead universities and states to reassess their expectations." *Chronicle of Higher Education*, July 3, A22–A24.

Bosch, T., and L. Levine (1985). "Technical communicators and the technical design process." *Proceedings of the 32nd International Technical Communication Conference*, MPD-28–MPD-31.

Bosley, D. (1988). "Writing internships: Building bridges between academia and industry." *Journal of Business and Technical Communication* 2(1):103–113.

Bradbury, F. (1978). "Technology transfer." In *Transfer processes in technical change* (107–118). Edited by F. Bradbury, P. Jervis, R. Johnston, and A. Pearson. Alphen aan den Rijn, Netherlands: Sijthoff & Noordhoff.

Bresko, L. L. (1991). "The need for technical communicators on the software development team." *Technical Communication* 36(1): 214–220.

Breuder, R. L. (1988). "Technology transfer and training." *AACJC Journal* (October-November):30–33.

Brooks, J. K., and B. A. Stevens (1987). *How to write a successful business plan.* New York: Amacom.

Bruce, B., and J. K. Peyton (1990). "A new writing environment and an old culture: A situated evaluation of computer networking to teach writing." *Interactive Learning Environments Journal* 1(3):171–191.

Buehler, M. F. (1986). "Rules that shape the technical message: Fidelity, completeness, conciseness." *Technical Communication* 33(3):130–132.

Carroll, J. M., R. L. Mack, C. H. Lewis, N. L. Grischkowsky, and S. R. Robertson (1988). "Exploring a wordprocessor." In *Effective documentation: What we have learned from research* (103–126). Edited by S. Doheny-Farina. Cambridge, Mass.: MIT Press.

Carroll, J. M., P. L. Smith-Kerker, J. R. Ford, and S. A. Mazur-Rimetz (1988). "The minimal manual." In *Effective documentation: What we have learned from research* (73–102). Edited by S. Doheny-Farina. Cambridge, Mass.: MIT Press.

Carter, J. F. (1985). "Lessons in text design from an instructional perspective." In *Designing usable texts* (145–156). Edited by T. M. Duffy and R. Waller. Orlando: Academic Press.

Carter, M. (1990). "The idea of expertise: An exploration of cognitive and social dimensions of writing." *College Composition and Communication* 4(3):265–286.

Charney, D., L. Reder, and G. Wells (1988). "Studies of elaboration in instructional texts." In *Effective documentation: What we have learned from research* (47–72). Edited by S. Doheny-Farina. Cambridge, Mass.: MIT Press.

Chay, R. F. (1989). "Discovering unrecognized needs with consumer research." *Research Technology Management* 32 (March-April):36–39.

Chisholm, R. M. (1988). "Improving the management of technical writers: Creating a context for usable documentation." In *Effective documentation: What we have learned from research* (299–316). Edited by S. Doheny-Farina. Cambridge, Mass.: MIT Press.

Cobb, B. K. (1990). "The Learning-support system: A unified approach to developing customer documentation and training." *Technical Communication* 37(1):35–40.

Couture, B. (1985). "Why an English department should join with industry in planning a professional writing program." *Technical Writing Teacher* 11(3):167–174.

Cross, G. A. (1988). "Editing in context: An ethnographic exploration of editor-writer revision at a midwestern insurance company." Ph.D. dissertation. Ohio State University.

Debs, M. B. (1986). "Collaborative writing: A study of technical writing in the computer industry." Ph.D. dissertation. Rensselaer Polytechnic Institute.

Debs, M. B. (1988). "A history of advice: What experts have to tell us." In *Effective documentation: What we have learned from research* (11–24). Edited by S. Doheny-Farina. Cambridge, Mass.: MIT Press.

Dobrin, D. (1989). *Writing and technique.* Urbana, Ill.: National Council of Teachers of English.

Doheny-Farina, S. (1986). "Writing in an emerging organization: An ethnographic study." *Written Communication* 3(2):158–185.

Doheny-Farina, S. (1988). "A case study approach using conflict among collaborators." *Technical Writing Teacher* 15:73–77.

Doheny-Farina, S. (1989a). "A secret project at Softec." In *Collaborative writing and group projects for technical writing classes* (235–256). Edited by R. Louth and A. M. Scott. Association of Teachers of Technical Writing Series.

Doheny-Farina, S. (1989b). "A case study of an adult writing in academic and non-academic settings." In *Worlds of writing: Teaching and learning in discourse communities of work* (17–42). Edited by C. Matalene. New York: Random House.

Doheny-Farina, S. (1991). "Creating a text/creating a company: The role of a text in the rise and decline of a new organization." In *Textual dynamics of the professions: Historical and contemporary studies of writing in professional communities* (306–355). Edited by C. Bazerman and J. Paradis. Madison: University of Wisconsin Press.

Doheny-Farina, S., and L. Odell (1985). "Ethnographic research on writing: Assumptions and methods." In *Writing in nonacademic settings* (503–535). Edited by L. Odell and D. Goswami. New York: Guilford.

Duffy, T. M., T. Post, and G. Smith (1987). "Technical manual production: An examination of five systems." *Written Communication* 4(4):370–393.

Dunkle, S. B., and L. H. Pesante (1988). "Role of the writer on the software team." In *Proceedings of the 35th International Technical Communication Conference*, WE-51–WE-53.

Ede L., and A. Lunsford (1990). *Singular texts/plural authors: Perspectives on collaborative writing.* Carbondale: Southern Illinois University Press.

Fischer, W. A. (1980). "Scientific and technical information and the performance of R&D groups." In *Management of research and innovation* (67–89). Edited by B. V. Dean and J. L. Goldhar. New York: North-Holland Publishing Co.

Flower, L., J. R. Hayes, and H. Swarts (1983). "Revising functional documents: The scenario principle." In *New essays in technical and scientific communication: Research, theory, practice* (41–58). Edited by P. Anderson, R. J. Brockmann, and C. Miller. Farmingdale, N.Y.: Baywood Publishers.

Fowler, S. L., and D. Roeger (1986). "Programmer and writer collaboration: Making user manuals that work." *IEEE Transactions on Professional Communication* PC 29(4):21–25.

Freed, R. C., and G. J. Broadhead (1987). "Discourse communities, sacred texts, and institutional norms." *College Composition and Communication* 38(2):154–165.

Frieberger, P., and M. Swaine (1984). *Fire in the valley.* Berkeley, Calif.: Osborne McGraw-Hill.

Gates, R. L. (1989). "An academic and industrial collaboration on course design." *Journal of Business and Technical Communication* 3(2):78–87.

Ginn, M. E., and A. H. Rubenstein (1986). "The R&D/production interface: A case study of new product commercialization." *Journal of Product Innovation Management* 3:158–170.

Gould, E., and S. Doheny-Farina (1988). "Studying usability in the field: Qualitative research techniques for technical communicators." In *Effective documentation: What we have learned from research* (329–343). Edited by S. Doheny-Farina. Cambridge, Mass.: MIT Press.

Grassmuck, K. (1990). "Wariness dampens 1980's craze for building university-sponsored technology parks." *Chronicle of Higher Education*, June 27, A29–A30.

Grice, R. A. (1988). "Information development is part of product development—not an afterthought." In *Text, context, hypertext: Writing with and for the computer* (133–148). Edited by E. Barrett. Cambridge, Mass.: MIT Press.

Gupta, A. K. (1990). "Improving R&D/marketing relations: R&D's perspective." *R&D Management* 20(4):277–290.

Haas, C., and L. Flower (1988). "Rhetorical reading strategies and the construction of meaning." *College Composition and Communication* 39(2):167–183.

Harrison, T. M. (1987). "Frameworks for the study of writing in organizational contexts." *Written Communication* 4(1):3–23.

Harrison, T. M., and M. B. Debs (1985). "Organizations and technical writing internships: Addressing social context in the internship program." *Proceedings of the IEEE Professional Communication Society Conference*, 275–279.

Harrison, T. M., and M. B. Debs (1988). "Conceptualizing the organizational role of technical communicators: A systems approach." *Journal of Business and Technical Communication* 2(2):5–21.

Haselkorn, M. P. (1988). "The future of 'writing' for the computer industry." In *Text, context, and hypertext* (3–13). Edited by E. Barrett. Cambridge, Mass.: MIT Press.

Herndl, C. G., B. A. Fennel, and C. R. Miller (1991). "Understanding failures in organizational discourse: The accident at Three Mile Island and the shuttle Challenger disaster." In *Textual dynamics of the professions: Historical and contemporary studies of writing in professional communities* (279–305). Edited by C. Bazerman and J. Paradis. Madison: University of Wisconsin Press.

Hise, R. T., L. O'Neal, A. Parasuraman, and J. U. McNeal (1990). "Marketing/R&D interaction in new product development: Implications for new product success rates." *Journal of Product Innovation Management* 7:142–155.

Hisrich, R. D., and R. W. Smilor (1988). "The university and business incubation: Technology transfer through entrepreneurial development." *Technology Transfer* (Fall):14–19.

Hosier, W. J. (1989). "Achieving documentation quality through controlled process." *Proceedings of Technicom '89. Society for Technical Communication*, 9–14.

Houghton-Alico, D. (1991). "Side-by-side: A model for simultaneous documentation and system development." In *Perspectives on software documentation* (165–180). Edited by T. Barker. Farmingdale, N.Y.: Baywood Publishers.

"The incredible explosion of startups" (1982). *Business Week*. August 2, 53–54.

Johnson, B. (1990). "User-centeredness, situatedness, and designing the media of computer documentation." *SIGDOC '90 Proceedings*, ACM, 55–61.

Karis, B. (1989). "Implications of Foucault's 'discursive formations' on drafting a 'RAP': An environmental case study in progress." Paper presentation, Penn State Conference on Rhetoric and Composition.

Karis, B. (1991). "To be a bridge or to be a collaborator: A problem for professional writers in the 90's." Paper presentation, Conference on College Composition and Communication Conference.

Karis, B., and S. Doheny-Farina (in press). "Collaborating with readers: Empower them and take the consequences." *Technical Communication.*

Kaufer, D. S., and C. Geisler (1989). "Novelty in academic writing." *Written Communication* 6(3):286–311.

Kelly, R., and C. Barnum (1987). "A foot in both camps: Academe and workplace." *Technical Writing Teacher* 14(1):77–85.

Kernaghan, J. A., and R. A. Cooke (1990). "Teamwork in planning innovative projects: Improving group performance by rational and interpersonal interventions in group process." *IEEE Transactions on Engineering Management* 37(2):109–116.

Kidder, T. (1981). *Soul of a new machine.* Boston: Little, Brown.

Killingsworth, M. J., M. K. Gilbertson, and J. Chew (1989). "Amplification in technical manuals: Theory and practice." *Journal of Technical Writing and Communication* 19(1):13–29.

Killingsworth, M. J., and B. G. Jones (1989). "Division of labor or integrated teams: A crux in the management of technical Communication." *Technical Communication* 36(3):210–221.

Kleimann, S. (1989). "Negotiating to a new text: The review process in a bureaucratic organization." Paper presentation, Conference on College Composition and Communication.

Knight, R. M. (1987). "Corporate innovation and entrepreneurship: A Canadian study." *Journal of Product Innovation Management,* 284–297.

Kozmetsky, G. (1990). "The coming economy." In *Technology transfer: A communication perspective* (21–40). Edited by F. Williams and D. V. Gibson. Newbury Park, Calif.: Sage Publications.

Larson, C. E., and F. M. J. LaFasto (1989). *Teamwork.* Newbury Park, Calif.: Sage Publications.

Lay, M., and W. Karis, eds. (1991). *Collaborative writing in industry: Investigations in theory and practice.* Farmingdale, NY: Baywood Publishing Co.

Leonard-Barton, D. (1990). "The intraorganizational environment: Point-to-point versus diffusion." In *Technology transfer: A communication perspective* (43–62). Edited by F. Williams and D. V. Gibson. Newbury Park, Calif.: Sage Publications.

Levering, P., M. Katz, and M. Moskowitz (1984). *The computer entrepreneurs.* New York: New American Library.

Levine, L. B. (1988). "Corporate culture, technical documentation, and organization diagnosis." In *Text, context, hypertext: Writing with and for the computer* (149–174). Edited by E. Barrett. Cambridge, Mass.: MIT Press.

Lipson, C. (1986). "Technical communications: The cultural context." *Technical Writing Teacher* 13(3):318–323.

Lipson, C. (1987). "Teaching students to 'read' culture in the workplace: Reply to Gerald Parsons." *Technical Writing Teacher* 14(2):267–270.

Little, S. B. (1985). "Industry in the technical writing classroom: A preliminary report of a study." *Proceedings of the IEEE Professional Communication Society Conference*, 293–297.

Louth, R., and A. M. Scott (1989). *Collaborative writing and group projects for technical writing classes*. Association of Teachers of Technical Writing.

Lutz, J. A. (1986). "The influence of organizations on writers' texts and training." *Technical Writing Teacher* 13(2):187–190.

Lutz, J. A. (1989). "Writers in organizations and how they learn the image: Theory, research, and implications." In *Worlds of writing: Teaching and learning in discourse communities of work* (113–135). Edited by C. Matalene. New York: Random House.

McCarthy, L. P. (1991). "A psychiatrist using DSM-III: The influence of a charter document in psychiatry." In *Textual dynamics of the professions: Historical and contemporary studies of writing in professional communities* (358–378). Edited by C. Bazerman and J. Paradis. Madison: University of Wisconsin Press.

McDaniel, E., R. E. Young, J. Vesterager, K. Bergsson, S. Jensen, and E. Tveldt (1991). "Document-driven management of knowledge and technology transfer: Denmark's CIM/GEMS project in computer-integrated manufacturing. *IEEE Transactions on Professional Communication* 34(2):83–92.

Maguire, M. (1988). "Leap or sleep: Transferring technology." *Rensselaer* (September):14–16.

Mikulecky, L. (1990). "Basic skills impediments to communication between management and hourly employees." *Management Communication Quarterly* 3(4):452–473.

Miller, C. R. (1979). "A humanistic rationale for technical writing." *College English* 40:610–617.

Miller, C. R. (1989a). "The rhetoric of technology transfer: The buzz-word as trope and topos." *Paper* presentation, the Society for the social study of science conference, Amsterdam, Netherlands.

Miller, C. R. (1989b). "What's practical about technical writing?" In *Technical writing: Theory and practice* (14–24). Edited by B. E. Fearing and W. K. Sparrow. N.Y.: Modern Language Association.

Miller, C. R. (1990). "The rhetoric of decision science, or Herbert A. Simon says." In *The rhetorical turn: Invention and persuasion in the conduct of inquiry* (162–184). Edited by H. W. Simons, Chicago: University of Chicago Press.

Mirel, B. (1988). "The politics of usability: The organizational functions of an in-house manual." In *Effective documentation: What we have learned from research* (277–297). Edited by S. Doheny-Farina. Cambridge, Mass.: MIT Press.

Mirel, B. (1990). "Expanding the activities of in-house manual writers." *Management Communication Quarterly* 3(4):496–526.

Moenaert, R. K., and W. E. Souder (1990). "An information transfer model for integrating marketing and R&D personnel in new product development projects." *Journal of Product Innovation Management* 7:91–107.

Myers, G. (1990). *Writing biology: Texts in the social construction of scientific knowledge*. Madison: University of Wisconsin Press.

Norman, D. (1988). *The design of everyday things*. Garden City, N.Y.: Doubleday.

Odell, L. (1985). "Beyond the text: Relations between writing and social context." In *Writing in nonacademic settings* (249–280). Edited by L. Odell and D. Goswami. New York: Guilford Press.

Odell, L., D. Goswami, A. Herrington, and D. Quick (1983). "Studying writing in non-academic settings." In *New essays in technical and scientific communication: Research, theory, practice* (17–40). Edited by P. Anderson, R. J. Brockmann, and C. R. Miller. Farmingdale, N.Y.: Baywood Publishing Co.

Paradis, J. (1991). "Text and action: The operator's manual in context and in court." In *Textual dynamics of the professions: Historical and contemporary studies of writing in professional communities* (256–278). Edited by C. Bazerman and J. Paradis. Madison: University of Wisconsin Press.

Paradis, J., D. Dobrin, and R. Miller (1985). "Writing at Exxon ITD: Notes on the writing environment of an R&D organization." In *Writing in nonacademic settings* (281–307). Edited by L. Odell and D. Goswami. New York: Guilford Press.

Parsons, G. (1987). "The elusiveness of workplace culture: Response to 'Technical communication: The cultural context.'" *Technical Writing Teacher* 14(2):265–266.

Peters, T. (1987). *Thriving on chaos: Handbook for a management revolution.* New York: Harper & Row.

Peterson, J. D. (1989). "The technical communicator's role: The impact of professionalism and boundary spanning." Master's thesis. Colorado State University.

Peterson, J. D., D. Zimmerman and M. Muraski (in press). "Boundary spanning: A role of technical communicators?" *Technical Communication.*

Pinto, M. B., and J. K. Pinto (1990). "Project team communication and cross-functional cooperation in new program development." *Journal of Product Innovation Management* 7:200–212.

Porter, J. E. (1986). "Intertextuality and the discourse community." *Rhetoric Review.* 5(1):34–47.

Porter, J. E. (1990). "Ideology and collaboration in the classroom and in the corporation." *Bulletin* (June):18–22.

Raven, M. B. (1990). "New venture techniques in a communication class." *Technical Writing Teacher* 17(2):124–130.

Redish, J. (1988). "Reading to learn to do." *Technical Writing Teacher* 15(3):223–233.

Redish, J. (1989). "Composing real world documents: A conversation with Dr. Janice Redish." *Issues in Writing* 1(2):82–98.

Reich, R. B. (1987). "Entrepreneurship reconsidered: The team as hero." *Harvard Business Review* (May-June):77–83.

Reich, R. B. (1989). "The quiet path to technological preeminence." *Scientific American* (October):41–47.

Roberts, D. D. (1989). "Readers' comprehension responses in information discourse: Toward connecting reading and writing in technical communication." *Journal of Technical Writing and Communication* 19(2):135–148.

Roberts, E. B. (1991). "High stakes for high-tech entrepreneurs: Understanding venture capital decision making." *Sloan Management Review* 32(2):9–20.

Rogers, E. M. (1982). "Information exchange and technological innovation." In *The transfer and utilization of technical knowledge* (105–123). Edited by D. Sahal. Lexington, Mass.: Lexington Books.

Rogers, E. M., and J. K. Larsen (1984). *Silicon valley fever.* New York: Basic Books.

Rogers, M. (1991). "The right button." *Newsweek.* January 7, 46–47.

Rosenbaum, S., and R. D. Walters (1986). "Audience diversity: A major challenge in computer documentation." *IEEE Transactions on Professional Communication* PC-29(4):48–55.

Ross, S., and B. Karis (1991). "Communicating in public policy matters: Addressing the problem of non-congruent sites of discourse." *IEEE Transactions on Professional Communication.*

Rubens, P., and B. K. Rubens (1988). "Usability and format design." In *Effective documentation: What we have learned from research* (213–133). Edited by S. Doheny-Farina. Cambridge, Mass.: MIT Press.

Sankar, C. S., and W. H. Hawkins (1991). "The role of user interface professionals in large software projects." *IEEE Transactions on Professional Communication* 34(2):94–100.

Scherer, A., and D. W. McDonald (1988). "A model for the development of small high-technology business based on case studies from an incubator." *Journal of Product Innovation Management* 5:282–295.

Schmitt, R. W. (1989). "Universities of the future." *Research Technology Management* (September-October):18–21.

Schrage, M. (1990). *Shared minds.* New York: Random House.

Schriver, K. A. (1989). "Document design from 1980 to 1989: The challenges that remain." *Technical Communication* 36(4):316–331.

"Seeing red at big blue" (1991). *Newsweek,* June 10, 40.

Shirk, H. N. (1989). "Humanists versus technologists: New challenges for publications managers." *Proceedings of the 36th International Technical Communication Conference,* MG-4–MG-6.

Smallwood, M. S. (1986). "Including writers on the software development team." *Proceedings of the 33rd International Technical Communication Conference,* 387–390.

Smilor, R. W., and D. V. Gibson (1991). "Accelerating technology transfer in R&D consortia." *Research Technology Management* (January-February):44–49.

Souder, W. E. (1988). "Managing relations between R&D and marketing in new product development projects." *Journal of Product Innovation Management* 5:6–19.

Southard, S. G. (1990) "Interacting successfully in corporate culture." *Journal of Business and Technical Communication* 4(2):79–90.

Spilka, R. (1988). "Studying writer-reader interactions in the workplace." *Technical Writing Teacher* 3:208–221.

Spilka, R. (1990). "Orality and literacy in the workplace: Process- and text-based strategies for multiple-audience adaptation." *Journal of Business and Technical Communication* 4(1):44–67.

Stewart, A. (1989). *Team entrepreneurship.* Newbury Park, Calif.: Sage Publications.

Stewart, G. H., and D. V. Gibson (1990). "University and industry linkages: The Austin, Texas study." In *Technology transfer: A communication perspective* (109–131). Edited by F. Williams and D. V. Gibson. Newbury Park, Calif.: Sage Publications.

Sticht, T. (1985). "Understanding readers and their uses of texts." In *Designing usable texts* (315–340). Edited by T. M. Duffy and R. Waller. Orlando, Fla.: Academic Press.

Suchan, J., and R. Dulek (1990). "A reassessment of clarity in written managerial communication." *Managment Communication Quarterly* 4(1):87–99.

Sullivan, D. L. (1990). "Political-ethical implications of defining technical communication as a practice." *Journal of Advanced Composition* 10(2):375–386.

Szakonyi, R. (1988). "Dealing with a nonobvious source of problems related to selecting R&D to meet customers' future needs." *IEEE Transactions on Engineering Management* 35(1):37–41.

Tebeaux, E. (1985). "Redesigning professional writing courses to meet the communication needs of writers in business and industry." *College Composition and Communication* 36(4):419–428.

Tebeaux, E. (1991). "The shared document collaborative case response: Teaching and research implications of an in-house teaching strategy." In *Collaborative writing in industry: Investigations in theory and practice* (124–145). Edited by M. M. Lay and W. M. Karis.

Tushman, M. L., and D. A. Nadler (1980). "Communication and technical roles in R&D laboratories: An information processing approach." In *Studies in the management sciences* (91–112). Edited by B. V. Dean and J. L. Goldhar. New York: North-Holland Publising Co.

Udell, G. G. (1990). "Are business incubators really creating new jobs by creating new businesses and new products." *Journal of Product Innovation Management*, 108–122.

Vliegen, H. J. W., and H. H. Van Mal (1990). "Rational decision making: Structuring of design meetings." *IEEE Transactions on Engineering Management* 37(3):185–190.

Von Hippel, E. (1988). *The sources of innovation*. New York: Oxford University Press.

Walker, J. (1987). *The autodesk file*. Thousand Oaks, Calif.: New Riders Publishing.

Walton, K. R., J. P. Dismukes, and J. E. Browning (1989). "An information specialist joins the R&D team." *Research Technology Management* 32(5):32–37.

Williams, E. E., and S. E. Manzo (1983). *Business planning for the entrepreneur*. New York: Van Nostrand Reinhold Company.

Williams, F., and D. V. Gibson (1990). *Technology transfer: A communication perspective*. Newbury Park, Calif.: Sage Publications.

Wimberly, L. W. (1983). "The technical writer as a member of the software development team: A model for contributing more professionally." *Proceedings of the 30th International Technical Communication Conference*, G/P-36–G/P-38.

Winsor, D. A. (1990a). "Engineering writing/writing engineering." *College Composition and Communication* 41(1):58–70.

Winsor, D. A. (1990b). "Joining the engineering community: How do novices learn to write like engineers?" *Technical Communication* 37(2):171–172.

Winsor, D. A. (1990c). "How companies affect the writing of young engineers: Two case studies." *IEEE Transactions on Professional Communication* 33(3):124–129.

Yee, C. (1990). "The brain/mind and document design." *IEEE Transactions on Professional Communication* 33(4):168–171.

Index

DATE DUE

MAY 1 4 2000			
JAN 2 3 2002			